PRAISE FOR *THE MENTOR'S FIELD GUIDE*

"Two deeply experienced mentoring leaders have created a rich and practical resource for our country's most powerful public servants, mentors. They have put the best of research, existing tools, and the everyday experiences of mentors into this new asset for the mentoring field."
— **David Shapiro, CEO of MENTOR: The National Mentoring Partnership**

"Having researched for fifteen years the effects of youth mentoring programs and program practices that help make programs effective, I was surprised, when I first became a Big to a Little two years ago, how many questions I had about how to be a mentor. *The Mentor's Field Guide* addresses my questions and many others in ways not found in other available resources. To be sure, *The Mentor's Field Guide* will help mentors feel more connected to the larger movement of youth mentoring and part of the community of volunteers who drive it. *The Mentor's Field Guide* is a resource that can help mentors be more informed consumers of programmatic supports available to them through their programs and their staff and will certainly help many mentors enhance the lives of youth."
— **Michael J. Karcher, Ed.D., Ph.D., co-editor of *The Handbook of Youth Mentoring* and professor, College of Education and Human Development, University of Texas at San Antonio**

"*The Mentor's Field Guide* is a well-organized comprehensive compilation of resources and useful suggestions for both beginning and experienced mentors. This is a powerful reference tool offering research-based and practical suggestions for mentors and for leaders coordinating mentor programs in all settings. The authors spared no sensitive issues while addressing 67 pertinent questions about mentoring programs making this guide a must-have resource for all mentoring programs. Every mentor will benefit from this valuable information, but more importantly, every child will benefit from a better relationship supported by the ideas in this guide."
— **Jay Smink, D.Ed., former executive director of the National Dropout Prevention Center at Clemson University**

"Packed with research and case examples, The Mentor's Field Guide demonstrates a remarkable blend of empirical science and the 'art' of the youth mentoring process. The authors draw on their collective years of experience in the field and their deep sensitivity to both research and practice wisdom to offer common sense approaches to the challenges facing mentors. The result is a balanced approach that encourages mentors to develop strategies based on sound science, while also recognizing and drawing on their own intuitive skills. Volunteer mentors, practitioners, and researchers will value this book for its rich up-to-date coverage, clear writing, and common sense guidance. This book is gift to the many mentors whose generous commitment to our nation's youth will be enriched with stronger, more effective relationships."

—Jean Rhodes, Ph.D., MENTOR: The National Mentoring Partnership
Professor of Psychology and Research Director,
Center for Evidence-Based Mentoring

"The future of mentoring lies with those who build strong relationships, with or without formal program supports. Manza and Patrick have provided natural mentors with insight and tools they need to succeed. I urge them to get this book and keep it handy. "

—David E. Van Patten, president and CEO of Dare Mighty Things

"Any mentor on the fence or who has already taken the leap has all the answers in this handy guide. It is a straightforward, sensible compilation of advice, counsel, tips, scenarios, and strategies to ensure that mentors are successful in their mentoring relationships. . . . Every question that a mentor has ever asked me has been addressed. This user-friendly guide is not only essential for mentors who want to be effective, but it is also a fun read!"

—Susan G. Weinberger, EdD., a.k.a. Dr. Mentor,
President, Mentor Consulting Group

"A field guide for mentors! A brilliant concept for those of us in the field who know how important high-quality tools are for the dedicated souls who mentor deserving young people. This guide is a unique and valuable resource for mentors and for others who mentor less formally, including teachers, youth group leaders, and national service volunteers."

—Barbara Lehrner Canter, president and CEO Emeritus, Los Angeles Team
Mentoring and co-founder, 1000 Women for Mentoring

THE MENTOR'S FIELD GUIDE

The Mentor's Field Guide

ANSWERS YOU NEED TO HELP KIDS SUCCEED

Gail Manza and Susan K. Patrick

SEARCH
INSTITUTE
PRESS

The Mentor's Field Guide
Answers You Need to Help Kids Succeed
Gail Manza and Susan K. Patrick

The following are registered trademarks of Search Institute: Search Institute®, Healthy Communities • Healthy Youth®, and Developmental Assets®.

Search Institute Press, Minneapolis, MN
Copyright © 2012 by Search Institute

At the time of publication, all facts and figures cited herein are the most current available; all telephone numbers, addresses, and website URLs are accurate and active; all publications, organizations, websites, and other resources exist as described in this book; and all efforts have been made to verify them. The authors and Search Institute make no warranty or guarantee concerning the information and materials given out by organizations or content found at websites that are cited herein, and we are not responsible for any changes that occur after this book's publication. If you find an error or believe that a resource listed herein is not as described, please contact Client Services at Search Institute.

Printed on acid-free paper in the United States of America.

Search Institute
615 First Avenue Northeast, Suite 125
Minneapolis, MN 55413
612-376-8955 • 800-888-7828
www.search-institute.org

ISBN-13: 978-1-57482-286-1

Credits
Book Design: Percolator
Edited by: Mary Byers
Production Supervisor: Mary Ellen Buscher

Library of Congress
Cataloging-in-Publication Data
Manza, Gail.
The mentor's field guide : answers you need to help kids succeed / Gail Manza and Susan K. Patrick.
    pages cm
    Includes bibliographical references and index.
    ISBN 978-1-57482-286-1 (pbk.)
    ISBN 1-57482-286-1 (pbk.)
1. Youth—Counseling of—United States.
2. Mentoring—United States. 3. Youth development—United States. 4. Social work with youth—United States. I. Patrick, Susan K. II. Title.
    HV1431.M359 2012
    362.74'860973—dc23
                    012001395

The authors and publisher would like to gratefully acknowledge the permission to reprint material from *The Handbook of Youth Mentoring* by David L. DuBois and Michael J. Karcher (Thousand Oaks, CA: Sage, 2005), a condensed version of the Mentoring Application Form from Mentoring U.S.A. (2011), definitions of abuse and neglect from the American Academy of Pediatrics (2011), excerpts from *Elements of Effective Practice for Mentoring* by MENTOR (2009), and excerpts from "First Do No Harm: Ethical Principles for Youth Mentoring Relationships" by Jean Rhodes, Belle Liang, and Renée Spencer, in *Professional Psychology: Research and Practice* (2009, Vol. 40, No. 5, 452–458).

About Search Institute Press
Search Institute Press is a division of Search Institute, a nonprofit organization that provides catalytic leadership, breakthrough knowledge, and innovative resources to advance the health of children, youth, families, and communities. Our mission at Search Institute Press is to provide practical and hope-filled resources to help create a world in which all young people thrive. Our products are embedded in research, and the 40 Developmental Assets—qualities, experiences, and relationships youth need to succeed—are a central focus of our resources. Our logo, the SIP flower, is a symbol of the thriving and healthy growth young people experience when they have an abundance of assets in their lives.

To the founders and leaders of MENTOR,
with admiration and affection

and

for our hubands,
William Aramony and Bob Gallagher

Remembering Dr. Peter L. Benson (1946–2011)

Dr. Peter L. Benson, former President and CEO of Minneapolis-based Search Institute, was one of the world's leading authorities on positive human development. Dr. Benson's international reputation emerged in the 1990s through his innovative research-based framework of the Developmental Assets. His vision, research, and public voice inspired a "sea change" in research, practice, and policy, shifting away from trying to "fix" what's wrong with kids, toward identifying and building on kids' strengths.

Dr. Benson was 65 years old when he died in 2011. His accomplishments were significant, including his work as the author or editor of more than a dozen books on child and adolescent development and social change. He co-authored *What Kids Need to Succeed*, which has sold more than 800,000 copies. His other books include *Parent, Teacher, Mentor, Friend; Vision: Awakening Your Potential to Create a Better World; Sparks: How Parents Can Ignite the Hidden Strengths of Teenagers;* and *All Kids Are Our Kids: What Communities Must Do to Raise Caring and Responsible Children and Adolescents* (2nd Edition).

CONTENTS

LIST OF QUESTIONS

CHAPTER 1. QUESTIONS ABOUT 21ST-CENTURY MENTORING

CHAPTER 2. QUESTIONS ABOUT THE MENTORING RELATIONSHIP

CHAPTER 3. QUESTIONS ABOUT ISSUES THAT COMMONLY COME UP IN MENTORING RELATIONSHIPS

CHAPTER 4. QUESTIONS ABOUT ISSUES THAT RARELY ARISE

CHAPTER 5. QUESTIONS ABOUT SPECIAL CIRCUMSTANCES SOME MENTEES FACE

Introduction

USING *THE MENTOR'S FIELD GUIDE*

If you are prepared, you will be confident and do the job.
TOM LANDRY, DALLAS COWBOYS COACH AND FOOTBALL LEGEND

You have opened *The Mentor's Field Guide*, so odds are that you either are a mentor or are thinking about becoming one. If you are a mentor, congratulations for taking on the challenge of playing an important role in a young person's life. In truth, it may be quite a while before the young person you are working with thanks you for the effort. But we do. You are part of a remarkable fraternity of adults who have a special gift for what Ron Suskind (1998) calls "hope in the unseen." And we firmly believe that if you take the time to learn how to be a skillful mentor, you are sure to find your gift for believing in a young person's future rewarded in ways large and small, and always meaningful.

If you are an aspiring mentor, we are delighted that you are considering joining millions of other adults who are transforming their interest in America's young people into real action on their behalf. But consider carefully. Mentoring a young person is a process in which neither deeply felt kindness nor the best of intentions are a substitute for energy, ability, and perseverance. So read on and use this resource to strengthen your mentoring skills. Or use it to discover whether you are ready for an assignment that—as one incandescent young mentee at a program sponsored by Morgan Stanley assured us—will bring you joy.

This introduction provides all that you need to make the most of *The Mentor's Field Guide* (hereafter the *Field Guide*). We address its purpose, how it is organized, two ways readers can approach its use, the sources of our material and ideas, and our dedication to evidence-based mentoring. By intention, this is the shortest chapter in the book. General information about mentoring is widely available, but few readily accessible resources speak directly to the interests and needs of mentors themselves. Consequently, our goal is to move quickly through user essentials and then on to what mentors tell us they want most: straightforward answers to the questions that intrigue, concern, or confound them.

PURPOSE

The aim of the *Field Guide* is to provide current and would-be mentors with *practical* counsel that can be used to initiate, strengthen, and maintain mentoring relationships that are worth the time (and hope) invested in them. The book begins and ends with mentors' needs in mind and is designed to deliver on its promise to provide "answers you need to help kids succeed." This is the essence of what all good mentors hope to achieve: success as the young people in their lives come to define and redefine it, time and time again.

We also bear in mind that while many adults mentor through formal mentoring programs, an equal or even larger number mentor informally. The *Field Guide* is intended to be a comprehensive, reliable, and reusable resource for *all* kinds of mentors, regardless of the degree of formality that characterizes their involvement. This is a resource to which any mentor can turn to test her or his ideas and inclinations, deal with a particular challenge, or simply revisit the practices that tend to make mentoring relationships endure and thrive. And readers of the guide should be able to do so easily, since the book has a handy-to-use format.

HOW *THE MENTOR'S FIELD GUIDE* IS ORGANIZED

The *Field Guide* has a straightforward format with two main sections:

> Part I. Our Answers to Mentors' Questions
> Part II. Resources for Strong Mentors

Part I contains the heart of the book and offers answers to questions that are on many mentors' minds. Some are questions that we have heard over and over again. Others have been raised just a few times, but with an intensity or on a subject that we think makes them especially noteworthy. The 67 questions that constitute part I are organized into five chapters that capture key dimensions of mentoring: (1) the nature of 21st-century mentoring; (2) the mentoring relationship; (3) issues that come up in almost every mentoring relationship; (4) issues that rarely but sometimes arise; and (5) special life circumstances some mentees face.

Chapter 1, "Questions about 21st-Century Mentoring." This chapter covers the basics of modern mentoring. What is it? Who mentors? How does one become a mentor? How do I know mentoring really helps kids? How exactly does mentoring "work"? Are there different types of mentoring programs? The program I am mentoring in requires a background check: is this routine? I don't think I need to attend mentor training; should I go? What if a young person asks me to mentor her or him? This chapter also includes our favorite question and the one that most genuinely effective mentors invariably ask of themselves: Will I be a good mentor?

Chapter 2, "Questions about the Mentoring Relationship." Jean Rhodes of the University of Massachusetts, Boston, taught us that because mentoring's benefits typically emerge from the relationship that develops between a mentor and mentee, the quality of that relationship matters a great deal (Rhodes, 2002). Chapter 2 concentrates on this pivotal relationship, tackling questions that address what it takes to build a strong one, for example: How much time should I be spending with my mentee? How do I build trust in our relationship? What about connecting with my mentee online: should we e-mail, text, tweet, or "friend" each other? What are the typical stages in the life cycle of a mentoring relationship? I'm just not connecting with my mentee; is it me? Will talking about my own life and beliefs help my mentee open up to me? What should I do if my mentee keeps "standing me up"? How deeply should I be involved in my mentee's life or that of my mentee's family?

Chapter 3, "Questions about Issues That Commonly Come Up in Mentoring Relationships." At some point during their mentoring experience, most mentors will deal with at least a few of the issues addressed in chapter 3. They relate to the aspirations mentees hold for themselves, whether short term (get more out of the school day, have a nice Saturday) or long term (be a more confident person, find a satisfying career). They also relate to obstacles that may thwart efforts to bring a mentee's aspirations to life, for example: My mentee is a whiz at school (or not). How do I help her make the most of her school experience? My mentee wants to talk about what seems like a sensitive issue (fill in your own blank), and I don't. Help! My mentee comes from a different economic, cultural, racial, or ethnic background. How can I honor and accommodate these differences? How do I tell what things should be kept between my mentee and me and what things I should share with my program coordinator or another responsible adult?

Chapter 4, "Questions about Issues That Rarely but Sometimes Arise." We are glad to report that the challenges addressed in this chapter are based on questions that don't come up in most mentoring relationships. But they arise more frequently than they should in any child's life, and the answers to questions in chapter 4 can help mentors be prepared to deal with them effectively: My mentee has a chronic health condition (such as diabetes, asthma, obesity). Do I need to make special provisions for that? My mentee is being bullied and doesn't want to go to school anymore. How can I help? My mentee has been put in a juvenile detention facility. What do I do now? I think my mentee and I have differences (regarding culture, gender, socioeconomic status, and/or race) that can't be bridged. Is it time to walk away from the relationship?

Chapter 5, "Questions about Special Circumstances Some Mentees Face." This chapter offers guidance related to questions that emerge from the context of a young person's life. We're not fans of the term "at-risk youth," but there are times when children will routinely find themselves at risk of real harm because of the situations in which their parents and family—or the larger community—place them. That jeopardy may come from their day-to-day living conditions or from their parents' status, say, as undocumented immigrants or as adults who are unfit or unavailable to provide a home and care. This chapter addresses such risks, including the following: My mentee is in foster care. What does that mean? My mentee has a parent in prison. Should I ignore this or bring it up with my mentee? The school my mentee attends is appalling. Is there anything I can do?

Finally, we think mentors can benefit from information that puts their mentees' experience into a larger context. Be sure to check out the Data Points which appear throughout the book. They are drawn from the nation's leading repositories of data on American children and youth and can help illuminate how common (or rare) your mentee's life experiences may be.

Part II, "Resources for Strong Mentors," offers considerable supplementary information, as well as materials that *every* mentor should be familiar with and know where to find. The three chapters in part II cover standards for quality mentoring; introductory information about the stages of youth development and Search Institute's framework of 40 Developmental Assets® that make positive youth development more likely; and resources for active mentors.

DATA POINT
America's Children

There are 74.2 million children ages 0–17 in the United States. They account for 24 percent of the total U.S. population. Roughly 55 percent are White, non-Hispanic; 15 percent, Black; 4 percent, Asian; 5 percent, all other races; and 23 percent, Hispanic (of any race).

Source: Federal Interagency Forum on Child and Family Statistics (2011).

Chapter 6, "Essential Guideposts." This chapter offers readers an introduction to the mentoring field's most important standards and practice guidelines. Highlighted are *Elements of Effective Practice for Mentoring*, Third Edition (MENTOR: The National Mentoring Partnership, 2009), and "First Do No Harm: Ethical Principles for Youth Mentoring Relationships" (Rhodes, Liang & Spencer, 2009).

Chapter 7, "Understanding What Young People Need and When They Need It." Many mentors, like many parents, say they wish they had more information about the phases and pace of child and youth development. Chapter 7 is designed to help mentors appreciate what young people need and at what stage of their development they need it. Search Institute's important work on youth development is highlighted here, with special emphasis on the 40 Developmental Assets. This chapter also suggests how mentors can play a role in the developmental process, as well as presents specific ideas about age-appropriate activities that mentors and mentees can do together.

Chapter 8, "Finding Additional Help and Providing Feedback on the Field Guide." The final chapter introduces still more people and places to which mentors can turn for ideas and advice or to take action on behalf of the young people they care about. Expertise and resources are available through MENTOR: The National Mentoring Partnership, a national organization dedicated to expanding the world of quality mentoring and through Mentoring Partnerships that operate in many states and communities throughout the United States. Also highlighted are several large mentoring organizations (like Big Brothers Big Sisters and Communities in Schools) that offer materials or advice tailored to specialized forms of mentoring, such as school-based or electronic- or Internet-based mentoring. Website addresses and other contact information for all are noted.

WAYS TO USE *THE MENTOR'S FIELD GUIDE*

There are two different ways mentors can use the *Field Guide* to best advantage. You can approach it as you would a much-anticipated or long-loved novel, carefully reading it cover to cover. Or you can direct your attention to the questions or supplementary materials that most interest you, read them first, and then move on to other sections as your needs or interests dictate. Our guess is that most readers will choose the selective approach, so we have tried to make it easy to find what you want when you want it. There is also a comprehensive subject index, and we have supplied clear cross-referencing when the answer to one question relates to, and will be enhanced by, an answer in another question or topic category.

Overall, consider the *Field Guide* as more like an encyclopedia than a textbook. It is likely to be most useful to readers who look at what is covered and take note of how to access information when they want it. This brings us to the question of the value of the information provided and why we think it will prove to be information you will want, need, and very probably enjoy having.

SOURCE MATERIAL

The advice the *Field Guide* offers is direct and frequently directive, which will naturally lead many readers to wonder about its validity. In turn, many readers will want to know "the sources" on which we base our advice. Our view is that the practical counsel mentors want is best drawn from three complementary sources: (1) research; (2) the experience of mentors and mentees; and (3) the expertise of those dedicated to supporting successful mentoring relationships.

Research

Although mentoring is still a young field, it has been the subject of considerably more research than many other areas of youth development.

Irv Katz, president of the National Human Services Assembly, summed it up this way in remarks he made at a meeting of MENTOR's Research and Policy Council: "During the past 20 years, mentoring has set the pace for many areas of youth development. There has been a consistent, perhaps even relentless concentration on tackling a challenge that bedevils many human services—identifying, generating or advocating for the development of strong research." One result is a robust and growing body of scholarship on the nature of mentoring, outcomes that mentoring relationships may influence, and factors that support and undermine mentor-mentee matches. An even more pertinent result is that research can now make a considerable contribution to refining the day-to-day mentoring practices that can increase mentor effectiveness, as well as something that should never be underrated—enjoyment of the mentoring experience.

Experience

Active mentors have a great deal to tell us about what motivated them to become mentors, how they initiated a mentoring relationship, and what kept them going once their mentoring relationships were under way. As a group they are unusually generous and candid in sharing insights drawn from their experiences. Although often overlooked, the experiences of mentees offer another important stream of information about what they think mentors should (or shouldn't) do. It is advice that can be eye-opening and invaluable. An example: Ten years before Ean Garrett became an attorney and a mentor, he was a 13-year-old mentee living in Lincoln, Nebraska. Ean's repeatedly unreturned phone calls to set a time to meet with his first would-be mentor clearly and powerfully underscored the value of what has become a hallmark of good mentors: the simple and absolutely impossible-to-overrate quality of reliability.

Expertise

Youth development experts drawn from many fields—education, social work, psychology, sports, and juvenile justice—play a pivotal role in mentoring by providing support to mentors, to mentees, and to mentoring relationships themselves. In formal mentoring programs, program coordinators (a term we will frequently use) come from these fields, and it is these men and women who form mentoring's front line. They perform one or more key functions: they recruit mentors; help train them; match mentor and mentee pairs; provide support both to the mentor and, many times, to the mentee during the course of the mentoring experience; and, finally, manage the process when the experience ends. The expertise program coordinators have gained from their day-to-day and year-to-year experiences is a rich resource for active mentors, as well as for those thinking about becoming one. It was a program coordinator, says mentor Shawn Pearson, who provided a straightforward piece of advice that changed the course of his mentoring relationship. The program coordinator's advice: stop talking so much.

The *Field Guide* draws on each of these three sources of guidance, integrating all we find most relevant to active or would-be mentors. Please read our acknowledgments for a more complete review of the experts on whom we most heavily relied. Note that the *research* of the nation's leading mentoring scholars constitutes a foundational resource and is cited throughout the book. Real-life *experience* is derived from a remarkable group of mentors and mentees who provided fresh thinking for use in the *Field Guide*. For professional *expertise*, or what is sometimes called practice wisdom, we relied on several key sources, the first being the dedicated team of human service professionals drawn from MENTOR: The National Mentoring Partnership (hereafter MENTOR) and the aligned network of local Mentoring Partnerships.

A second key source of professional expertise: the counsel of and material developed by the eminent group of men and women who pioneered targeted uses for mentoring (e.g., dropout prevention); new types of mentoring (e.g., faith based, Internet based, and school based); new ways to deliver mentoring (e.g., through a team-based approach); and new ways to recruit mentors (e.g., equip kids, especially of a certain age, to recruit their own mentors). We want you to know their names and their innovations:

Daniel F. Bassil and **Marc Freedman**—mentoring blended with tutoring

Shay Bilchik—mentoring for delinquency prevention

Jeb Bush—peer mentoring for academic success

Duncan Campbell—intensive, full-time mentoring

Barbara Lehrner Canter, Suzanne Spero, and **Patrice Theard**—team mentoring

Robert Craves—mentoring that blends scholarships and mentorships

Matilda Raffa Cuomo—mentoring for children in foster care

W. Wilson Goode Sr.—mentoring for children of prisoners

Andrew Mecca and **James Kooler**—mentoring for drug and alcohol abuse prevention

David Eisner and **David Neils**—e-mentoring

Jay Smink—mentoring as dropout prevention

Arthur Tannenbaum and **Phyllis Tannenbaum**—reading focused mentoring

Andrea Taylor and **Marc Freedman**—intergenerational mentoring

David E. Van Patten—youth-initiated mentoring

Susan Weinberger, **Thomas McKenna**, and **Tom Osbourne**—school-based mentoring

Harry Wilson—voucherized mentoring (or mentorships)

Harris Wofford and **John Bridgeland**—mentoring as national service

The third and final source of expertise is our more than 40 years of combined experience in leading initiatives that supported mentors as they worked to help young people envision a positive future—and find the means for getting there. Susan is a community psychologist, founder of the Connecticut Mentoring Partnership, and former president of the Governor's Prevention Partnership in Connecticut; Gail is a social worker, advocate, and former CEO of MENTOR. Both of us have also been mentors. We learned a great deal during the course of our enormously happy work and have incorporated every lesson that we think today's mentor will find genuinely useful. We learned even more by being mentors ourselves. There is no doubt that a Danish proverb applies: "He who knows the water best has waded through it."

DEDICATION TO EVIDENCE-BASED MENTORING

We are firm in our conviction that experience is a peerless teacher, but we hold another firm conviction as well. We believe that experience becomes especially valuable when it is systematically captured, analyzed, and interpreted by skilled researchers. Captured experience is transformed into something of equal value—evidence. And evidence brings us to the concept of *evidence-based practice*.

Many readers will have heard of or even be quite familiar with the term evidence-based practice. Although there is considerable variation in how the term is defined and debate about its value, many scholars and practitioners agree that evidence-based practice constitutes an approach to delivering services that requires that practices be based on three things: the best available research, practitioner expertise, and the needs and interests of the client (Shlonsky & Gibbs, 2004). Further, the prevailing view is that evidence-based practice is client-centered practice (Sackett, Rosenberg, Gray, Haynes & Richardson, 1996). It can be applied to mentoring in this way: the client is the mentee and her or his interest is always paramount. Further, evidence-based practice best advances the primacy of the mentee's interest by ensuring that mentoring is conducted in a way that acknowledges and integrates creditable research, the knowledge and wisdom of practitioners, and, of course, the interests of the mentee.

As the *Field Guide* makes clear, we are believers in the principle of evidence-based practice. We think mentors can benefit from understanding the approach, how it applies to their own mentoring relationship, and ways they can (and cannot) leverage its benefits. It is the dedication to evidence-based practice that led us to rely on the same three sources of guidance that drive evidence-based practice. We emphasize research findings and honor practitioner wisdom throughout the book. And, not surprisingly, a dedication to the primacy of the interests of mentees comes easily to us. We are educators and social workers, so mentee interests are our North Star, and you will see that view reflected throughout the book. As much as we are concerned about you and all the other caring and intrepid adults who mentor, we care even more about the young people who are depending on you to live up to the principle that "a mentor is a trusted guide and friend" (MENTOR, 2009). We know that the best mentors feel this way, too.

It is also important to acknowledge the potential weaknesses of evidence-based practice. First and foremost, all research is not equal. The quality of available research varies dramatically, and it is frequently difficult for those who are either untrained in research methods or not natural data junkies to separate strong studies from weak or misleading ones. This raises a second issue: the task of translating strong research into language that all of us can understand is, at present, an underfinanced and underpracticed art. A third challenge is that conducting strong, scientifically valid research is rarely an inexpensive undertaking, and in human services (including youth development and mentoring), it remains an undercapitalized function. Furthermore, a number of important issues in mentoring practice remain largely unexplored. For example, while research can tell us a great deal about what represents best practice in traditional one-on-one mentoring, it has considerably less to offer to the practice of newer forms of mentoring.

Despite weaknesses, there is reason to believe that the quality and quantity of research available for use in evidence-based practice will continue to grow. Our optimism is based on the continued leadership of the mentoring movement in highlighting its import, as well an accelerating appreciation for evidence-based practice (U.S. Department of Education/ Office of Safe and Drug-Free Schools, 2009). One prime example is the recently launched UMASS/MENTOR Center for Evidence-Based Mentoring.

In summary, although we may not be in the midst of what Jenson (2005) calls an "evidence-based practice revolution," it seems undeniable that evidence-based practice has gained a society-wide momentum in the United States that is unlikely to abate soon. In fact, many worry that the enthusiasm for evidence-based practice may be growing at a faster pace than the evidentiary base that supports it (Nutley, Walter & Davies, 2003). But, as we have said, we are optimists and believe that continuing momentum will concentrate the minds of mentoring and other youth development practitioners. We expect that they will continue to press for the advance of evidence-based practice, as well the high-quality research and practice wisdom on which it depends. We therefore urge readers to familiarize themselves with the term evidence-based practice. You are likely to hear more about it, and you and your mentees could be the beneficiaries of both its current offerings and future promise.

A FINAL WORD BEFORE THE QUESTIONS AND ANSWERS

We hope you will keep reading and that you will find many good answers to questions your current or planned mentoring experiences raise. Mentors have a unique place in our hearts. We admire your kind nature, respect the skills and dedication you bring to mentoring, and are invariably moved by your willingness to take the risk of entering young persons' lives in order to help them achieve their ambitions and, sometimes, even their dreams. You are our inspiration. And, if you are not already, you *can* be an inspiration to a young person who, in every way, deserves your interest and support.

PART I

Our Answers
to Mentors'
Questions

QUESTIONS ABOUT 21ST-CENTURY MENTORING

Mentoring . . . I think about it as a great opportunity to be an integral part of a young person's success.

MICHELLE OBAMA, FIRST LADY OF THE UNITED STATES

The questions in this chapter focus on the basics. We start with a definition of mentoring, then address the first questions that typically occur to adults as they begin to think about what it means to be a mentor, as well as what it takes to establish a relationship with a young person they are—in most instances—meeting for the first time. As you consider the answers in this chapter and throughout the book, you will see that we have highlighted some differences in the ways our advice may be applied by those who are mentoring through organized programs and those who are mentoring informally. If you are unclear about which category best fits your mentoring experience, begin with Question 2 (Formal and informal mentoring: what's the difference?), and then return to Question 1 and take Questions 3–14 in order. Otherwise, start with Question 1 and read on.

QUESTION 1. *Mentoring—I generally get it but am in search of a good, jargon-free definition. What have you got?*

Mentoring is an ancient form of social interaction that has modern applications, one of which is youth mentoring. Definitions of *modern youth mentoring* abound, but the one we have come to favor was introduced by former MENTOR CEO, Larry Wright: "Mentoring is a means to an end, with the end being any objective that a mentor and mentee agree is important to a child's development."

Commonly agreed-upon *ends* include broadly cast objectives like exposure to new experiences, stronger relational skills, improvements in overall or selected aspects of academic achievement (e.g., reading, math, music, language skills), exploration of work or career options, and opening doors to new worlds and new opportunities. Ends can, and often do, embrace much more limited aspirations: getting to school on a regular basis, learning to deal with bullies, navigating new cultural or social environments, getting (and keeping) a summer job, or identifying and completing the many steps involved in applying to a technical school or college. An even more targeted end of interest to many young people living in disadvantaged circumstances is simply getting to know people and places beyond the narrow boundaries of their worlds. Mentees from South Central Los Angeles participating in the Los Angeles Team Mentoring program wanted, quite literally, to see the Pacific Ocean, just eight miles away. Still other children may, as Cyndi Lauper sings, "just want to have fun," something that can be in surprisingly short supply in many young lives.

Broadly defining mentoring as a means to a young person's ends has several advantages. It concisely captures the essence of good mentoring: helping a young person get to where he or she wants to go. It is easily applied by mentors who are called upon to respond to questions from friends, colleagues, or family members. "You're mentoring?" they ask. "What's that?" The answer: "Mentoring is a way for me to team with a young person to _____" (*with the blank being yours—along with your mentee—to fill in*). We emphasize that this definition is widely applicable, regardless of the age of a mentee. Even the youngest participants in targeted mentoring programs, such as a reading mentoring program like Everybody Wins, will be able to give you some idea of what they are after: learning to improve their reading, being able to read the kinds of books *they* like, or just having someone nice to sit with during lunch. All are good places to start.

In fact, we have found that the most essential feature of whatever ends are identified is that they are explored and mutually agreed upon by the mentor and mentee—and then revisited and refined as the mentoring relationship evolves. There are few things more disappointing (and, potentially, more damaging) than finding out that your mentee wanted a mentor to help him learn how to talk comfortably with new people (including college admissions officers or potential employers), while you spent your time together focusing on trying to improve his math, even though, of course, you could have done both.

Although we think you'll find "mentoring as a means to a young person's ends" to be an accurate and consistent definition of mentoring, we want you to be aware of more formal alternatives. We provide several very good ones. Also note that most dictionaries define mentoring by relying on its root word: *mentor*. Admirers of Greek mythology will recall that when Odysseus set sail in Homer's *The Odyssey*, he left the care of his son Telemachus in the worthy hands of his wife, Penelope. Odysseus also asked his trusted friend, Mentor, to provide watchful support, as well as the challenge and counsel his young son would inevitably need in his absence. This makes Mentor the first mentor; it further established the idea that a mentor is both a friendly adviser and thoughtful teacher who knows when to challenge a mentee, when to help, and when to let go (McEwan, 2000).

HIGHLIGHT
Definitions of Mentoring and Mentor

"Mentoring is a structured and trusting relationship that brings young people together with caring individuals who offer guidance, support and encouragement aimed at developing the competence and character of the mentee" (MENTOR, 2000a).

". . . a relationship between an older and more experienced adult and an unrelated, younger protégé—a relationship in which the adult provides ongoing guidance, instruction and encouragement aimed at developing the competence and character of the protégé" (Rhodes, 2002, 3).

". . . a powerful emotional interaction between an older and younger person, a relationship in which the older member is trusted, loving and experienced in the guidance of the younger. The mentor helps the growth and development of the protégé" (Merriam, 1983, 162).

"The mentor is ordinarily several years older, a person of greater experience and seniority in the world the young mentee is entering. The person acts as teacher, sponsor, counselor, developer of skills and intellect, host, guide, exemplar and one who supports and facilitates the realization of a young person's dream" (University of South Florida, 2003; adapted from Levinson, Darrow, Klein, Levinson & McKee, 1978).

Source: DuBois and Karcher (2005); reprinted with permission.

In keeping with this lineage, *The Oxford English Dictionary* (2009) defines a mentor to be "a trusted guide and advisor." *Webster's American Dictionary* (2010) defines a mentor "as a trusted friend and guide" and mentoring as "the act of being a trusted friend and guide." Finally, MENTOR, the leading champion for youth mentoring in the United States, defines a mentor as "a wise and trusted friend and guide."

While all of these definitions are clearly correct and consistent with mentoring's genesis, the average mentor is not entirely or even remotely comfortable describing her- or himself as a "wise and trusted friend and guide to a young person." So we suggest building on the versatile idea that mentoring is a means to help reach a young person's ends. It will surely make talking about mentoring, as well as your role as a mentor, more comfortable and, very probably, more engaging. It also will make you less of a target for any of your family, friends, and colleagues who may see you as slightly less than manifestly "wise." More importantly, it will remind you that the central focus of mentoring remains the dreams and aspirations of young people. Your assignment is to make the mentoring experience meaningful to them, to become—as First Lady Michelle Obama and the Corporation for National and Community Service suggest—an integral part of their success (nationalservice.gov).

QUESTION 2. *Formal mentoring and informal mentoring: what's the difference?*

In our view, the terms *formal mentoring* and *informal mentoring* leave a lot to be desired as descriptives. Formal mentoring invariably makes us think of dinner-jacketed mentors at long dining tables, while *informal mentoring* evokes the image of a kind of drive-by mentoring where an adult says, "You go, girl!" to a nice kid she runs into every once in a while in the neighborhood McDonald's. Although we can't account for these flights of definitional fancy (or for a certain fixation on food), we can say that formal mentoring simply means you are mentoring as part of a structured program operating under the auspices of an institution, such as a nonprofit organization, a school, a place of worship, or a business enterprise. Formal mentoring programs typically have either paid or volunteer staff who will help you through the process of becoming a mentor and then a strong mentor by providing solid training, making a well-considered match with a young person, and ensuring you have ongoing support during the experience. You are in a formal mentoring program if you are mentoring through organizations like Best Buddies International, Big Brothers Big Sisters, Experience Corps, Goodwill Guides, Everybody Wins, Mentoring the 100 Way, or any one of thousands of mentoring programs that operate throughout the United States and elsewhere. You also may be formally mentoring if you are involved in a youth development program (e.g., an after-school or recreation center program) that explicitly adds mentoring to the service mix and prepares adults to mentor. Good examples are the programming of the U.S. Dream Academy and more than 60 after-school programs that the Afterschool Alliance estimates have a mentoring dimension.

In contrast, informal mentoring, which researchers often call natural mentoring, is mentoring that happens outside the bounds of formal, structured programs. In many families, aunts, uncles, grandparents, and close family friends often mentor a young person a generation or two younger. A common example: parents find adults in the family circle who are involved in a sport or career that interests their child and encourage a sustained connection that allows the exploration of new territory. A real-life example: the course of Gail's husband's life was shaped by the imagination and vigor of an informal mentor, his beloved uncle Mitre. Teachers also frequently mentor informally, not as part of their job description or contract or formal school-based program, but because it is a part of their personal mission or they are moved by particular children's talents or needs. This is true for a host of caring adults, including clergy, coaches, supervisors of student interns or part-time workers, or family friends who have been drafted into service by parents and caregivers, by their own interest in the well-being of a child who simply crosses their path or by young people themselves.

In our experience, strong mentoring can occur in either a formal or informal context. Research on this subject seems to bear this out (DuBois & Silverthorn, 2005; Lerner, Zimmerman, Bingenheimer & Behrendt, 2005). And we may eventually find that following the example of the National Guard Youth ChalleNGe Program, which blends techniques drawn from formal and informal mentoring, delivers meaningful outcomes for young people by capitalizing on the strengths of both approaches. Meanwhile, it is important to note that there is far more informal mentoring occurring in the United States than the more formalized, institution-based alternative (DuBois & Silverthorn, 2005; McLearn, Colasanto & Schoen, 1998; MENTOR, 2002, 2005).

This point is equally important: although we believe that both types of mentoring can be effective in terms of the one index that matters most (the needs of the mentee), this rarely happens serendipitously. But much can be done to enhance the quality of either formal or informal mentoring. It is an entirely doable assignment and is becoming more so with each new development that brings mentors—formal and otherwise—in contact with the information and expertise they need to make the most of their mentoring relationships. For more on this point, read on.

QUESTION 3. *Who mentors?*

A great many adults in the United States mentor and many young people do, too. Here's an aerial view. In 2009, the Corporation for National and Community Service reported that nearly 11 million American volunteers (or 17 percent of the 63.4 million Americans who volunteered) engage in some youth mentoring activities each year (Corporation for National and Community Service, 2010). Four years earlier, MENTOR found that nearly 3 million American adults were in *formal* one-to-one mentoring relationships (MENTOR, 2005), while the corporation reported that the number of volunteers who spend time mentoring in a variety of ways stood at 11.5 million (Corporation for National and Community Service, 2006a). Highlights from these two surveys, which comprehensively assess the rate of mentoring in the United States, as well as the characteristics of those who mentor, appear on pages 9 and 10. Take a look and see how they compare with your "personal profile."

Also note that the numbers underscore that interest in and dedication to mentoring have grown substantially during the past couple of decades, spurred by the exceptional leadership of MENTOR co-founders Geoffrey Boisi and Raymond Chambers and all the leaders they, in turn, engaged in creating what has become a broad-based national mentoring movement. Other notable champions are the current and past presidents and their first ladies, Barack and Michelle Obama (2009–present) and George W. and Laura Bush (2001–2008), along with Colin and Alma Powell, founders of America's Promise: The Alliance for Youth, many sitting and past governors, corporate and faith-based leaders, and human services leaders operating at the federal, state, and local levels in the public, private, and nonprofit sectors. If you are mentoring or interested in becoming a mentor, you, too, are part of a large cadre of Americans who have come to believe that mentoring can play a meaningful role in a young person's development and success.

DATA POINTS
Volunteers Mentoring Youth

- Age: Volunteers under 24 are the likeliest group to mentor; those over 65 the least likely. Also, 41 percent of those who mentor are baby boomers.

- Gender: Among U.S. volunteers, men and women mentor at similar rates (18 percent and 17 percent, respectively). Fewer men than women volunteer, however, which means that in 2009, more women than men were mentors.

- Race: Minorities (including Blacks and Latinos) volunteer at lower rates than Whites. However, among Americans who do volunteer, more Blacks (24 percent) engage in mentoring than do Whites (17 percent).

- Work status: Of all volunteers who engage in mentoring work, 59 percent work full-time and are more likely than nonworking volunteers to mentor.

- Intensity of commitment: Volunteers engaged in mentoring serve a median of 80 hours annually, while those volunteering in other ways serve a median of 40 hours annually.

- Institutions in and through which mentors mentor: The top two types of organizations in which or through which American volunteers mentor are religious institutions (43 percent) and educational organizations (31 percent).

Source: Corporation for National and Community Service (2006b).

QUESTION 4. *How does someone become a mentor?*

You can become a mentor in one of two ways: you can volunteer or you can be drafted. Let's start with volunteering. Once you have made a decision to explore mentoring, you will find many ways to identify an opportunity that may be right for you. A good place to start is MENTOR's Volunteer Referral Service. If you visit www.mentoring.org/get_involved, you can search for mentoring opportunities within a radius of your ZIP code and find profiles. Other useful sites, including those hosted by the Corporation for National and Community Service (serve.gov/mentor.asp) and United Way's Live United Campaign (liveunited.org).

If you prefer talking with someone in your community who is knowledgeable about current mentoring opportunities in your town or workplace, there are three excellent places to start. First, find out if there is a Mentoring Partnership in your state and, if so, call, e-mail, or visit for an

---

HIGHLIGHT
Mentoring in America

• Age: Middle-aged adults (34–54) and young adults mentor through formal mentoring programs at the highest rate. Older adults (especially those over 65) are least likely to be engaged in formal mentoring.

• Gender: In 2005, men were more likely to mentor (31 percent) than women (27 percent).

• Race: Non-Whites are more likely to mentor (35 percent) than Whites (28 percent).

• Education: Those with higher levels of formal education mentor at higher rates (35 percent) than those with a high school education or less (26 percent).

• Work status: Those working full-time are more likely to mentor (32 percent) than those who are retired or unemployed (23 percent and 22 percent, respectively). Part-time workers are most likely to mentor (37 percent).

• Duration of mentoring relationships: Most mentoring relationships last an average of 9 months. Thirty-eight percent of mentors spend at least 12 months with their mentees.

• Types of organizations through which mentors mentor: Of those polled, 21 percent connect through a Big Brothers Big Sisters or Boy Scouts organization; 20 percent through or at a school; 20 percent through a faith-based organization; 14 percent through a workplace; and 9 percent through an after-school program.

• Motivation to mentor: Want to help young people succeed (82 percent); want to make a difference in someone's life (76 percent); want to give back to the community (43 percent); religious and spiritual reasons (27 percent); and because someone helped them when they were young (22 percent).

In 1990, a national poll of agencies providing mentoring found that collectively these organizations were supporting 500,000 formal mentoring relationships (MENTOR, 2002).

Source: MENTOR (2005).

---

overview of what's available in your community (see chapter 8 for a state-by-state list and contact information for Mentoring Partnerships). Also, virtually every community in the United States has a United Way or Volunteer Center (or Hands On Action Center) that tracks volunteer opportunities, including mentoring opportunities (again, see chapter 8). As a third option, you can touch base with your place of worship or your workplace's human resources or volunteer services department. A substantial amount of mentoring happens through religious organizations, and many workplace groups support mentoring programs in their communities and even sponsor mentoring programs within their walls. The latter opportunities are likely to grow as many more U.S. companies respond to the Corporate Mentoring Challenge issued in early 2011 by First Lady Michelle Obama and the Corporation for National and Community Service.

In short, if you want to mentor, there are lots of organizations and people who will help you find the right opportunity. Your job is to find it and then contact the sponsoring agency. Once you do, you are likely to be asked to move through a screening and application process (described in Question 11). As we say there, embrace the process. It is essential for ensuring that young people are matched with the right mentors, and it should be invaluable to you, too.

What if mentoring finds you? There are three ways you are likely to be recruited to be a mentor. First, a young person may ask you to be her or his mentor. This sometimes happens within families or a circle of close family friends and is what often prompts the kind of informal mentoring relationships described in Question 2. If you are drafted by a young person, consider it an honor and review our advice on how to respond in the discussion of Question 17. Second, an adult in your personal or professional network may ask you to mentor one of his children, in ways large (a sustained relationship) or small (help the child explore activities or professional realms where you have expertise). Finally, you may be moved to respond by one of a number of national campaigns dedicated to generating more mentors for America's children.

First and foremost is the National Mentoring Month campaign, spearheaded by the Harvard School of Public Health in partnership with MENTOR and the Corporation for National and Community Service. This broad-based campaign has taken place each January since 2002. In 2012, the theme was "Invest in the Future, Mentor a Child," and the campaign offered a wide range of opportunities for Americans in every community throughout the country to do three things: learn more about mentoring, become a mentor, and—through an especially inspired element of the campaign—thank someone for being a mentor (for more information on National Mentoring Month and Thank Your Mentor Day, visit national mentoringmonth.org). Jay Winsten, National Mentoring Month's principal architect and dedicated advocate, calls the campaign "a way to do what it takes to persuade more Americans to mentor: Ask them to be a mentor."

In turn, National Mentoring Month has encouraged the development of more targeted campaigns, like the National Cares Mentoring Movement and One Million Mentors Campaign to Save Our Kids, which in 2011 joined together to sponsor mentoring forums in 72 communities in partnership with affiliates of Big Brothers Big Sisters, 100 Black Men of America Inc., and other organizations. Another recent initiative—Fatherhood Incorporated's *weMentor* outreach campaign to African American men. If any of these great efforts manage to reach you, we hope you will listen to what they have to say and consider saying yes to an appeal for more mentors. As Michael Baisden, the radio personality who is the force behind One Million Mentors, said in announcing the start of the campaign, "I knew I needed to step up and get involved personally . . . with young people who need caring adults . . . in their lives." Maybe the timing is right for you to do the same.

QUESTION 5. *Does mentoring work?*

This is the single most frequently asked question by potential mentors, active mentors, program designers, service advocates, and policymakers, along with their budget-focused counterparts. In fact, the only group not raising this question is researchers, because they know it is the wrong question. We agree with the researchers but nonetheless address the issue here because of the immense level of interest. In response, we offer what we think is an undeniably effective answer delivered by Alan Schwartz, an influential banker, philanthropist, and longtime mentor: "Mentoring *doesn't* work. [Pause] *Quality* mentoring works."

Alan is noted for having a way with words, including an exceptional ability to penetrate to the core of a point by using just a few of them. His response does that by concentrating listeners on the central message of mentoring advocates, practitioners, and researchers: mentoring works under certain conditions. Those conditions embrace a host of variables, starting with the expectations of the adult and young person involved and including the quality of the supports available to a mentor and mentee pair during the course of their mentoring experience. So in short, the best way of responding to "Does it work?" is to consider the two closely related questions we address next.

QUESTION 6. *How does mentoring "work," and under what conditions does it work best?*

Based on the seminal research of Jean Rhodes, we know that mentoring is a mediated process in which the relationship itself serves as a development tool (Rhodes, 2002, 2005). This means that mentoring works *through* the vehicle of the unique relationship that develops between a particular mentor and a particular mentee: in other words, through the relationship that develops between you and your mentee. It also means that mentoring works when your relationship works. Since the mentor-mentee relationship stands at mentoring's core, it is vital to understand three things: what a good mentoring relationship looks like, what helps to create productive mentoring relationships, and what is likely to do the opposite.

This is an area where researchers have a great deal to offer current and aspiring mentors. Compelling research tells us that a meaningful relationship between a mentor and mentee is one marked by trust and mutual regard and understanding (Rhodes, 2002, 2005). Our experience tells us that productive mentoring relationships have another essential ingredient, namely, opportunities to have fun. Very few enduring mentoring relationships seem to last without it. There is also a strong and growing body of knowledge telling us that mentoring relationships are more likely to take root and thrive if (1) mentor-mentee expectations are aligned; (2) mentors and mentees are well matched, especially with respect to shared interests; (3) mentors have access to a support system that can help them prepare for the mentoring experience; (4) mentors are able to adopt a good mix of authority and friendship in their relations with their mentees; and (5) mentors have a source for and ongoing access to "advice and counsel" from those with the experience and expertise to help them employ best practices, avoid common pitfalls, and handle any rough spots that emerge.

In contrast, factors that we believe thwart the development of good working relationships relate to the most practical of considerations (Are you reliable?) and the decidedly personal (Are you mentoring to *help* a young person succeed or to *direct* his development?). Good working mentoring relationships rarely result when mentors find it hard to be where they say they will be . . . *when* they say they will be there. No doubt about it, reliability is key. Even more rarely do strong relationships result when mentors simply don't enjoy the company of young people or fancy themselves as drill sergeants assigned to shape kids up. Good mentoring is unlikely to be the product of a relationship in which the adult doesn't appreciate that young people are young people, with all the hopes, anxieties, energy, and routine highs and lows that attend the passage from childhood to young adulthood. In contrast, the mentors who are considered most successful are those characterized as "accepting young people on their own terms" (Philip & Hendry, 2001).

DATA POINT
Match Quality Matters

• Shared Interests: New research underscores that it is important to take account of similarities in the interests of potential mentor/mentee pairs *before* a mentoring match is made. Positive outcomes (measured by what researchers call "effect size" or "ES") doubled (from ES of .21 to ES of .44) when matching was based on shared interests.

• Mentor's Role: Researchers also found stronger effects in mentoring programs that are designed for mentors to serve as advocates for their mentees, as well as offer mentors active support if they take on the role of tutor, information resource, and so on.

Source: Dubois, Portillo, Rhodes, Silverthorn & Valentine (2011): 77 & 78.

• Mentor's Attitudes Toward Young People: Mentees paired with high school mentors with positive attitudes about young people were more emotinoally engaged with their mentors than those paired with those with negative attitudes toward their peers. In addition, young people paired with mentors who had negative attitudes were less emotionally engaged and experienced more negative outcomes from the mentoring experience.

Source: Karcher, Rhodes, Herrera & Davidson (2010).

So, it's important to reflect upon your inclinations before plunging in. It is equally important to note that research and longtime experience indicate that good mentoring relationships are a product of two things: doing and accomplishing things together (Hamilton & Hamilton, 2010) and time. In fact, the *duration of a mentoring relationship* may be the single best benchmark of mentoring effectiveness (Rhodes, 2002). Mentoring relationships that last less than a year generally produce few benefits for young people. But, of course, there are exceptions. These include mentoring programs that make it clear from the start that the mentoring relationship has a definite start and finish date or are quite narrowly focused, for instance a mentoring initiative designed to help a young person navigate the college application process (Keller & Pryce, 2010; Larose, Tarabulsky & Cyrene, 2005). Because of the centrality of the mentoring relationship, we devote a full chapter to the subject. Head to chapter 2 if you'd like to explore more detailed thinking now. Otherwise, read on.

QUESTION 7. *How do I know that mentoring really helps kids?*

Most adults mentor for one reason: they want to help kids. In fact, 82 percent of volunteers who responded to a national poll conducted by the Corporation for National and Community Service (2006) reported that what motivated them to mentor was a "desire to help young people succeed." This impulse is well placed, because research and experience tell us that mentoring can deliver important benefits to young people. And due to its inherent flexibility, mentoring can also create a close fit between the benefits that are delivered and those that young people actually want and need. Twenty years of research demonstrates that mentoring can help young people in two related ways. First, as Peter L. Benson, Richard Lerner, and others in the field of positive youth development (PYD) have established, mentoring fosters a young person's overall social and emotional development. As Lerner and his colleagues at Tufts University say, "In all settings, people are the most important developmental asset associated with PYD" (Theokas & Lerner, 2006).

Second, mentoring can help bring about changes in a young person's behavior, attitudes, health, and academic performance. For example, carefully done studies show that effectively mentored young people have fewer absences from school, better attitudes toward school, fewer incidents of hitting others, reductions in substance abuse and other high-risk behavior, better relations with peers, and more positive attitudes about helping others (Cavel, DuBois, Karcher & Rhodes, 2009; Jekielek, Moore, Hair & Scarupa, 2002). Two important megastudies, which gather and synthesize evidence from a large number of research studies, also support the contention that mentoring can improve outcomes for young people. The studies, led by David DuBois, University of Illinois at Chicago, are highlighted on the next page.

Our experience underscores these findings. Throughout both our personal and professional lives, we have seen scores of indelible examples of the impact that mentors have had in young people's lives. We will surely never forget our own mentors and have rarely met adults who are living

---

HIGHLIGHT
The Effectiveness of Mentoring Programs for Youth

"As in our prior review, the weight of the evidence we have reviewed supports the value of mentoring as an intervention strategy for enhancing young people's development. We find it particularly noteworthy that mentored youth have often benefited in more than one broad area of their development (e.g., social and academic), that program effects have tended to reflect a combination of both forward gains and avoidance of declines on outcomes, and that areas of positive impact have encompassed not only outcomes that tend to be seen as "soft" or subjective (e.g., attitudes) but also those typically regarded as "harder" or more objective (e.g., behavior, academic performance)." (73–74)

Source: DuBois, Portillo, Rhodes, Silverthorn, and Valentine (2011).

"From a development standpoint, we also find that benefits of participation in mentoring programs are apparent from early childhood to adolescence and thus not confined to a particular stage of development. Similarly, although programs typically have utilized adult volunteers and focused on cultivating 1-to-1 relationships, those that have engaged older peers as mentors or used group formats show comparable levels of effectiveness." (57)

Source: DuBois, Portillo, Rhodes, Silverthorn, and Valentine (2011).

"Findings of this investigation provide support for the effectiveness of youth mentoring programs. . . . Favorable effects of mentoring programs are similarly apparent across youth varying in demographic and background characteristics such as age, gender, race/ethnicity, and family structure and across differing types of outcomes that have been assessed using multiple sources of data. Although included in only a minority of studies, follow-up assessments that have been conducted also offer at least a limited basis for inferring benefits of mentoring that extend beyond the end of program participation. Cumulatively, based on available findings, it thus seems that youth mentoring programs do indeed have significant capacity to reproduce through more formal mechanisms the types of benefits that have been indicated to accrue from so-called natural mentoring relationship between youth and adults."

Source: Dubois, Holloway, Valentine & Cooper (2002).

---

satisfying lives who cannot point to the pivotal role a mentor (or mentors) played in their growing-up years. These were the adults, beyond their parents or caregivers, who took a special interest in them, recognized and encouraged an emerging talent, offered guidance at important turning points in their young lives, and last, but decidedly not least, cheered them on through the simple act of believing in and just plain liking them a lot. Most readers can cite similar examples of this phenomenon in their own lives or the lives of those close to them.

Yet, it is the exceptions to this pattern we remember most: people who told us they didn't have mentors, wished that they had, and regretted the lack to this day. Wintley Phipps, internationally recognized gospel artist, told an audience that he had no mentors when growing up and did what he now thought of as mentoring himself by listening to and learning from the recordings of great musicians. He added that he now recognized this as an important childhood void, and it was one of the things that motivated him to establish the U.S. Dream Academy, a respected source of tutorial and educational programming that includes mentoring opportunities. "The most important part of the program is really the caring, loving adults who surround these kids," Phipps has said.

Closer to home, we've had young people—especially those who have had a very hard time finding a place in the world—tell us how much they wanted a competent adult (or even a reasonably competent one) who would take an active interest in them. And this applies to the very young people few would guess actually *want* more adults in their lives. In a sea of tremendously bright and articulate young people assembled at a conference sponsored by Dorothy Stoneman of YouthBuild USA, the one who moved us most was a young girl with the least polished delivery: "I'm in a school filled with adults who walk by us every day," she said. "Can't they see? Can't they see we need help?" Have no doubt, adults who *can see* know that pairing a caring adult with a young person really can help.

Nonetheless, we also want to underscore that while we believe both experience and research illustrate that strong mentoring relationships can deliver real and meaningful benefits to young people, *any* activity of *any* quality that operates under the term "mentoring" does not automatically lead to positive outcomes. Nor, as the same megastudies cited earlier demonstrate, does mentoring typically lead to sea changes in a young person's attitudes or behavior. In fact, changes that do occur are typically modest in scope and intensity, particularly in short-term relationships (DuBois et al., 2011). Furthermore, poor-quality mentoring not only fails to make good on the promise of benefits, it may cause real harm (Rhodes, 2002).

Bear these points in mind when embarking on a mentoring relationship. We expect you will find that most mentoring relationships deliver for kids, especially if they are carefully established and guided. Nonetheless, few will dramatically *transform* young lives. It is a mistake to expect this outcome. Instead, mentors should expect to *contribute* to a young person's life in meaningful and frequently important ways that advance a young person's development and interests—an outcome that in and of itself is worth a mentor's time . . . a mentee's, too.

Finally, when mentors ask, "Does mentoring help kids?" what they are most interested in is whether mentoring helps their own mentees. If that is a question that interests you, take a look at Question 28.

QUESTION 8. *Are there different kinds of mentoring . . . or different kinds of mentoring programs?*

There are not different kinds of mentoring. Mentoring is a process that works as we describe in Question 6. But there can be differences in what mentoring aims to achieve, as well as differences in the contexts in which mentoring takes place. In fact, these contexts are quite diverse, and we regard that fact as one of the strengths of mentoring. Such diversity provides for the widely varying needs and interests of mentees and the equally wide and varying abilities and interests of mentors. It also has resulted in many different kinds of mentoring programs—a bonus for mentors and mentees alike. A summary of program aims and important contextual factors follows.

Program Aims

The terminology used by youth development experts to describe mentoring's aim generally divides the subject into two categories: *personal* or *instrumental.* While these descriptors leave much to be desired, they do give you a way to think about whether the mentoring you are engaged in (1) aims to help a young person develop specific skills or abilities or achieve a specific objective *or* (2) aims to help them to develop more general traits like competence and character. If you are concentrating on overall youth development, you are engaged in personal mentoring. If your goal is more narrowly focused skill development, you are engaged in mentoring with instrumental aims. And if—as is often the case—your mentee is aiming toward general and specific developmental objectives, you are doing both. Here are a few examples:

> *Personal mentoring*: Big Brothers Big Sisters' traditional model and that of the Across Ages program, an intergenerational program that pairs young people with older adults (that is, seniors).

> *Instrumental mentoring*: Communities In Schools of Peninsula's Math Mentor Program (Vaughn, Washington), which matches trained adult mentors with middle school students who are at risk of academic failure in math.

> *Hybrid of personal and instrumental mentoring*: Mentoring USA's mentoring program, which aims to improve both academic achievement and a young person's overall social and emotional well-being.

Contextual Factors

> *Age* of the mentee. Clearly, mentoring an 8-year-old will be very different from mentoring a 17-year-old. The developmental needs of children vary dramatically by age group, and we explore this vital topic more thoroughly in chapter 7. Typically, mentoring younger children tends to focus on doing things together in order to develop certain skills or just have fun, while mentoring older young people is likely to focus on helping them explore the world of work or prepare for further schooling or a transition to the work force.

> S*pecial characteristics* of the mentee or the mentee's circumstances. Some mentees, because of their status as members of any number of minority or special-interest groups, are most interested in mentoring or mentoring programs that are particularly mindful of or knowledgeable about their life situations. So, you will find mentoring experiences geared, for example, to the science minded; the sports minded; gifted and talented kids or those with intellectual or physical disabilities; African Americans, American Indians, Latinos, and Asian Americans; gay, lesbian, and transgender young people; or young people who, like Wintley Phipps, are moved by music and the arts. You also will see some mentoring programs intentionally target young people who are facing particularly tough circumstances—children who are placed in foster care, have parents who are in prison, or have been assigned to a group home or juvenile detention facility.

> *Site*: If you are involved in a formal mentoring program, you might hear it referred to as a school-based, workplace-based, or online- or e-based program; a faith-based program; or a community-based program. The first three terms tell you just one thing: where the programs take place. They don't tell you anything about the nature of the programs. "Faith based" indicates one or two things: the program takes place in a church, mosque, synagogue, or other place of wor-

ship, and/or is grounded in or geared toward either a general (in the case of the Salvation Army) or particular (in the case of the mentoring programs of Prison Fellowship) set of religious beliefs. Despite its apparent breadth, the term "community based" usually means that the mentoring experience takes place wherever the mentor and mentee agree to meet (in keeping with parameters set by particular formal mentoring programs) and applies, of course, to the site(s) of informal mentoring. Community-based programs also include mentoring that takes place within the context of child development agencies and organizations. A prime example would be mentoring in after-school or other positive youth development programs, like 4-H or the Scouts. We are especially keen on mentoring that takes place in this context, since these programs can augment mentoring with other resources young people want and enjoy.

> *Ratio of mentors to mentees*: Most mentoring programs, along with mentoring done informally, pair one mentor with one mentee. But there are variations. As the names suggest, *group or team* mentoring programs pair either one mentee with a group of adults or pair a group of adults with a group of young people. One excellent example is LA Team Mentoring.

> *Level of formality*: As discussed in Question 2, some mentoring occurs within the context of a formalized mentoring program while other kinds occur outside the bounds of any formal institutional ties.

As you can see, there are lots of options and ways to help young people develop to their fullest potential. To get a sense of the full range of mentoring programs operating today, we again recommend you visit MENTOR's Volunteer Referral Service at www.mentoring.org/get_involved. Even if you don't intend to volunteer right now, the profiles MENTOR offers on nearly 5,000 mentoring programs provide an up-to-the-minute picture of what modern youth mentoring looks like.

QUESTION 9. *What do mentors do with their mentees?*

This question worries a lot of mentors because they imagine themselves stranded in a room with a young person who either just stares at them or can, at best, manage only a one- or two-word response to any attempt at conversation. This scenario does arise, but believe us, it is preventable—or at the least is one you can successfully negotiate, especially with help of Michael Karcher and those who have studied the "I dunno, what do you want to do?" syndrome (Karcher, 2010; Karcher, Herrera & Hansen, 2011). We discuss this more in Question 22 and in chapter 7 (in the context of stages of youth development) in part II, "Resources for Strong Mentors."

At this stage, we hope you will bear three things in mind. First, forget yourself for a bit. Many mentors worry that they will fail the kids they are mentoring or that their mentees will think they are "uncool." On the latter count, harbor no doubt. All but the youngest mentees will not think you are cool (happening, hip, groovy, awesome, da bomb, sweet, or whatever word applies in your own generational lingo). "Cool," however, is not what most young people seek. They are looking for adults who have a genuine interest in them and are competent enough in the ways of the world to help them get where they want to go. If you listen, they will find a way to tell you what they want to do. Let their interests be your guide. The same caution applies to your fear that you will fail them. If you are genuinely dedicated and prepared, you will not let them down. Second, if you are in a formal mentoring program, have confidence in the structured training and activities offered by your program coordinator. Most are good, and many are getting even better at ensuring that you get the training and ongoing support needed to address the "what to do" question. And, finally, for those readers who are now mentoring, review the material in chapters 2 and 8 extra carefully. There's a lot to be learned from the experience of other mentors and those who support them.

QUESTION 10. *We live in a lawsuit-happy world. Should I be worried about liability issues?*

Do not worry, but do be prudent. Prudence requires that that you take the following actions. First, if you are mentoring in a formal mentoring program or are planning to be, actively participate in a screening process. *Elements of Effective Practice for Mentoring,* Third Edition (2009), recommends that all prospective mentors be screened to determine whether they have the time, commitment, and personal qualities to be good mentors. This process typically starts with the completion of a written application and includes at least one face-to-face interview and a personal and professional reference check, although in workplace mentoring programs the

MENTORING U.S.A. VOLUNTEER MENTOR APPLICATION (Excerpt)

Name: _____

Home Address (Street Address, City, State, Postal Code): _____

_____

Home Phone No. _____ E-mail Address: _____

Affiliation/Employer: _____ Title/Position Held: _____

Work Address (Street Address, City, State, Postal Code): _____

Work Phone No. _____ E-mail Address: _____

Supervisor's Name: _____ Years at current employer: _____

Does your employer promote volunteer activities? ☐ yes ☐ no

Previous Employer (if less than 3 years at current position): _____

Address: _____ Years at this employer: _____

How do you identify yourself: gender and/or religious and ethnic heritage (optional)?

_____

_____

High School Attended: _____ Year of Graduation: _____

College Attended: _____ Degree: _____

Other Education and/or Special Training: _____

_____

Do you speak any languages other than English? If so, please indicate:

_____

Do you have prior Volunteer Experience? ☐ yes ☐ no

Have you applied to be a mentor with Mentoring USA in the past? ☐ yes ☐ no

Mentoring Site Preference

Please list 3 locations from the Site List where you would like to mentor. Please consider the type of program you would like to join (General, ESL, Foster Care), and the meeting time/location most convenient for you.

_____

_____

_____

Application Questions

Your responses to the following questions will help us determine whether you are a good fit for Mentoring USA's program and match you with a mentee.

1. Do you have any previous experience volunteering or working with youth?
2. What qualities, skills, or other attributes do you feel you have that would benefit a youth?
3. What do you think will be most challenging about being a mentor?
4. What do you hope to gain from becoming a mentor?
5. Do you have an age preference for your mentee?
6. Do you have any disabilities that may affect your involvement in the program?
7. Are you an adopted adult or have you been through the foster care system?
    If so, do you have an interest in working with kids in care?

References

Please list 3 references who you have known for at least 1 year. One of these references must be your current supervisor, if applicable. Relatives or family members cannot be used as references. Please give complete addresses and phone numbers. References will be contacted by phone or mail. The information furnished to us by your references will remain strictly confidential.

_____

_____

_____

Background Screening

Mentoring USA's mentors work with children. Therefore, we are required to screen our volunteers. Please respond to the following questions, read this Agreement and Consent and sign below.

Name: _____   Date of Birth: _____

Gender: _____   Driver's License # _____

Have you ever been charged/indicted for any crime? If yes, please supply details (date, charge, disposition). _____

_____

Have you changed your name? If so, please provide previous name: _____

Have you lived at your current residential address for less than one year? If so, please provide previous address(es): _____

_____

Signature: _____   Date: _____

Source: Mentoring USA (2011). Reprinted in condensed form with permission.

latter is sometimes replaced by the employee screening process that applies. For a complete list of the screening benchmarks in the *Elements,* see chapter 6. For an idea of the kind of application form you may be asked to complete, see the Mentoring USA form highlighted on pages 22–23. It is also important to note that many mentoring programs now also conduct criminal background checks (more on this in Question 11).

The second action you should take is to be sure that the program you are working with provides liability insurance for its mentors *and* that you fully understand the extent of your liability and dimensions of any coverage that is offered. Strong mentoring programs cover this subject in mentor orientation sessions. If your program or program coordinator does not do so, raise the question and get an answer that satisfies you. We can only cite two instances during our long careers in which a mentor was sued by the mentee or the mentee's family (in both instances, very sadly, the suits related to sexual harassment or assault), but that doesn't mean you should feel released from the obligation of understanding the liability issue. Doing so is likely to ease rather than exacerbate concerns, since you are likely to find that the liability issues that most worry mentors (e.g., that their mentee will be hurt in an accident in their company) rarely occur and are almost always covered by either the program or your personal liability insurance, which most adults now have.

If you are mentoring informally (remember, this means mentoring outside the boundaries of any mentoring program or youth development program that incorporates mentoring), the liability issues you face are exactly the same as those you face in everyday life and everyday relationships with family members, friends, and colleagues—young or old. If you have given sufficient thought to liability matters generally, liability concerns should not be a reason to avoid mentoring a young person informally. Embrace the opportunity to mentor a young person, as long as you can spend the time required to be a good one.

QUESTION 11. *The program I am mentoring in (or want to mentor in) requires a background check. Is this common?*

Almost all mentoring programs require a background check and, as noted earlier, these typically rely on the contents of a formal application to mentor (as discussed in Question 10), along with personal and professional references that prospective mentors (or their places of employment) provide.

Many mentoring programs in the United States also require a criminal background check. If your program does, it is representative of the mainstream. Some criminal background checks are cursory (asking you to list charges filed and explain their disposition); others are quite comprehensive. A comprehensive criminal background check includes a fingerprint check, with the best ones using a national fingerprint-based FBI criminal background check system.

Sadly, criminal background checks are an important and necessary precaution. Analyses show that it is vital to gain access to both state and national criminal records for the simple reason that people move, and state registries may not provide a complete picture of a potential mentor's criminal history (MENTOR, 2011). We favor a criminal background check called SafetyNET, but, regrettably, as of March 31, 2011, it was no longer operating. Efforts are under way in the U.S. Congress to restore SafetyNET programming through the Child Protection Improvements Act of 2011; this legislation was introduced by a bipartisan group of dedicated sponsors in both the U.S. House of Representatives and the U.S. Senate. We look forward to the day when Congress will make permanent a system of timely and inexpensive checks for mentors and other volunteers who work with young people. Meanwhile, you can keep track of developments via MENTOR's Advocacy Network (mentoring.org/get_involved/advocate).

DATA POINT
Results of the SafetyNET Pilot Project

In a test of a fingerprint-based FBI background check system (i.e., the former SafetyNET system operating under the auspices of the PROTECT Act and coordinated by MENTOR), 6.1 percent of the 105,000 prospective mentors who submitted applications had criminal records of concern. This includes serious offenses like rape, murder, and child sexual abuse. Also, 42 percent of those with negative results had criminal records in a state other than the one where they were applying, while 23 percent showed a different name on their record from the one used to apply.

Source: MENTOR (2011).

QUESTION 12. *My mentoring program requires that I participate in training sessions, which I don't think I need. Should I go?*

No matter how brilliant, experienced, and well intentioned you are, you will benefit from the mentor orientation and training sessions offered by the program in which you are participating. This is true even if you find the training weak, amateurish, or in any other respect not what you hoped it would be. Even flawed training provides the opportunity to meet other mentors and get to know your program coordinator. Happily, most mentoring programs offer strong training, especially those that are guided by MENTOR's *Elements of Effective Practice for Mentoring,* Third Edition (2009). The *Elements* recommends that mentors participate in a minimum of two hours of pre-match, in-person training grounded in evidence-based methods and materials; and it urges mentoring programs to offer additional training (either in person or online) to all active mentors. Basic mentor training should include an overview of program rules and mentor obligations; mentors' goals and expectations for the mentoring relationship; appropriate mentor roles; how best to develop and maintain a relationship with a mentee; ethical issues that may arise; how to effectively close the mentoring relationship when its agreed upon course has been completed; and sources of ongoing assistance to support mentors, including the name and contact information for the program coordinator.

Those mentoring in formal mentoring programs and those who are mentoring informally also have access to a growing number of mentor training opportunities that focus on the "what if" and "how to" issues that interest many mentors. For example, many mentoring programs and some community colleges offer "beyond the basics" mentor training that is open to any interested mentor (or potential one), focusing on mentoring children and adolescents in certain age groups. If you live in a state or region that has a Mentoring Partnership (see listing in chapter 8), find out whether they offer training sessions that are open to mentors from many different programs. One good example: the offerings of the Mentoring Partnership of Long Island's Mentoring Academy.

Online training also is available on a limited basis—directly through some mentoring programs (e.g., iMentor.org) and through Innovation Research & Training (IRT) and Education Northwest (check out "Talking it Through: Communication Skills for Mentors" at talkingitthrough.educationnorthwest.org). IRT's training, called Mentoring Central, is an especially strong resource for those who are either thinking about becoming a mentor or just starting a new mentoring relationship. This Web-based interactive training is based on *Elements of Effective Practice for Mentoring, Third Edition*, has benefited from rigorous testing, and is likely to grow even better over the next few years as new topic areas are added. Find out more about Mentoring Central by visiting mentoringcentral.net.

In summary, good training to help you become a strong mentor is available, and both the scope and the quality of training are on the rise. If training is not presented to you through a formal mentoring program, find it elsewhere, and make use of it. Both you and your mentee will be beneficiaries.

QUESTION 13. *I want to connect with other mentors. How do I do that?*

First, follow your impulse to connect with other mentors. Doing so is important, and it is almost always rewarding. According to MENTOR, when mentors and potential mentors are asked, they invariably say they rely on other mentors—especially more experienced mentors—when they want to think through an issue or get advice about a specific challenge or need that arises in their mentoring relationship.

We view other mentors as one of three sources of support and advice that can be very useful to you as you embark on a mentoring relationship and move through it. Two others are a mentoring program coordinator (if you are mentoring through a formal program and one has been made available to you) and people in your personal or virtual network who are willing to be sounding boards or offer counsel when you need it. For more on how to activate all three resources, see the "People to Talk To" section in chapter 8. For additional thinking about what you can expect from the person who can play a supporting role in the life of a mentor, see Question 14. It outlines exactly what you can expect from a mentoring program coordinator. And, finally, look once again to your Mentoring Partnership if you have one in your state (see chapter 8 for a listing). Many can offer ideas— or actual opportunities—to connect with other mentors. And, check out what they offer online: two great examples: the Mentoring Partnership of Minnesota's website, which has a dedicated section for mentors (www .mpmn.org/Resources/ForMentors.aspx); and the Mentoring Partnership of Long Island (mentorkids.org) for highly practical downloadable resources like "SAT Test Prep for English Language Users."

> **⊹ DATA POINT**
> ## Mentors Look for Expertise
>
> Of those considering becoming mentors, 83 percent reported that getting expert help when needed—including from other mentors—would encourage them to become a mentor.
>
> Source: MENTOR (2005).

QUESTION 14. *I'm involved in a formal mentoring program. What should I expect from the program coordinator?*

Most formal mentoring programs have a volunteer or paid staff person who will be a mentor's principal connection to the mentoring program. While the *program coordinator* in your program may carry a different title, he or she is the key player on mentoring's front line: among the first people you meet when you sign up to be a mentor and the last you are likely to see at the conclusion of your mentoring assignment. And whether your program coordinator is a great professional or leaves a lot to be desired, the role that person fills is pivotal. You are right to be interested in what you can expect from the program coordinator and should know how to fill in the gaps if the help you need isn't there to be had.

Typically, a program coordinator handles most of the best practices outlined in *Elements of Effective Practice for Mentoring.* He or she plays a role in mentor recruitment, screening, orientation, and training; frequently takes the lead in making the match between you and your mentee; and is almost always the person who monitors your ongoing relationship and offers support (or avenues to support) throughout. You can use the information excerpted from the *Elements* that appears in chapter 6 to assess whether your mentoring coordinator is performing these functions in keeping with evidence-based practices. And bear in mind that while all the functions are important, once you begin mentoring, ongoing support will be the one that matters most. Whether mentors take advantage of the available support, most agree that it is vital to know they have someone to turn to if they can't get their relationship off the ground, could use a sounding board, need a referral for a service they think their mentee needs, want help in resolving a specific issue, or just need to double-check that their mentoring relationship is on the right track.

Be assured that most program coordinators live up to their billing: they are resources who can actually be counted on to provide support. They are not only skilled at performing all the tasks outlined here, but many also have been mentors and bring big hearts and real-life mentoring experience to their assignments. But two caveats apply. Most mentoring program co-ordinators have more mentor matches to support than is optimal, which means the level of support they can offer sometimes may be less than optimal as well. You might also get a coordinator who is neither skilled enough to handle the job nor motivated enough to ask for help and learn how. If that is the case, we urge you to let your program coordinator know that you are not getting what you think you need. Most coordinators genuinely want to know, and those who don't want to know especially need the feedback. If that doesn't help, head up the staff or volunteer chain to ask for whatever assistance you need. And, if that doesn't yield the required results either, we return once again to ideas about forming and using your ongoing personal support network (see chapter 8).

QUESTION 15. *I mentor informally. Is there any support out there for me?*

Mentors typically rely on three sources of ongoing support: their program coordinator, other mentors, and their personal and professional networks. If you are mentoring informally, your backup system is necessarily limited to two of the three. You won't have a program coordinator to call upon (and that is generally an inestimable loss). But you can—like all mentors— look to other mentors and your own networks for the help you are likely to want and may need, such as good sounding boards and some voices of experience, as well as advice tied to resolving a specific challenge (or op-portunity) facing you and your mentee.

Ideas about how to engage and activate these resources were covered in Questions 12 and 13 and are addressed in chapter 8 (see the sections "People to Talk To" and "Organizations That Can Help"). We hope you will take a close look. Other mentors and family members, friends, and col-leagues can be tremendously useful resources as you initiate and move through the experience of mentoring a young person. And don't overlook the growing number of mentor training opportunities (see Question 12). Many are now open to those who are mentoring informally, as well as to those who are mentoring through formal mentoring or youth develop-ment programs. Once again, material in chapter 8 provides specifics.

QUESTION 16. *Where can I get specialized advice on a specific issue if I need it?*

Almost all mentors reach a point when they need help with a specific situation or issue affecting their mentee. So what's important here is preparedness: knowing ahead of time where to turn or to whom to turn to find specialized advice. We refer you back to Questions 13, 14, and 15 for ways to establish your own support network, as well as the sources of specialized advice offered in chapters 3, 4, 5, and 8.

QUESTION 17. *What if a young person asks me to be her or his mentor?*

Your first response should be to say that you are honored. Treat the request with the responsiveness and respect it deserves, letting the young person know that you are pleased to be asked and want to know more about what he or she has in mind. Then pitch right into that conversation. Once you do and have made—either on the spot or over time—an assessment of the obligations such a role will entail and whether you can fulfill them, you have two equally good options. You can deliver an enthusiastic yes. Or you can explain why you are not the right person for the role but can help the young person think it through and find someone who is a good match (assuming you can actually provide this sort of assistance). There is also a third option that allows you to treat the request with the seriousness it deserves. If, whether for personal or professional reasons, you just can't serve as a mentor or offer the young person help in finding one, be direct and explain why in as much detail as the situation allows. In this circumstance, as in many others, we subscribe to the principle that a short no is better than a long maybe.

It is also important to note that formal mentoring programs that rely on young people to recruit their own mentors are building track records of success. David Van Patten, president and CEO of Dare Mighty Things and an expert in the field of youth-recruited mentors, explains the thinking behind this approach: the odds are greater that a young person will connect with a person he chooses, since it is highly likely that the possible mentor will be someone he already likes and respects. To date, one major test of this approach is being conducted by the National Guard Youth ChalleNGe Program. Findings suggest mixed results for this dimension of the program (Millenky, Bloom & Dillon, 2010; Millenky, Bloom, Muller-Ravett & Broadus, 2011), but it is a concept worth watching.

QUESTION 18. *Will I be a good mentor?*

We love this question and love the would-be mentors who ask it, because we are convinced that if you are putting thought into this issue, the odds are high that you can be a great mentor to a young person. Why? Experience tells us that the very worst mentors are those who move into the mentoring experience with supreme confidence and the unyielding belief that they are exactly the kind of "adult influence" that young people need. And, as we noted in Question 4, research underscores this point.

All potential mentors should ask themselves, and ask seriously, whether they will be good mentors. There are several ways to explore this question:

1. Turn the research on the attributes of good mentors into questions. For example, consider the following: Do I have the time to be a reliable partner to a young person? Do I enjoy (or think I will) spending time with a young person? Am I able to set boundaries on the relationship in a way that keeps it on track? Do I want to mentor because I want to help a young person find and pursue her own ambitions or because I have important lessons I think every young person needs to hear?

2. Tell a friend or family member whose judgment you trust that you are thinking about becoming a mentor, and listen to that person's feedback.

3. Talk with mentors and see whether their experiences make you want to participate in mentoring firsthand.

4. Read a published account of a mentoring experience, for example, Ron Suskind's *A Hope in the Unseen.*

If you are in a formal mentoring program, review the application and screening process described in Questions 11 and 12 to continue to explore the question. The opportunity to do so is one of the great benefits of mentoring through a formal program. Bear in mind that if you didn't give yourself an A+ on any of these self-administered tests, it doesn't mean you don't have what it takes to be a terrific mentor. It probably bodes well. Kids aren't perfect and aren't looking for perfection in their mentors. They are looking for people who have a genuine interest in them, like them, and are willing to learn about them and about how to be helpful to them.

Finally, remember that even if you decide mentoring isn't for you, your desire to help young people is a wonderful and well-aimed one. There are many ways to act on that impulse, starting with taking on a different kind of volunteer assignment at a mentoring program that interests you (e.g., organizing data that tracks the mentoring program's operations and outcomes or helping to set up training and other events for mentors and mentees). Most programs are keenly interested in building their corps of dedicated volunteers and will warmly welcome you in a supportive capacity.

HIGHLIGHT
Will I Be a Good Mentor?

Basketball legend and mentoring leader Bill Russell firmly believes and has always demonstrated that "it takes a strong man to be kind." Of course, he applies that thinking to women, too, and he frequently askes would-be mentors if they have the "strength to be kind." So, if you are thinking about becoming a mentor, consider this: do you have the kind of strength it takes to be kind?

Source: Bill Russell, 2004.

QUESTIONS ABOUT THE MENTORING RELATIONSHIP

I love my relationship with Coach Vermeil because
it is one of the few genuine relationships I have.

DANTE HALL, NFL GREAT AND ACCLAIMED RETURN SPECIALIST

This chapter concentrates on factors that help build effective mentoring relationships. As we discussed in the preceding chapter (see especially Question 6 on how mentoring works), mentoring depends on a *relationship* between a mentor and young person (mentee) undertaken for the express purpose of supporting that young person's social, emotional, and intellectual development. Like all relationships, its quality depends on a strong foundation of trust, respect, and feelings of connection to one another. It is further enhanced by enjoying each other's company, having fun together, and being able to negotiate and agree on the basics of how the relationship will function. As we all quickly learn, relationships of this caliber rarely just happen, so let's turn to what helps things along.

Research, along with our own experiences as mentors—Gail as a mentor with Everybody Wins! USA and Susan as a mentor (with her husband) of five inner-city minority kids—tells us that mentoring works best when the following five conditions prevail:

> The relationship lasts long enough and contact is frequent enough for a strong feeling of connection to develop.

> Mentors go into the relationship with realistic expectations. They take the commitment seriously and understand that the relationship should be focused on the needs of the mentee, not those of the mentor.

> Mentors respect the integrity, culture, and rights of their mentees and their mentees' families.

> Mentors understand that their role is to be a "coach" or "guide," not to replicate the roles of parents, guardians, or teachers.

> Mentors are trustworthy, consistent, patient, and willing to be persistent in the face of setbacks or feelings of discouragement.

A mentor's efforts to establish each of these conditions typically lead to questions like the ones that follow. You will note that our answers assume you have access to a program coordinator (as described in Questions 8 and 14) for support and advice. If you are mentoring informally or if the program through which you mentor is loosely organized and lacks a designated program coordinator, we recommend that you identify a knowledgeable adult you can turn to for support and advice—an educator, youth worker, or member of the clergy, for example. While many mentoring relationships proceed without significant challenges, you will benefit from someone who can provide perspective and guidance if you hit a rocky patch or face a tough problem (see more on these in chapters 4 and 5). We also hope you will seek out the opportunities to participate in a training program to prepare for your mentoring experience (see Question 12). And don't fail to take full advantage of the supplementary resources described in part II.

QUESTION 19. *What should my expectations be for my relationship with a mentee?*

Like most mentors, you probably went into this out of a desire to make a difference in a young person's life. Your desire to help is truly a gift to your mentee, but chances are that you were not exactly sure what "making a difference" looks like. You may have had very modest expectations, such as exposing your mentee to new experiences, or you may have had visions of your mentee achieving high levels of success as an adult. You also may be in a mentoring program that has explicit goals on which you are expected to focus, such as improving school performance or supporting the transition from foster care to independent living. There are many areas in which you can support your mentee. You may find it helpful to refer to chapter 7 and review Search Institute's framework of 40 Developmental Assets for some ideas.

No matter how long you have been in a mentoring relationship, it helps to step back now and then to examine your expectations: What do you want from the relationship, and what do you think your mentee wants? What exactly are you hoping to achieve? How do you or your mentee want your mentee's life or behaviors to change because of you? How do you or your mentee define success? How does your role as a friend or "coach" call for a different approach to "helping" than that used by a parent, teacher, or professional youth worker?

The more specific you can be in answering these questions, the better you can assess whether your expectations are realistic. In "It's Not What I Expected" (2007), Boston College's Renée Spencer demonstrates how counterproductive it can be when mentors fail to establish reasonable expectations for themselves, for their mentee, and for their relationship. But always remember, it is your mentee's expectations that should drive the relationship, not yours.

Depending on the age of your mentee, you can also mutually set expectations for the relationship. You can ask questions such as, "What would you like to get out of our relationship?" "What kinds of things would you like to do with me?" "Is there anything in your life right now that I can help you with?" "What are your dreams?" "What are your biggest frustrations?" These discussions can set the stage for helping you focus your expectations and helping your mentee think about how to benefit from the relationship with you. These questions can be explored even if the mentoring program already has specific goals like the ones mentioned earlier.

It is also particularly important to focus your expectations on developing feelings of trust and closeness in the early stages of your relationship (see additional information in Question 20 about stages of the mentoring relationship). Building the relationship is the most important work you will do as a mentor, and the most successful relationships are those in which mentors take their lead from their mentees.

While it is natural to have goals for the child you want to help, trying to push your mentee to achieve your goals will not only make you seem more like a teacher or parent than a friend, it may also impede the development of the very type of relationship that can be most helpful. There is a further risk, too. Mentors who go into mentoring with an agenda to "change" the mentee run the risk of feeling frustrated, disappointed, and rejected if the hoped-for changes do not materialize. These feelings, in turn, can lead the mentor to conclude that she is being ineffective or that the relationship is not working. Such feelings may be unintentionally conveyed to the mentee, or worse, may lead the mentor to give up on the relationship, thus inadvertently hurting rather than helping the mentee.

One mentor referred to expectations as the Achilles' heel of mentoring. What he meant was that your expectations and the reality of mentoring may not be in sync after you are in an actual relationship. This discrepancy can lead to feelings of inadequacy on your part and to feelings of frustration or defensiveness in your mentee. And it makes it easy to forget that it is the relationship that is the transformative element in your mentee's life, not actions you take to improve your mentee's life. Further, it is possible you will never know about the real changes that have taken place unless you happen to see your mentee many years later, and he or she thanks you.

You will be most successful when you keep your goals "on the back burner" so that you can focus on helping your mentee establish his own goals and then provide the support and guidance needed to achieve them. This is a fine balancing act, since you may see possibilities for your mentee that he would not see. If you do want to help your mentee raise his aspirations, you can do this most effectively if you "guide" rather than push. Check out resources like the *K–12 Journey Map* (www.mpmn.org /Resources/ForMentors.aspx). It is also very important to remember that mentoring cannot take the place of professional treatment that a troubled young person may need.

QUESTION 20. *Are there typical stages in the life cycle of a mentoring relationship?*

Most mentoring relationships go through predictable stages, although these stages can take differing amounts of time and do not necessarily proceed in a straight line. The length of the relationship also will influence how far you get in these stages, which is why researchers recommend that the relationship last at least a year.

There are many ways to describe stages of development. We have used a six-stage framework developed by Susan Murphy and Ellen Ensher, as outlined in *Stand by Me* (Rhodes, 2002) and described in the following pages: introductions, relationship building, growth, maturation, transition, and termination. Another good overview of mentoring stages, by Thomas Keller of Portland State University, appears in *The Handbook of Youth Mentoring* (Dubois & Karcher, 2005). Both models make it clear that each stage has its own challenges, tasks, and rewards. And although the issues from one stage may continue to surface in the next, you should feel some sense of progress in the relationship. As in all relationships, there will be rough patches and problems that arise during which your commitment and persistence will be tested. If, no matter what you do, you continue to be uncomfortable with the way things are going, consult your program coordinator sooner rather than later.

The Introductory Stage: The primary objectives are for you and your mentee to get to know one another and begin establishing a sense of trust and connection. Because you are just learning things about each other and a low level of trust is likely, you may experience feelings of discomfort with one another in this early stage. If your mentee is shy, it may take weeks or even months before she is comfortable talking much with you.

Two things are particularly important at this stage: for you to be reliable, predictable, and consistent in showing up for meetings and to involve your mentee in deciding how you will spend your time together. However, mentees in this stage may be less reliable and may forget to show up or call you. The reason for this may be as simple as just forgetting a new routine in their lives, or it may be that they are "testing" you to see whether you are really committed to the relationship. Young people who have had prior disappointments with adults may take longer to begin to trust and may engage in more testing behavior.

It can be helpful if you think about some fun, structured things for your mentee to choose from during these early sessions of getting together, such as "getting to know you" activities, playing a game together, or doing something active like going to a park. Be flexible in changing plans and activities if they don't seem to be working. Try to avoid bombarding your mentee with questions, and be particularly careful not to dominate the conversation. Ask open-ended questions about what he likes (music, TV shows, games, sports) to better understand his interests, and encourage him to think about things he would like to do with you. Try to find common ground in things you both enjoy.

It is also important to be nonjudgmental at this and all subsequent stages, even though you may be surprised by or uncomfortable with your mentee's language or behaviors. It is OK to be clear about appropriate behavior and to set simple consequences for misbehavior—ending an activity that is producing the misbehavior, for example. Your mentee will almost certainly test you to see what behaviors you are willing to accept, so be consistent in your responses. Avoid canceling get-togethers as a punishment; it is counterproductive and likely to delay relationship development significantly. At the right moment, it is also appropriate to explain, in terms the mentee can understand, the boundaries of your relationship (see Question 21 on boundaries).

Once your mentee begins to open up a little, you can talk about the special nature of your relationship and convey that you will not be telling your mentee's parents or teachers about your conversations. If your mentee is old enough to understand this point, explain the few circumstances in which you would have to break confidentiality, specifically if your mentee or someone else were in danger of being seriously hurt (see Question 43 on confidentiality). This conversation may occur in this or the next stage.

The Relationship-Building Stage: The primary objective in this stage is to solidify the sense of closeness and trust you began to establish in stage 1. This is best achieved by doing things together that are mutually enjoyable, foster a sense of attachment, and build shared memories. You may even go through a sort of "honeymoon" period as many relationships do when two people are growing closer.

You can begin to suggest things that will expand your mentee's range of experiences, such as going to a museum, but continue to let your mentee make decisions about how you spend time together. If you are mentoring in a school or other setting where some of the activities you do together are already defined, try to expand on these with other activities whose sole purpose is having fun. Never underestimate the power of having fun together!

By now you should have a regular schedule for getting together, although the mentee may still occasionally be unreliable. As in the previous stage, mentor consistency, reliability, and persistence will help carry the relationship through any rough spots that may occur.

Don't feel pressured to get your mentee to "open up," but rather do things together that naturally lead to opportunities for conversation. Each relationship progresses at its own pace; it may sometimes feel that you are going back a step for every two steps you move forward. And sometimes you will simply not see any external sign that your mentee is growing close to and being positively influenced by you. We have all heard the stories of the young person who comes back years later to tell an adult how much that person meant in her life, much to the adult's surprise.

If you are feeling that you are not connecting at this stage, it is important to speak with your program coordinator (see also Question 26 on not connecting).

The Growth Stage: During this stage, your objectives are to encourage and support your mentee's social, emotional, and cognitive (or intellectual) growth. By now you and your mentee should be pretty comfortable with each other and find that conversation comes easily. You will find yourself truly enjoying each other's company, and your mentee will be more comfortable opening up with you. Continue with activities you both enjoy, and add new age-appropriate activities that will help your mentee develop socially, emotionally, and intellectually.

You may also find that your mentee starts to talk to you about little problems he is having. If you can control the impulse to give advice or fix whatever is bothering your mentee, you have a wonderful opportunity to guide him in developing problem-solving skills he can use for the rest of his life. You can also be an advocate for your mentee, helping him access additional support or help that may be needed. Dan Mulhern, former First Gentleman of Michigan and chair of Mentor Michigan, has a terrific way to curb the impulse to pepper your mentee with streams of unsolicited advice. Say something like, "I had some experience with that problem myself. So if you want to talk about that at some point, just let me know." This gives the mentee more control over when to seek advice and helps him learn how to ask for help, rather than waiting for someone to deliver it.

Ironically, increased trust and closeness may cause your mentee to bring up sensitive topics for which you may feel unprepared. Your mentee may also want you to be involved in helping her address a more significant life challenge, such as being bullied or dealing with a family problem. This is where your role as a "sounding board" can be most valuable. Do not be tempted to solve the problem for your mentee, no matter how much it distresses you. Rather, guide your mentee to find solutions on her own. Your program coordinator can help you sort out how to respond to these situations if you feel unsure of how to proceed. He or she also can involve the family or other resources as needed and appropriate (see also Question 42 and chapters 3, 4, and 5 for ideas on how to deal with various situations that may come up).

Because a certain level of trust is now present, your mentee may also feel more comfortable challenging you or allowing conflicts to occur. For example, your mentee may make inappropriate requests, may seem bored with the things you have been doing together, may say he prefers to see a friend at the time you usually get together, or may pick fights with you. Don't take these behaviors personally, and don't assume they mean your mentee no longer needs or values the relationship; he may just be testing your commitment again, or he may need some space. It also could be that he has other problems in his life.

Such conflicts provide good opportunities for helping your mentee develop problem-solving and conflict-resolution skills. You can start by asking your mentee what he thinks the problem is and how he feels about it. Validate his concerns and feelings; if you disagree at this stage, you will shut off further conversation. Even if what he says upsets you, do your best to stay calm and do not react emotionally (i.e., with anger or blaming). It is OK to tell your mentee how you feel in response while still acknowledging his perspective and conveying how committed you are to the relationship. Ask your mentee what he would like to change, and be open to his ideas. If you have made any mistakes, it is better to admit them. See if you and your mentee can find solutions to the problem you can both live with, and stress that this is something that you can get through together.

Another possible challenge in this stage is that your mentee may become too dependent on you—not wanting your sessions to end or calling you frequently at home, for example. This may especially happen with young people who live in chaotic or stressful home situations (see Question 21 on relationship boundaries and chapters 3, 4, and 5 for more information on family situations). Consult your program coordinator if you feel stuck or in doubt about how to handle the situation.

The Maturation Stage: The mentoring relationship will continue to strengthen during this stage and you will truly feel like good friends. Continuing to let your mentee take the lead in what you do or talk about will assure that she stays engaged. You probably will also find that she turns to you more often for your opinion on things and may show increasing interest in understanding you better.

Working with your mentee on her life goals can be very productive during this period, and the activities you do together can begin to move in this direction. These goals may include everything from improving academically to mastering a sports skill to losing weight to navigating the challenges of peer relationships. They may also include beginning to plan for what the mentee wants to do with her life. Even elementary children like to talk about what they want to be when they grow up, and teens are beginning to think seriously about their life options. You can cultivate these interests through reading, field trips, computer-based activities, exposure to other people, movies, games, and other means.

Depending on your mentee's life circumstances and the nature of your mentoring relationship, you may find yourself being pulled into more of your mentee's family's issues. It is important to continue to observe the boundaries you established for the relationship or to renegotiate these boundaries in consultation with your program coordinator (see also Question 21 on boundaries and Question 31 on family involvement issues).

The Transition Stage: Transitions in mentoring relationships happen for a wide variety of reasons. For example, your mentee may be getting older, a physical move may occur, family issues may interfere, or your own life circumstances may change. Such transitions may lead to a redefinition of the relationship or to closure or termination. Examples of redefinition include adjusting the frequency and focus of your mentoring sessions and moving from an in-person to an e-mentoring relationship. It is important to work with your program coordinator to manage the transition in such a way as to not harm your mentee.

Termination: The final stage of your mentoring relationship is when it ends, at least in its present form. Either you or your mentee may initiate the termination, or life circumstances may lead to it. If you and your mentee have been together for many years, you may find that you remain friends for years to come, getting in touch periodically to catch up on each other's lives. (For more information, refer to Question 36 on ending your relationship.)

QUESTION 21. *What constitutes appropriate boundaries, and how do I establish them?*

You may have thought about the issue of boundaries when you were first considering becoming a mentor, wondering how much of your time it would take and how deeply involved you would have to become in a young person's life. Boundaries define what is appropriate and inappropriate in the relationship, and they clarify the limits of the mentoring relationship. Appropriate boundaries are crucial because they facilitate successful relationships and protect the mentee and mentor from harm. Some boundaries are self-evident, such as avoiding sexual or romantic contact, not engaging in illegal acts, not being physically abusive or violent, and not putting your mentee in dangerous situations; others are less evident, such as not imposing your own religious beliefs or political views. If you are mentoring an adolescent, it is appropriate to tell them that it is not OK with you if they use drugs before your sessions.

Other boundaries are defined in the specific context of each mentoring relationship and mentoring program requirements. Factors to consider in setting appropriate boundaries include (a) your mentee's developmental stage; (b) cultural, racial, and gender issues; (c) your mentee's family's situation, values, and beliefs; (d) the stage and length of the mentoring relationship; (e) the distinction between "friendship" (mentor's role) and "helping" (professional's role); (f) confidentiality issues; (g) your own circumstances and comfort zones; and (h) special circumstances in your mentee's life (see also chapter 5).

Some boundaries are spelled out by the mentoring program while others are jointly developed by the mentor, mentee, mentee's family, and program coordinator. Still others emerge and evolve as the relationship unfolds. It is your responsibility to define and observe appropriate boundaries, even when your mentee is "testing" such boundaries. For example, if you mentor in a school-based program, the boundaries of the relationship are probably limited to school meetings only, yet your mentee may want to come over to your house on the weekend.

Boundary issues are likely to come up throughout your relationship. Good examples include things such as deciding how involved to get with your mentee's family (see Question 31); decisions about spending money on your mentee (see Question 33); deciding what activities are appropriate for your mentee (e.g., attending a movie with a PG rating); putting limits on the amount of time you talk on the phone or spend together, or helping your mentee cope with challenging situations (see chapters 3, 4, and 5).

Remember, it is appropriate as well as necessary to redefine your boundaries as the relationship goes through various phases and presents new opportunities or as your mentee gets older.

QUESTION 22. *How much time should I be spending with my mentee?*

The Elements of Effective Practice for Mentoring (2009) recommends that mentors and mentees have face-to-face meetings an average of one time per week, one hour per meeting over the course of a calendar or academic year. This works out to a minimum commitment of 40 hours (for a school or academic year) to 52 hours (for a calendar year) each year. Some mentors meet less frequently for longer periods with their mentees, meeting once a month for a full day, for example. Other mentors and mentees may meet virtually through e-mentoring rather than face-to-face.

There's more about the *Elements* in chapter 6, but we want to highlight that these recommendations are based on research findings that demonstrate two things: longer-term mentoring relationships are associated with more benefits to young people (Grossman & Rhodes, 2002); and ending a relationship prematurely may result in negative outcomes (Grossman & Rhodes, 2002; Karcher, 2005). Researchers theorize, and have generated evidence that supports the view, that regular contact provides more opportunities for developing a close relationship simply because there is time to engage in shared activities and opportunities for mentors to offer social and emotional support to their mentees (DuBois & Neville, 1997; Herrera et al., 2007; Parra, DuBois, Neville & Pugh-Lilly, 2002).

Our own experience, and that of many other mentors, also supports the view that longer is better, as—undoubtedly—will your own mentoring experiences. It is hard to imagine how you would get to know, appreciate, and have the opportunity to help and guide someone in less time than that. Nonetheless, some compelling new research suggests that the extent to which mentee expectations about the relationship are met can influence mentoring outcomes (Keller & Pryce, 2009, 2010; Larose, Tarabulsby & Cyrenne, 2005). In other words, if the mentoring relationship endured for the period of time that the young person thought suitable (in the case of informal mentoring), or for as long as the program in which he or she was participating promised it would, then it was likely to be a positive experience for the mentee. Once again, *expectations* seem to play a key role.

QUESTION 23. *How can I establish a trusting relationship with my mentee?*

As answers to Questions 19–22 highlight, trust takes time to develop, with some young people requiring more time than others, depending especially on their prior experiences with adults. People often talk about "creating" trust as though it were something we conjure up at will. In reality, trust emerges slowly and tentatively from experiences that create the conditions for it. Such conditions include the following:

> Being reliable, consistent, patient, and persistent with your mentee.

> Encouraging your mentee to take the lead in deciding what you will do together.

> Telling your mentee what positive qualities or behaviors you see in her or him.

> Having fun together and creating shared memories.

> Listening to cultivate and communicate understanding rather than giving advice.

> Keeping your conversations with your mentee private; not telling parents or teachers the details of your conversations.

> Letting your mentee know how much you like and believe in her or him.

> Avoiding pushing your mentee to achieve goals you have set.

> Being trustworthy yourself: keeping your word, respecting your mentee's privacy, and keeping what your mentee tells you confidential unless there is a compelling reason to involve someone else (see Question 43 on confidentiality).

It can be tempting to equate the level of trust with the level of communication. But this can be misleading because some mentees are never going to be great "talkers." What is more important is whether you feel like a friendship is developing; if it is, trust is developing. As in any relationship, trust evolves slowly through the simple process of being together on a regular basis and liking the experience. We rarely take genuine pleasure in the company of people we don't trust.

QUESTION 24. *How do I handle it if my mentee doesn't talk much to me . . . or at all?*

Not all young people are talkative by nature; others can take a long time before they feel comfortable enough to talk to an adult they have recently met. Stop and think about it for a moment: how comfortable would you have been at your mentee's age talking to an adult you barely knew? This is why we recommend focusing more on activities you both enjoy doing rather than on talking for the sake of talking. It can be helpful to do activities that don't rely on talking but might be conducive to conversation afterward, such as seeing a movie or sports event together, reading a book together, or playing a board or computer game. Another strategy mentors use is to go for a walk or a drive with their mentees; something about being together in this nonthreatening way is conducive to conversation. Ask open-ended questions related to what you are doing together.

Once again, we strongly recommend a look at Michael Karcher's tools for solving the "I dunno, what do you want to do?" problem (available at www.michaelkarcher.com). Also bear in mind that another reason for the silence may be that your mentee just doesn't know what to talk about. One nonthreatening way to get young people talking is to ask what they and their friends or siblings like to do together and what they talk about. If you have access to other kids around your mentee's age, you can observe or interact with them to see what they do or talk about.

Sometimes mentees don't talk much because they have things going on in their lives that they are embarrassed about, and they may believe adults would think less of them if they were aware of them. You can frequently mention to your mentee that you are there for him if anything is ever bothering him, and remind him again that you will not share what he tells you with other people unless you feel that he is in danger. Express how much you care about him, and explain that it is up to him whether he talks to you.

Meanwhile, avoid pushing your mentee to talk, and try to avoid filling the silence yourself. If you can learn to be comfortable with silence, you are giving your mentee the space he needs to think on his own. Keep the focus on having fun together rather than talking.

QUESTION 25. *Will talking about my own life or beliefs help my mentee open up to me? If so, how much should I share?*

The answer to this question depends on the stage of your mentoring relationship and whether your mentee has expressed an interest in knowing more about you. In general, if you believe sharing certain information about yourself will strengthen the relationship, then it is probably appropriate to do so. Keep in mind, however, that the mentor should be more listener than talker. Talking about yourself just to get your mentee to open up may have the opposite effect—you are filling the silent spaces so she doesn't need to try. In general, wait for your mentee to initiate conversations in which you talk about yourself.

If your mentee initiates a conversation about your life or beliefs, a good first response is to ask why she is interested. Try to see whether the question is simply a way for your mentee to bring up a topic about her own life or beliefs. Remember, you want to keep the relationship focused on your mentee, so continue to encourage her to talk about her perspectives. Each

mentor must decide how open he or she wants to be in sharing information with a mentee. You have as much of a right to privacy as your mentee,
so you should not feel obligated to talk about any personal issues if it is
not your style or makes you uncomfortable.

It is also particularly important to avoid sharing details that might
unintentionally have a negative influence on your mentee, such as your
former drug use or other illegal activities. While it may seem at first that
sharing such information can be an opening to warn your mentee away
from such behaviors, in reality the mentee can walk away with the sense
that his mentor did it and is fine, so what can be so bad about it? The
mentee's family also might not be comfortable with you sharing such information. If asked, try to redirect the conversation back to the mentee by
saying, for example, "Why are you interested in knowing this?" Or, "What
would you think of me if I did—or didn't?"

One thing mentees always seem to enjoy hearing is stories—especially
funny stories—about your childhood. They can be a gateway to talking
about embarrassments and challenges you faced and how you handled
them. Keep it light and humorous to avoid sounding like you are preach-
ing. At least until you are well into a relationship, stay away from sensitive
topics such as your religious or political beliefs. But if you have a mentee
in his late teens, he may raise these topics, especially in the context of
current events. If your mentee brings up such issues, encourage him to
explore what he thinks, and wait for him to ask what you think. Remember once again, your role is to help the mentee develop critical thinking
skills, which will happen most effectively by exploring his beliefs, not
yours. You also should be aware of and sensitive to the cultural, religious,
or political views of the mentee's family if you enter into these discussions. Asking your mentee about his family's beliefs may also lead him
to discuss whether he agrees or disagrees and help him to examine how
he feels about any differences that may exist (see also Question 42 about
discussing various sensitive issues).

QUESTION 26. *I just don't seem to be connecting with my mentee. Is it me?*

Some mentoring relationships take longer to get established than others.
Some young people are just shy or are not used to interacting with adults
outside their family or school. Young people who come from circum-

stances in which they felt let down by the adults in their lives may take extra time to decide to trust another one. It can be especially challenging to connect with teenagers, at least in part because developmentally they are more oriented toward their peers than to the adults in their lives. Cultural, racial and ethnic, or gender differences can slow down the connection simply because it may take more time and effort to find common interests on which a relationship can be built (see Questions 37 and 38 for more on these issues). Family circumstances may also make it more difficult to establish a regular schedule for getting together. It is possible, too, that your expectations are out of sync with the reality of mentoring a young person. You may be looking for results in the first stage of your relationship that do not typically occur until later in the relationship (see Question 19 on expectations and Question 20 on relationship stages).

Here are some straightforward things you can do to establish a stronger connection with your mentee:

> Have fun together. Ask your mentee to make a list with you of 10 things she would like to do when you get together. For your suggestions, focus on fun things the mentee might not otherwise be able to do—going to a sports event or museum, for example.

> Let your mentee make the final decision on what you will do.

> Ask open-ended questions about your mentee's interests, and incorporate these interests into your activities.

> Listen more than you talk.

> Be patient and persistent in the face of setbacks.

> Keep telling your mentee how much you care about her.

> Affirm your mentee's good qualities and strengths.

> Take a look (or a second look) at resources that can help fine-tune your communication skills (e.g., Talkingitthrough.educationnorth west.org).

If, in spite of such efforts, this feeling of "not connecting" doesn't improve, inform your program coordinator sooner rather than later. The support he or she provides may help you get through this rough period. If a mentor loses interest and disengages from the relationship when she experiences this lack of connection, it may have unintended harmful consequences for the mentee, further impairing her ability to trust adults. If you and the program coordinator jointly determine that the relationship does not have a viable chance of working, you can collaborate to manage the relationship termination in a way that will minimize such harm (see Question 36 on ending a relationship).

QUESTION 27. *What should I do if my mentee keeps "standing me up"?*

Most important, try not to get discouraged, much less angry. You came into this relationship knowing it requires commitment, patience, and perseverance, all of which are now being tested. Some simple strategies can help: have your mentee write down when your next meeting is, be sure he has your phone number if he needs to cancel, and make a reminder call the night before. If your mentee is younger, ask if he is comfortable using the phone to call you.

It also can be helpful to talk to your program coordinator, or if mentoring informally, to your mentee's family about missed appointments. Many times, your mentee has little to no control over the situation because of other family commitments such as needing to babysit a younger sibling. It is also possible that your mentee wants to back off a little in the relationship and may be too embarrassed to tell you. When you see your mentee the next time, mention that you were disappointed about the canceled meeting and reiterate how much you care about him. Explain that you understand that he may need to cancel a meeting with you and let him know that it would be better for you if he did so in advance rather than just being a "no-show." Tell him you'd like to solve the problem, and brainstorm possible solutions together. Be open to the possibility that your mentee may want to see you less often. See if you can agree on a solution that works for both of you, and then make a plan for how you are going to follow through on the solution.

QUESTION 28. *How do I know that mentoring is helping my mentee?*

Most mentors have a keen interest in the answer to this question. While they want to know the benefits of mentoring in general, they are typically more interested in the specific value it has for their mentees. As noted in chapter 1 (see question 7), research has shown that mentoring can have many positive effects. Success is usually defined in terms of positive changes that occur in your mentee over the course of your relationship and beyond. You can also think of it in terms of helping your mentee get where she wants to go in her life. It is useful to ask your mentee and your mentee's parents, caregivers, and teachers what they would like to see happen as a result of the mentoring relationship. In addition, your mentoring program may have specific goals or outcomes it is seeking to achieve. These should be communicated to you during the orientation and training you receive, and you may also want to have this conversation with your program coordinator.

As we note many times throughout the *Field Guide*, the cornerstone of a successful mentoring relationship is realistic expectations. One of the best indicators of success is how you and your mentee feel about each other: Do you look forward to seeing each other? Do you have fun together? Is there a sense of warmth and connection between you? Can you talk openly about issues your mentee is facing? Do you and your mentee respect each other?

Other factors to consider in answering this question include the following:

> Are your mentee's social skills improving?

> Is your mentee more self-confident?

> Have your mentee's relationships at home improved?

> Does your mentee feel more motivated to do well at school?

> Have there been any improvements, however small, in behavioral issues your mentee might have?

> Is your mentee beginning to think about the future?

The more frequently you can answer yes to these questions, the more thoroughly you can be assured that you are being successful. Consider, however, that positive outcomes may not be immediately apparent and may not show up until years later in your mentee's life. There are also ways to measure what changes are occurring, and many formal mentoring programs have made great strides in doing exactly that. And bear in mind that your mentee's needs and goals may change over time, moving from short-term goals, like help with homework, to longer-term goals like choosing a career direction, so your definition of success is likely to change as well. In fact, that's a very good thing.

QUESTION 29. *Can I get together with my mentee outside of the times and places specified by the program we are involved in?*

This question only applies to those who are mentoring through formal programs, and our answer is a quick and direct no. It's best to stick with the guidelines established by your particular program. Going beyond the program policies and guidelines could expose you to personal legal liability should anything happen to your mentee and could also cause the program to terminate the mentoring relationship. Some examples of situations where mentors are tempted to break program rules include seeing your mentee more often outside of the program meeting times, taking him to an event in your community, or having him spend the night at your house. If you feel very strongly about wanting to do these kinds of things, your program coordinator may have the authority to make exceptions to the program guidelines and policies, so it is always worth talking with her or him about what you would like to do.

You may also want to consider whether the program you are mentoring in meets your needs and those of your mentee. For example, you, your mentee, and your mentee's family may desire greater flexibility in when and where you get together, yet you are constrained by the requirements of a site-based program. We recommend that you talk to your program coordinator to see if there are other programs in your community that would better meet your needs. It is sometimes possible to transfer the relationship from one program to another—from a school-based program to a community-based program like Big Brothers Big Sisters, for example.

QUESTION 30. *What about communicating with my mentee online? Should we e-mail, text, tweet, or "friend" each other?*

Online communication is here to stay, and its reach just keeps expanding. Chances are that unless you have a very young mentee or are quite tech-savvy yourself, your mentee is ahead of you in using social media and electronic means to form and sustain relationships. Even if you think the development of the Internet and all that it has spawned is one of the 20th century's worst developments, it is important to familiarize yourself with the nature and offerings of the online world because it is the world in which most mentees live. Technology is now embedded in school curricula, and even a significant percentage of kids living in our nation's most disadvantaged neighborhoods grow up with cell phones and other high-tech devices as routine parts of their lives.

We encourage mentors to be open to using electronic media unless they are involved in a formal mentoring program that discourages it. If you are mentoring through a program that is based online (like iMentor.org), one that encourages online contact, or you are mentoring informally, this arena offers opportunities to enhance the quality of both your communications and your relationship with your mentee. Keep in mind that some mentees may not wish to "friend" their mentors in social media sites because they want to maintain some privacy regarding their peer relationships and activities. If your mentee does friend you, these sites are a great way to get to know her better and learn more about her interests and daily life.

A good place to start in learning the basics is the straightforward article developed by the Corporation for National and Community Service (www.nationalserviceresources.org/files/Youth-Impact-vol-2.pdf). At a minimum, it will help you become familiar with the terms you're likely hear your mentee use. Mentor Michigan also has a useful one-page tip sheet on social media (www.michigan.gov/documents/mentormichigan/Social _Networking_Tips_for_Mentors_347569_7.pdf).

Finally, bear in mind that there is no need to become an expert in all matters related to the virtual world. Your objective is simply to be aware of the extent to which young people operate in that world and to become familiar with basic forms and forums for online communications. In fact, mentors who are largely untutored in this area have one bonus: your lack of knowledge and skill gives your mentee the chance to demonstrate competence by helping you gain your bearings in a world that is new to you. Cyberspace and its myriad Internet-based access points also provide op-

---

DATA POINT
Children and Internet Access

The U.S. Census Bureau stopped tracking computer use at home by children because the availability of home computing was so highly correlated with actual use. Today, the bureau tracks only children's Internet access. In 2009, nearly 77 percent of children lived in a household with Internet access, with markedly higher rates (more than 90 percent) for children with a parent holding a bachelor's degree or higher and lower rates for children whose parent holds a high school diploma (63 percent) or did not complete high school (39 percent).

Source: U.S. Census Bureau (2009).

portunities for you and your mentee to explore a wide range of interests together. One simple example: we think of our smartphones as 24/7 encyclopedias. Want to know who the sitting governor in your state is, how many games the Knicks won last year, or when Mozart was born? Google it and use the information you locate to enliven (and inform) on any subject that interests your mentee.

If you are interested in learning more about online mentoring, there is a good overview on the MENTOR website at mentoring.org/downloads/mentoring_1316.pdf. Or visit imentor.org. Finally, if you are concerned that your mentee has fallen into the "technology gap" that affects many young people living in tough circumstances, see Question 39a.

QUESTION 31. *How deeply should I be involved in my mentee's life or that of my mentee's family?*

The level of involvement you have in your mentee's life and that of her or his family will depend on a range of factors, beginning with the type of program in which you are mentoring. For example, friendship-focused programs (e.g., Big Brothers Big Sisters' original program) have different expectations of mentors than many school-based or career-oriented programs do. These differences will define how often and for how long you are expected to see your mentee, the settings in which you see your mentee, the kinds of activities you can engage in, and the extent to which you interact with your mentee's family, if at all. Ideally your mentee's family will have received some sort of orientation about what to expect from their child's mentoring experience and their role in it.

If you are in a site-based program, it is likely you will have more limited involvement in your mentee's life and little, if any, interaction with the family. However, your conversations with your mentee may touch on many aspects of his home life. In a community-based program, you are likely to be exposed to more dimensions of your mentee's life and may have more extensive and direct involvement with the family.

If your mentee comes from a disorganized or stressful family situation in which the family is not able to adequately address all your mentee's needs, it can be difficult to remember that your role is not to "fix your mentee's life." Some common situations in which you might be tempted to overstep your role include academic problems, financial problems that directly affect your mentee (no money to buy new school clothes, for example), health concerns, or specific problems your mentee may be having. It can be particularly challenging to avoid doing anything that would undermine or supplant the role of your mentee's family, even though their circumstances and behavior may concern you.

If you are seeing things that worry you, talk to your program coordinator or one of your informal advisers. Your coordinator can and should look into the situation, speak to the family, or take action if needed. And remember that if you suspect child abuse, you must report it immediately to your program coordinator, or if you are mentoring informally, to the child welfare authorities in your state (for more on this, see Questions 45 and 58).

It is also possible that your mentee's family will try to involve you in their problems. They may see you as an "outside expert" or as a "close friend" who can help them with things like school problems, legal issues, transportation, child care, job contacts, money problems, or immigration issues. If this happens, let the family know, as nicely as you can, that you cannot really help but that you will discuss the situation with your program coordinator, who may be able to connect them with someone who can help. To avoid role confusion and possible ethical issues, you should take this approach even if you have professional expertise related to the request. As tempting as it may be, especially if you believe you could help, it is important to maintain appropriate boundaries. Your role as mentor is not to take on these problems, but together with your mentoring coordinator, you might be able to point the family in the direction of more appropriate helping resources.

You also could have the opposite problem: your mentee's family doesn't ask for help but tries to make you an extended family member. For example, they may invite you to all their family events, give you gifts, turn to you for advice, or ask you to "take on" other children in their family. If you have been mentoring a child for many years in a program where you also interact with their family, you may well feel like an extended family member and may be entirely comfortable being involved with the family as well as with your mentee. But if your relationship is newer or if you are feeling uncomfortable, it is best to discuss these types of situations with your program coordinator to determine the appropriate boundaries and to help facilitate discussions with the family about these boundaries.

QUESTION 32. *Are my mentee's parents comfortable with my role in their child's life?*

As noted in Question 31, you may or may not have direct contact with your mentee's family, depending on the type of program in which you are mentoring. All programs should make every effort to assure parents' or guardians' comfort by involving them during and after the match process. However, even though the family may have requested a mentor for their child and signed a permission form for participation, they may still have ambivalent feelings—wanting to help their child but also feeling uneasy about this "stranger" entering the child's life.

If you put yourself in the parents' shoes, it is easy to imagine that the fact that your child has a mentor might make you feel inadequate in some way. Or, you might feel jealous of the mentor's relationship with your child, especially if your own relationship has been characterized by conflict or lack of time to spend together. Parents also can be nervous if you, as a mentor, come from a different cultural, racial, religious, or socio-economic background, wondering if you are going to turn their child away from her family heritage. To avoid these concerns, it can help to engage parents as "partners" from the beginning. If your program allows, you can talk to them or drop them a note telling them what a wonderful child they have and thanking them for trusting you, reiterating how you can never take their place in your mentee's life.

When talking with your mentee, it is very important that you avoid any criticism of her family (even though your mentee might be critical) and that you show respect for the family's culture, values, and beliefs. If your mentee needs to talk to you about family conflicts or frustrations, avoid taking sides; put yourself in "sounding board" mode. Help your mentee figure out why she is upset, and guide her in problem-solving discussions. In general, avoid speaking to your mentee's parents on her behalf, but rather help your mentee develop a plan for such a talk. If she is willing, role playing can be a fun activity with your mentee being the parent and you being the child. This can help you both see things from a different perspective. If these issues come up frequently or persist over time, talk to your program coordinator and together develop a plan to increase the family's comfort level with the mentoring relationship.

QUESTION 33. *How should I respond to my mentee's request for gifts?*

Most formal mentoring programs have specific guidelines about how to handle gifts and spending money on your mentee, so check with your coordinator first. Some programs strongly discourage or even forbid gifts. Programs that have "no gift" policies typically put them in place to avoid offending a mentee's family or putting mentors in situations they can't afford. Other programs leave the decision to give or not give entirely to the mentor's discretion.

Some factors to help you make a decision about how to respond to your mentee include your own financial situation, the type and length of the relationship, the nature and amount of the request, the boundaries you have set for the relationship, the mentee's family's feelings and financial situation, and the type of activities you and your mentee do together.

Deciding not to spend money on your mentee: If you decide not to buy things for your mentee, you should not feel guilty. If you wish, you can explain why but it is not necessary. A simple response (such as, "I don't have the money for that right now") may just end the matter. Try to avoid getting into a discussion of whether your mentee "needs" the item; it sets up an adversarial tone between you.

If you *have* been spending money on your mentee for activities you do together, you can say that you prefer to spend your money on activities you can do with each other rather than on things. Of course, if the requested item is related to your activities, such as a baseball mitt or a new book, you might consider talking with your mentee about how he could earn the money, or you could take him to a thrift shop or garage sale to find the item at a cheap price.

Deciding to spend money on your mentee: Before you decide to spend money on your mentee, consider the family's feelings. You do not want to make parents or guardians feel unable to provide for their child. If you are thinking of giving your mentee a birthday gift, for example, ask the family for advice on what your mentee may like. This will help them feel included and will give you some spending parameters.

Doing some activities with your mentee will most likely involve money, such as going to a movie or sports event or having a meal out, but be low-key about it. If you would like to work with your mentee on financial literacy, you can establish a monthly spending budget for doing things together and ask your mentee to make decisions about how you will spend it.

QUESTION 34. *I think my mentee needs more than I can give, and I am worried that I am letting her or him down. Am I?*

Every mentoring relationship goes through its ups and downs, and it is a rare mentor who doesn't get discouraged at times. Sometimes a mentor has unrealistic expectations and is not seeing the changes she had hoped for, or she might worry about how slowly the relationship is progressing. A mentor may also become concerned when the mentee appears to withdraw from the relationship or engages in provocative or inappropriate behavior. It can be natural for the mentor to conclude in such circumstances that she is not being effective when in reality the mentee is just testing her mentor's commitment.

It is also true that some mentees have more needs than others and that these needs may be beyond the scope of a mentoring relationship. It is not unusual for a mentoring program to either recruit or be faced with referrals for troubled young people with multiple life challenges. Your mentee's life circumstances may also change significantly during the course of your relationship, placing him under more stress and challenging his coping skills (for more on this, see chapter 5).

One place to start in thinking about your capabilities with your mentee is to examine your expectations and boundaries (see Questions 19 and 21). You may be taking on too much responsibility for your mentee's problems. As we have observed, your role is to be a friend. And friendship itself is an important source of support for your mentee, especially if he or she has multiple needs. Your program coordinator may have ideas about strategies you can use with your mentee and can also provide additional moral support as you try them out. It might help to review the first three mentoring stages (Question 20) about the principles for making your relationship work.

It is possible, however, that your mentee needs professional help to cope with stressful situations. Talk to your program coordinator, who can consult with your mentee's family and school to discuss what services might be needed. Chapters 3, 4, and 5 provide additional information on issues your mentee might be facing and how to handle them.

If you are patient and persistent, you are likely to find that the situation improves. It also helps to remember that you are "planting seeds" that may not bear fruit until years later. So, it is difficult to tell right now if you are giving your mentee what she needs.

QUESTION 35. *Because of a geographical move, my mentee and I will not be able to get together. Is there a way we can continue our relationship in some form?*

If you are the one who is moving, it is essential to discuss the transition with your program coordinator as soon as possible so that you have enough time to plan for how to end the relationship—at least in its present form. If you are mentoring informally, have this discussion directly with your mentee and his family. Express your wish to stay in touch with your mentee, and talk about how that might happen. (The ideas in this section also are applicable to summer vacation periods in school-based mentoring programs that allow continued contact.)

There are various options for continuing the relationship, depending on the policies of your mentoring program, your mentee's age, the distance of the move, and access you and your mentee have to computers or affordable phone use. Be sure that you are able to honor any commitment to stay in touch before you make it. Some options to consider include the following:

> Regular phone calls: You can have regular phone calls either using a dial-up phone or using a computer with Skype. Skype is a video calling service that is free when it is installed on your and your mentee's computers. Mentors like Skype because the phone call is more personal when you can see each other, and it also allows you to do things like read together.

> A reduced but regular meeting schedule: If you or your mentee are moving within a reasonable distance, it might be feasible to continue seeing each other on a less frequent schedule. For example, instead of seeing each other for an hour a week you might see each other once a month for several hours.

> An e-mentoring experience: Depending on your mentee's age and computer access, you also can have an e-mentoring relationship. For more information on e-mentoring, see Question 30 and chapter 8 on resources. In addition to communicating by e-mail, you can communicate through social media such as Facebook if your mentee is willing to "friend" you. Facebook and similar programs are a great way of staying in touch with what is going on in your mentee's life on a daily basis.

If continuing the relationship is just not feasible, work with your program coordinator and your mentee's family to end the relationship in a supportive way. Also be clear that you have appreciated the chance to get to know your mentee. For more on this point, see the next question.

QUESTION 36. *I need to end my mentoring relationship. Is there a "good way" to do that?*

We hope you are not thinking of ending your relationship in its early stages unless it is absolutely necessary. As we have noted, this can have unintended but nonetheless harmful consequences for your mentee. If you are feeling challenged or discouraged, there may be ways to address the issues that make you think you need to terminate the relationship. Your program coordinator can help.

There are many reasons why mentoring relationships end, but in the final analysis, the reason is less important than how the ending is handled. Like most mentors, you take your relationship seriously and want to conclude it in a way that does not harm your mentee. Sometimes, because a mentor feels guilty or sad, she puts off telling her program coordinator and/or mentee. Instead, allow as much time as possible for planning and managing the transition. If you handle the termination well, it can be a learning experience for your mentee. If it comes as a last-minute surprise with little or no explanation, your mentee may well conclude that there is something wrong with him. Further, it may impair his ability to trust adults in the future.

One exception is a mentoring relationship that is set up from the start to be time limited, with an expectation on both sides that it will stop at a designated point. Examples include a career mentoring program or some school-based programs. Care still should be taken in these situations, and there will still be feelings of loss. But if it is anticipated, the end of the relationship is less likely to have harmful effects.

Although your mentee will undoubtedly be disappointed, there are ways to help her through the process such that she develops further life skills and does not lose trust in other adults. Adolescents may have a harder time letting go of mentoring relationships than younger children, and the longer you have been together, the stronger the feelings of loss will be. Don't be offended if your mentee seems angry or acts in ways that show she is rejecting you. These may be defense mechanisms to help her cope, especially if she has had prior disappointments with important adults or if she has vulnerabilities that the termination triggers. If this happens, tell your mentee what you are observing, and encourage her to talk about how she is feeling. Tell her how much you care for her and how disappointed you feel too.

Allow time, if at all possible, for a transition phase to prepare your mentee for the end of the relationship. During this phase you can take the following actions:

> Share your own feelings of loss and disappointment, telling your mentee how important she has been in your life.

> Encourage your mentee to talk about how she feels, letting her know that all her feelings are normal and OK.

> Reminisce about the things you have done together, and ask your mentee what she liked about and learned from these experiences.

> Tell your mentee how much you like her, and reiterate your belief in her and your confidence in her strengths and capabilities; express positive aspirations for her future.

> Be concrete in setting a last get-together date, and plan a special last activity together that your mentee chooses.

> Do a project to help you remember each other, such as creating a photo album or memory book.

Finally, refer to Question 35 if you want to maintain some level of contact with your mentee after your formal relationship is ended.

3

QUESTIONS ABOUT ISSUES THAT COMMONLY COME UP IN MENTORING RELATIONSHIPS

It's simple, not easy.
ALBERT EINSTEIN, THEORETICAL PHYSICIST AND NOBEL PRIZE WINNER

In this chapter we address some of the most common issues that surface during a mentoring relationship. While some are applicable to mentees of any age, others are more relevant for adolescents. Not all situations will arise in your mentoring relationship, but we encourage you to read through each question so that you can be prepared if they do come up. The world has changed so significantly in the past two decades, you might not have experienced some of these situations or perhaps you have experienced them in different ways. Read on and be prepared to help your mentee face 21st-century challenges in a way that makes the most of every single one.

As you read, bear two things in mind. First, a number of our answers include lists of optional ways to respond to a situation. The purpose of the lists is to provide a range of ideas so that you can consider what is likely to work best with your mentee, then choose (or craft) the right approach. Second, some mentees will confront obstacles or life circumstances that are considerably more serious than those addressed here. You will find ideas on how to successfully overcome or learn to cope with these in chapters 4 and 5.

QUESTION 37. *My mentee and I come from different economic, cultural, racial, or ethnic backgrounds. How can I honor and accommodate these differences?*

Although research shows that shared interests are an important component of successful mentoring relations (see Question 6), research also suggests that successful relationships can and do form when the mentor and mentee come from backgrounds that are different in major ways (Sánchez and Colón, 2005). As a mentor, you can view such differences either as barriers or as opportunities. We hope you will choose the latter approach. In fact, your positive attitude about these differences will go far in limiting any discomfort they could cause in your relationship and will certainly put your mentee's family more at ease if they have any concerns.

The most significant differences in your relationship may well be those related to culture and socioeconomic status rather than race and ethnicity. Having similar backgrounds can initially make it easier to connect with your mentee because you will have similar experiences, views on life, and even language. But you can expect to find that you have other things in common on which to build your relationship even if you have different backgrounds. And when you stop to think about it, if mentoring is about expanding children's horizons, raising their aspirations, and fostering their positive development, the prospects for emotional and cognitive growth are very rich when you come from different backgrounds.

Of course, your success will depend on your ability to set aside any preconceived notions and judgments you may have (harder than it sounds), to embrace and learn from your mentee's culture, and to be a guide to help your mentee build bridges between his world, your world, and the larger world around you. In fact, many families want their child to have a mentor from a different background because they think their child will benefit from these differences.

We explore the terms *race, ethnicity, culture,* and *socioeconomic status* here because although they are often used interchangeably, there are meaningful distinctions among the terms. The following outline will help you understand and frame key differences.

Race: The word race has traditionally been used to encompass the concept of biologically based physical characteristics, such as skin color and hair type, that have been used to divide human populations into distinct groups. In our increasingly global world of multiracial births, and with DNA studies showing that all human beings probably came from a common ancestor that is theorized to have evolved in East Africa roughly 2 million years ago, the concept of race has become much harder to define and apply. It still carries powerful connotations in the United States, however.

Ethnicity: The term ethnicity has traditionally been used to denote groups that stress common ancestry, as well as shared language, heritage, and customs that are learned and passed on, but not genetically based. People from the same race may have totally different ethnic identities and customs. Sometimes, but not always, religion is a distinguishing characteristic of different ethnic groups. Ethnicity can be thought of as culture passed on through generations of a given group.

Culture: Culture has traditionally been used to encompass the concept of norms and behavior formed on a foundation of the shared beliefs, values, and traditions within a group of people. Culture defines a way of life that includes day-to-day living practices, food, faith, marriage practices, holidays and celebrations, and expectations for children in the family. People from a common ethnic group may have quite different cultures. A good example of this is immigrant groups. Some families will hold on to their native land's culture through generations while others assimilate quickly to the American culture.

Socioeconomic status: Socioeconomic status defines a person's social and economic standing relative to others based on their financial worth, education level, and occupation. Socioeconomic status can become ingrained into a family's culture, setting up expectations for what children can—or cannot—achieve in life.

While we offer several ideas about things you can do as a mentor to bridge and work within racial, cultural, and ethnic differences, we strongly recommend that you also take advantage of training and reading on cultural diversity that your program coordinator can provide or suggest (or you can locate in your community or at your workplace). If you have no program director to whom you can turn, check out chapter 8 for resources that may be available to both formal and informal mentors.

> Think carefully about any prejudices or preconceived notions you might have related to your mentee's background. It is almost impossible to grow up in the United States without such influences, but the more you are aware of them, the better you can set them aside in your relationship.

> Do research on the Internet to better understand your mentee's racial, ethnic, and cultural background.

> Show a strong interest in learning about your mentee's ethnic and cultural identity, focusing on things such as family history, beliefs, traditions, food, holidays, and living customs. Share the same information about your family.

> Discover similarities and common interests you share. For example, both your cultures/families may like similar sports, foods, and television shows and may have similar ways of celebrating holidays.

> Try some elements of your mentee's culture when you are together, such as eating new foods, listening to different music, or adopting new words.

> If invited, participate in cultural events, celebrations, or meals with your mentee and her family.

> Be sensitive to and nonjudgmental about prejudices your mentee may have acquired related to race and culture. Become a sounding board to help her understand the source of those prejudices, and expose her to experiences that may help her overcome those prejudices.

> Consult your program coordinator if there are conflicts or "disconnects" between you and your mentee that you have been unable to resolve; they could have a cultural basis. For example, your mentee may be disinterested in school and even want to drop out despite all your efforts to help her academically. You could conclude that she just doesn't care when, in reality, she simply does not see college as a real-life option because no one in her family or neighborhood has ever gone to college. Or perhaps her family expects her to get a job to help economically.

Socioeconomic differences can be especially challenging because they often are attended by assumptions and expectations that might be less transparent than those associated with race, ethnicity, and culture. Furthermore, poverty is so often intertwined with race and ethnicity that it may be difficult to distinguish what is at the heart of issues you are experiencing. It is best to approach socioeconomic differences with the same sensitivity and respect for your mentee's family as you have for the other types of differences. One caution: you may feel compelled to "save" your mentee if he is living in poverty. It's a good impulse. But, once again, remember that your role is not to fix your mentee's life but to support him in developing the critical thinking, social, and other skills every person needs to succeed. A number of challenges other mentors have experienced are noted in the following list. If you are facing the same issues, recall that in this instance it is especially important to show respect for your mentee's family, and at the same time encourage your mentee to think about what these challenges mean for his own life and future.

> Your mentee may find it harder to trust you, especially initially, if he thinks you are judgmental about his life circumstances.

> You may find that things you take for granted, such as access to books, writing materials, a phone, a computer, or transportation, are things that your mentee doesn't have and can't easily get.

> If you bring your mentee to your house, he may become envious of your possessions or even critical of his own family.

> Your mentee may think you have unlimited amounts of money to spend on him.

> Your mentee's family may ask for financial favors.

On the other hand, your lifestyle might encourage your mentee to raise his aspirations for their future. Seeing what you have achieved in your life, especially if you talk about the effort and self-discipline that went into it, can be a powerful motivator. This is an opportunity to make the connection between education, hard work, and life goals.

QUESTION 38. *I have been matched with a child whose gender is different from mine. How should I take this into account in our relationship?*

Studies of gender in relationships in general seem to suggest that gender may influence the types of relationships young people form, the types of activities they are interested in, and the ways in which mentoring can benefit them (Bogat & Liang, 2005). Some gender differences to consider are described in the following list. Please take them as general principles that won't apply to all young people. While social scientists have identified social gender differences between boys and girls, our society has been quick to turn these differences into stereotypes that can limit opportunities for young people. Mentors should always look at mentees as unique individuals, encourage them to follow their own interests without regard to gender, and support them to move beyond gender stereotyping. This last point is especially critical in the area of academic achievement.

> Both boys and girls are capable of having close and long-lasting mentoring relationships.

> Girls seem to prefer mentoring that is relationship focused (psychosocial mentoring) while boys seem to prefer mentoring that is goal focused (instrumental mentoring).

> Girls seem to be more comfortable with conversation-based activities, while boys enjoy activities that involve doing things.

> Boys are more likely to express upset feelings through behavior, while girls are more likely to bring up and talk about sensitive issues and ask for help.

> Boys and girls mature at different rates, with girls slightly ahead of boys in general.

Seeing your mentee as a unique individual without applying gender stereotypes allows you to stay open to your mentee's unique needs, strengths, and capabilities. That said, the experience of parents, teachers, and mentors does indicate that you may face different issues and challenges with girls than with boys. Examples of issues that have been identified as being specific to girls or boys follow; however, we want to stress that these are generalizations and not applicable to all girls or boys. Some things you might face with girls include body image, self-esteem, assertiveness, peer relationships and rejection by peers, maintaining academic performance into the teens, dating relationships, decisions about sexual activity, pregnancy, and dating violence. Issues that might surface with boys include the need to be physically active (and consequent dislike of sedentary activities like reading), academic performance issues, disciplinary issues, a tendency to act out rather than talk about negative feelings, and a willingness to take risks like experimenting with alcohol and drug use.

QUESTION 39. *My mentee is a whiz at school (or not). How can I help her or him make the most of the school experience?*

It is wonderful (and important) that you care about your mentee's academic success. It is an area where help is often needed, and parents and teachers may be hard pressed to provide the extra attention a young person needs. Some mentoring programs, particularly those in school or after-school settings, or those with a career development focus, have explicit goals aimed at improving student achievement and attendance, helping students stay in school, or helping students with post–high school options. In addition, children who are having school-related difficulties or who could be considered at risk for school failure often are recommended for participation in mentoring programs. Some mentoring programs expect their mentors to engage in academically oriented activities, such as helping with reading, math, homework, or study skills, and this assistance can be quite helpful to young people.

It is important to remember, however, that these academic activities should not come at the expense of relationship development. Both research and mentors' experiences show that mentoring can improve mentees' attitudes toward school achievement and belief in their ability to do well in school (Rhodes, Grossman & Resch, 2000). Your belief in your mentee and your encouragement can help him be more willing to make the effort to do well. Mentoring can also increase your mentee's aspirations for his future, and when he has goals he would like to achieve, he is more likely to appreciate the role education plays in attaining them.

Deciding how to help your mentee academically and how involved to get will depend on her current academic performance and challenges, the wishes of her parents or guardians, suggestions from her teachers or your mentoring program, and conversations with and observations of your mentee. This is also an area where realistic expectations are important. As noted earlier, avoid taking on a role that more properly belongs to your mentee's family and teachers. In fact, if you do take on a parental or teacherlike role, you will be missing a unique opportunity to allow your mentee to open up about school-related problems without feeling judged or criticized. At the very least, your encouragement and interest will plant seeds to help your mentee see the importance of doing well in school.

You can do specific things to support your mentee's academic performance:

> Reinforce the importance of education for future success when discussing what your mentee would like to do with his life.

> Be specific when talking about ingredients for school success, such as going to school every day, being an active participant in class, doing assignments on time, and asking for help when needed.

> Explore whether your mentee knows *how* to study. Many young people don't, and providing help with study techniques and methods can be an invaluable gift.

> Show interest in what your mentee is doing at school by, for example, reading together, asking to see her artwork, talking about a story she has written or talking about a science project.

> Ask about the books he is reading in school; you may have read some of the same books when you were younger.

> Encourage her to keep trying, and express confidence in her when she seems frustrated or wants to give up on school.

> Provide specific help with schoolwork, making sure that you stay in your role as "guide," not "doer."

> Incorporate educational enrichment activities into the time you spend together, such as doing a project together that builds on something your mentee is learning.

> Help your mentee engage in problem solving about issues that come up at school or at home about school.

> Explore whether your mentee doesn't care about school because he believes he isn't smart enough or can't afford to go on to higher education.

Also, most mentors find it helpful to consider school-related issues by placing them in one of three categories: a) academic achievement issues, b) school adjustment issues, and c) life and career issues. Examples of each type, along with actionable recommendations, appear in the following lists. As you reflect on any that apply to your mentoring experience, think about what your role might be in a "team approach" to addressing them—with the team consisting of you, your mentee's family, and your mentee's teacher(s). Keep in mind that addressing these concerns is best accomplished through small, achievable steps rather than large, longer-term goals. Most young people can generate the latter, but have a much harder time figuring out to get there. Finally, don't overlook the considerable number of free online resources that can support your work. For example, check out the U.S. Department of Education's *Helping Your Child Series* (www2 .ed.gov/parents/academic/help/hyc.html?src=rt), the offerings of the Khan Academy (www.khanacademy.org), and tools available through your local Mentoring Partnership (see list and contact information in chapter 8).

A. ACADEMIC ACHIEVEMENT ISSUES

If your mentee is achieving below their ability level, you can:

> Communicate your belief in his ability and encourage him to talk about what is getting in the way of his success.

> Have your mentee list things she is interested in and does well. Reinforce that she has skills and abilities. Ask her if any of her skills could be used in the present situation.

> Avoid making him feel guilty about not doing better.

> Focus on helping her raise her aspirations by talking about what she would like to do with her life.

> Help him with strategies for good study habits and specific study techniques.

> Help her learn how to use a computer.

> Problem-solve with him by identifying two or three small steps he can take to get better grades.

If your mentee is reading below grade level, you can:

> Incorporate reading together into your mentoring sessions.

> Take her to the library to check out books to read at home.

> Read a story together and tape-record it.

> Play a dictionary game to learn new words.

> Ask him to think of something he would really like to do with you and use it as an incentive for reading a book or two (or three).

If your mentee has been kept back a grade and is in danger of being held back again, you can:

> Talk to your mentoring program coordinator and your mentee's family to see what steps are being taken to address the issue, asking how they think you can best help.

> Support your mentee's family by being an additional advocate for your mentee to access supportive services such as tutoring.

> Set aside some time in each of your mentoring sessions to do some homework or review for a test, making sure the whole session is not focused on schoolwork.

If your mentee says it is too loud and chaotic to get any homework done at home, you can:

> Brainstorm with her about how to find a quiet space and time.

> Talk to his teacher about options for doing assignments before leaving school.

> Help her share this concern with her family.

If your mentee is gifted or has a talent you would like to see the school encourage, you can:

> Look into relevant programming your mentee's school (or after-school program) may have.

> Check out the resources of the National Association for Gifted Children (nagc.org).

> Ask your mentee how you can help him talk to his family or teacher about to encourage the talent.

> Encourage the talent yourself, incorporating related activities into your mentoring sessions.

> Help your mentee find resources or activities on the Internet that will allow her to develop her talent.

DATA POINT
Number of Gifted Children in the United States

There are approximately 3 million academically gifted children in grades K–12 in the United States. This represents 6 percent of the student population. No federal agency collects statistics on gifted children, nor on the incidence of children who have exceptional artistic talents.

Source: National Association of Gifted and Talented (2011).

If your mentee has fallen on the wrong side of the digital divide, you can:

> Explore to what degree your mentee possesses "Internet literacy."

> Find out what resources exist in his home or school to develop or enhance these skills. For example, does he have or have access to a computer with Internet access at home or at school? Does he use

a laptop in school? Does he get and perform homework assignments online?

> Find ways to use some of your time together to explore subjects on the Internet.

> If your program permits, introduce your mentee to high-tech environments or demonstrate how to use Internet services that are available in school or in a local library.

> If you have the means and your relationship is a fairly long-standing one, consider giving your mentee a computer as a gift on a special occasion; or make a contribution to her "technology fund."

> See also Question 67.

If you feel your mentee is not being challenged enough at school, you can:

> Talk to your mentoring program coordinator and your mentee's family to see what steps are being taken to address the issue, asking how they think you can best help.

> Talk to your mentee about why he is bored or disinterested in school and brainstorm things he can do to make school more interesting or challenging.

> Identify other activities your mentee might participate in after school to challenge her.

> Provide academic enrichment opportunities in your mentoring sessions.

B. SCHOOL ADJUSTMENT ISSUES

If your mentee just doesn't seem to care about school, you can:

> Make a list together of all the things he likes and dislikes about school. Then ask him to think of one thing he is willing to do to increase the number of "likes" and decrease the number of "dislikes." Make a plan together to take action on his ideas, and provide ongoing encouragement and positive reinforcement for what he does.

> Focus on things she might like to do with her life, and help her make the connection between these goals and what she is learning in school.

> Expose him to things that will enrich what he is learning about in

school, for example, seeing a movie about the Civil War if he is studying about that or playing math games together.

If your mentee says he or she hates his or her teachers, you can:

> Allow her to vent with you about what she dislikes in her teachers.

> Help him make a list of what he dislikes and likes about each teacher and discuss.

> Brainstorm with her about things she could do to improve her relationship with at least one teacher. Make a plan to follow up, encourage her to act on the plan, and check to see how she is doing.

If your mentee is having disciplinary problems at school, you can:

> Talk to your mentoring program coordinator and your mentee's family to see what steps are being taken to address the issue, asking how they think you can best help.

> Encourage your mentee to talk about what is happening.

> Have a talk about what he could have done differently each time your mentee gets in trouble at school. Ask what positive things he has learned from the situation. Keep the conversation light; don't turn it into a lecture.

> Role-play the situation that led to the disciplinary action with you taking the mentee's part and your mentee being the teacher. Talk about each of your perspectives and how your mentee might have responded differently in the situation.

If your mentee is frequently staying home from school because of illness and other reasons, you can:

> Talk to your mentoring program coordinator and your mentee's family to see what steps are being taken to address the issue, asking how they think you can best help.

> Explore whether it is appropriate for you to see your mentee after school on a day she has stayed home from school. Don't make this a punishment, however.

> Also see Question 40, which addresses a range of health issues.

If your mentee is reluctant to go to school out of fear of being teased by other students, you can:

> Encourage your mentee to talk about what is going on, allowing him to vent without offering advice.

> Ask your mentee what her family or the school has done about it and what she would like to see them do.

> Talk to your mentoring program coordinator and your mentee's family to see what steps are being taken to address the issue, asking how they think you can best help.

> Work with your mentee on options to deal with the teasing, including brainstorming and role-playing possible responses.

> Encourage your mentee to talk to his teacher every time a teasing incident occurs.

> Also see Question 42a, which addresses bullying.

C. LIFE AND CAREER ISSUES

If your mentee has asked you to help him or her determine a career direction, you can:

> Help her make a list of what she likes to do and dreams of being when she grows up, using it as a basis to identify her interests.

> Use the computer to answer questionnaires about career interests and to identify possible careers. There are now a number of websites designed for this purpose. A good one is Quintessential Careers, sponsored by American University (quintcareers.com).

> Help him identify and access resources at school or in the community that can provide career development support, including clubs he might join, classes he might take, and internships he can pursue.

> Take her to visit a local college or business.

> Make career options a frequent discussion point and take advantage of online resources to bridge the divide between aspirations and paths to achievement.

If your mentee would like to go to college, but the family has no financial means to send her or him, you can:

> Ask the family for permission to help their child explore college and financial aid options (and visit collegeaccess.org/accessprogramdirectory).

> Talk to your program coordinator or your mentee's school about resources they can provide; suggest connections and help your mentee make them; find online SAT/ACT exam support.

> Help your mentee research colleges and financial aid options.

> Help him apply to college and apply for scholarships and financial aid.

> Also, take a look at Question 42f if your mentee's family can't or won't apply for financial aid.

If your mentee wants to drop out of school, you can:

> Encourage her to talk about why she wants to drop out (what needs it will fill) and help her think about whether there might be other ways to meet these needs.

> Avoid giving lectures about staying in school, but rather help him explore the concrete effects this will have on his life. This could include doing research on annual incomes for dropouts vs. high school graduates, building a "what I need to live on" budget, and doing research on what jobs might be available to him.

> Identify and help her connect with supportive resources at school or in the community. Many school districts have dropout prevention programming, including alternative education programs.

QUESTION 40. *My mentee is sick a lot. Should I intervene?*

(See also Question 44 for guidance on how to respond if your mentee has a chronic health condition or disease.) After observing the frequency and severity of the symptoms your mentee is exhibiting, contact your program coordinator. If you are mentoring informally, you can contact another helping professional, such as the school nurse, for advice. He or she can then contact the mentee's family to further discuss the situation and help them access medical services to address the health issues. Under no circumstances, except a life-threatening emergency, should you take direct action to seek medical care for your mentee.

Your program coordinator, with parental consent, can inform you about the medical conditions or needs your mentee might have, and you can appropriately adapt your relationship to accommodate these needs. If your mentee is a teenager, federal and state laws may allow him to seek medical services without parental consent. Consequently, you may be able to provide information to them about options for medical services he can seek on his own, such as substance abuse or family planning services, mental health services, or HIV testing. The rights of teens to seek such medical services will differ from state to state, so it is imperative that you speak first with your program coordinator about the wisdom of this action and to be sure you are sharing accurate information with your mentee. As one of our mentors frequently observed, "It is one thing to have an opinion on an important matter; it is something else entirely to have an informed opinion."

QUESTION 41. *My mentee wants to talk about what seems like a sensitive issue to me, and I don't want to. Help!*

It is not necessary to discuss any and every topic your mentee raises, but sometimes questions or comments on a sensitive issue may indicate an underlying problem that you should bring to the attention of your program coordinator. If at all possible, you should try to determine why your mentee raised the topic, rather than just avoiding it, by asking why she is concerned about the issue. Try to put your mentee at ease by telling her you appreciate her coming to you about this issue. Ask her if she has talked to anyone else about it. Tell her that you do not feel able to help her with the issue, but offer to connect her with someone else more prepared to help.

The following examples describe reactions you might have to sensitive topics and how you can respond to maintain the trust you've established while staying within appropriate boundaries and reasonable comfort levels. If your mentee repeatedly brings up sensitive topics, you should seek guidance from your program coordinator.

The topic seems inappropriate within the context of your relationship or is especially sensitive or uncomfortable for you. For instance, your mentee asks for advice on whether to become sexually active or wants to know how someone can get an abortion.

Keep calm and thank your mentee for approaching you. Tell your mentee that you are not the best person to talk to about the issue, and ask if there is anyone else with whom she thinks she could talk. Offer to help your mentee connect with this person, who might be a school nurse or other health professional, a school counselor, a coach, a clergyperson, an extended family member, or another adult in her life. Also consider whether you would be comfortable acting as a sounding board to help your mentee clarify her values and needs without feeling like you have to offer an opinion or advice (which is the best approach to take anyway).

The topic is a "hot button issue" for you. For example, your mentee starts talking about how much he likes or dislikes the current U.S. president or says he does not believe in God.

Try to ask open-ended questions about why your mentee feels that way. Once you are satisfied that he has had the opportunity to express himself, try to steer the conversation to other topics. If he persists, and depending on his age, you can try to convey that this is an uncomfortable subject for you and tell him you want to talk about something else.

The topic seems developmentally inappropriate for your mentee. For example, your young mentee talks about a specific drug-using behavior or wants to know at what age someone can get pregnant.

Ask open-ended questions to determine why your mentee is curious about this issue, and try to ascertain whether there is a problem that should be brought to the attention of your program coordinator. Ask why she wants to know about the topic and, if appropriate, ask whether this situation involves her personally in any way. Remember, if there is any suspicion of abuse, it must be reported to the program coordinator or other professional. See also Questions 42 and 58.

The topic raises alarm bells for you. For example, your mentee asks if taking a bottle of Tylenol would be enough to kill someone or makes a comment about taking a knife to school for protection.

Ask open-ended questions to determine why your mentee wants the information and if he appears to be planning to act. See if you can find out if this is a situation in his life or in the life of one of his friends (see also Question 46 about school safety and Question 52 regarding potential suicide). Bring topics such as this one to the immediate attention of your program coordinator or other resource person.

The kinds of topics your mentee is raising make you question whether you are equipped to handle the mentoring relationship. For example, your mentee talks about feelings of extreme rage or wanting to get revenge for something.

Approach your program coordinator or resource person as soon as possible to discuss any situations that you feel are too serious for you or pose a risk to your mentee or others. This person can help you with strategies for handling the immediate situation, meet with the mentee and/or the mentee's family to determine whether these issues need to be addressed through other helping resources, and assess the mentoring relationship to see if further action is required (see also Question 42 and chapters 4 and 5 for additional information).

QUESTION 42. *What is the best way to approach a discussion about . . .*

The willingness to deal with sensitive issues is one hallmark of what makes a mentor particularly valuable. If you are mentoring a young person in middle school or beyond, chances are that you will have opportunities to demonstrate value by helping your mentee deal with a tough issue or common yet challenging life transition. We've identified a dozen such issues in sections 42a–42l. They range from teasing or bullying to grooming; parental job loss; chronic health issues; the death of a parent, close family member, or friend; and dating and relationship issues.

You may be proactive and bring up potential situations your mentee could face, but sensitive issues typically will surface in the context of a question or comment your mentee makes or in things you observe. For example, you may observe changes in your mentee's personality or behavior and have no sense of what is causing them. Encourage her to talk about it. Tell her what you have noticed and that you are concerned. Some common warning signs you might encounter include:

> Withdrawing emotionally, not wanting to talk about things.

> Acting out and aggressive behaviors accompanied by a high or persistent level of anger.

> Pervasive sadness or depression over a period of weeks.

> Academic and/or behavioral problems at school.

> Fatigue and loss of energy, which may result from sleeping difficulties or depression.

⟩ Loss of interest in eating.

⟩ Loss of interest in things you usually do together.

⟩ High levels of anxiety that do not appear to be solely situational.

⟩ Anxiety about being away from family, which may reveal itself through canceling or cutting short your mentoring sessions.

As you read the following discussions of specific situations, you will note similarities in the warning signs for different concerns, so you may not always be sure about the issue you are facing unless your mentee tells you. This is where program coordinators can be particularly helpful. They are likely to have seen similar situations in other young people's lives, so they have a frame of reference for understanding what is happening. They may also have additional information about your mentee and his family that will inform their advice to you.

If your mentee brings up a sensitive issue, you may be caught off guard, so it helps to have thought through in advance how you might handle certain situations. It is also important to know the limits of confidentiality (see Question 43) and the requirements and process for reporting things like suspected abuse (see Question 45) or suicide risk (see Question 52). If you think you have to break confidentiality, you should speak with your program coordinator as a first step. He or she can help you figure out your next steps and provide guidance on what to say to your mentee about the need to get help, which will involve breaking confidentiality.

Sometimes, because you can feel so close to your mentee, or because you have concerns about her family life, it can be easy to forget that the primary responsibility for your mentee lies with her family (or designated caregivers). They may have values and desires for their child that differ from yours, and they may pursue a course of action that makes you uncomfortable. At the same time that you are respectful of your mentee's family, you are in a unique situation to provide support that helps your mentee handle a given situation. You can also focus on your mentee's strengths and assets to help her develop healthy coping skills.

Once again, remember that your role is not to solve the problem, or take action on your mentee's behalf, but rather to be a sounding board and coach to help your mentee resolve the issue. Some general principles for dealing with sensitive situations include the following:

> Stay calm.

> Ask age-appropriate questions to better understand why your mentee has brought up the topic.

> Try to get at the feelings your mentee is having about the issue; watch for nonverbal clues as to how he is feeling.

> When you talk with your mentee about situations she could handle on her own, focus on her strengths and capabilities.

> When facing complex situations, focus on your mentee's feelings and needs rather than jumping to problem solving. Show that you want to understand things from his perspective.

> Avoid offering your opinions. You want to encourage your mentee's critical thinking skills. Say things like, "I'm not sure what I think. What do you think?" Even younger children can solve problems with age-appropriate guidance.

> Ask questions like, "What would be an ideal solution to this situation?" Or, "What do you think you can do about it?"

> Help your mentee assess the pros and cons of her suggested solutions. If you are not comfortable with the solution she likes best, try to figure out why you are uncomfortable and share your thoughts with your mentee. Ask if she is willing to consider other solutions and do more problem solving.

> If you are comfortable with his proposed course of action, convey your belief in his ability to handle the situation, and ask how he would like you to help.

Finally, bear in mind that your mentee's age and life situation will influence how she reacts to the issues we have tagged. So, please review the stages of youth development outlined in chapter 7 for additional perspectives on how best to add real value.

A. TEASING AND BULLYING

No doubt you've noticed a considerable uptick in news coverage of bullying in recent years. It is, in fact, a pervasive problem that can begin in elementary school.

Bullying is typically defined as an intentional pattern of behavior rather than a one-time incident. It may take different forms, among them *psychological bullying,* which includes ostracizing or shunning someone, spreading rumors, and intimidating someone; *physical bullying,* which includes pushing and hitting; *verbal bullying,* which includes teasing, name-calling, and mocking; and *cyberbullying,* which takes place on the Internet.

It is not unusual for several types of bullying to be used on the same target. An example: bullying that takes the form of extortion in which a child is psychologically and physically forced to give up money or possessions. There is a growing problem of cyberbullying starting around the middle school years, using social media to spread lies and rumors, make hurtful negative comments, and attack someone's character.

DATA POINT
Bullying

A 2009 study by the Office of Juvenile Justice and Delinquency Prevention within the U.S. Department of Justice found that "overall, 13.2 percent of those surveyed reported having been physically bullied within the past year, and more than one in five (21.6 percent) reported having been physically bullied during their lifetimes." The study also found that "about one in five children (19.7 percent) reported having been teased or emotionally bullied in the previous year, and nearly 3 in 10 reported having been teased or emotionally bullied in their lifetimes."

Source: Finkelhor, Turner, Ormrod, Hamby & Kracke (2009); ncjrs.gov/pdffiles1/ojjdp/227744.pdf.

Your mentee may be affected by bullying in several ways: as a bully, a victim of bullying, or a bystander in bullying incidents. If your mentee brings up the topic of bullying in general, ask open-ended questions to find out what aspect of bullying he wants to talk about. You also should bring the issue to the attention of your program coordinator; either that person or you should follow up with your mentee's family as appropriate.

If your mentee talks about being a bully, listen nonjudgmentally and ask open-ended questions to better understand what he is doing and why. Kids engage in bullying behavior for a variety of reasons, such as wanting to feel important and powerful or to increase their popularity and social standing. They may also come from a family background where this type of behavior is normal or encouraged. Or, they may come from a tough neighborhood where such behavior becomes a survival tactic. Depending on the severity of the bullying behavior your mentee describes, it may be necessary to say that you need to tell someone else about what is happening because he needs help before he gets hurt or ends up in serious trouble. If your mentee is upset by your response, it sometimes helps to negotiate whom you will tell and to offer to have your mentee come with you to talk to someone.

If your mentee is a victim of bullying, encourage her to talk, listen empathetically, and ask open-ended questions to better understand the situation. Ask, for example, "Where does the bullying occur?" And, "What is being done, and who is doing it?" Ask her how she feels and support her emotionally. She may be ashamed that this is happening to her, and she will most likely find it very embarrassing and hurtful. She may also believe that the bullying is her fault or believe there is something wrong with her and become hypercritical of her own appearance or personality. Depending on the form of bullying, she may also be afraid. Reassure her that the problem is not about her; it is about the bully who is behaving very badly. And reinforce for her that it is not her fault. You also should ask whom she has told about the bullying and what actions those people have taken to stop it.

Your mentee may want you to tell him how to stop the bullying, and under no circumstances should you tell him to "do it back" to the bully. Rather, engage in problem solving and role playing with your mentee to help him discover some solutions he can try. This might include strategies for avoiding the bully, always having another friend with him when he might encounter the bully, ignoring the bully and walking away, or going immediately to an adult. Discuss the importance of talking to his family and telling other adults where the bullying occurs. Be prepared that your mentee may be resistant to telling anyone what is going on out of fear of even worse treatment from the bully, so explain that the point of telling someone is to stop the bullying altogether.

If your mentee is a frequent bystander in bullying incidents, encourage her to talk about what she has seen and how it makes her feel. She may talk about feeling ashamed about not doing anything, or she may be afraid that she will be the next victim. She may even have joined in. For example, she may have gotten involved in a new peer group and, in the process, excluded and made fun of a former friend or laughed when the bully was making fun of the victim. Be nonjudgmental as you listen, and move the conversation into problem solving: What are some things your mentee could have done to be helpful in the situation? Are there other kids she could partner with to speak out when they see bullying? How could adults who are around help? Your goal is to empower your mentee with strategies to take action with which she feels comfortable. In fact, many experts believe it is the bystanders who hold the key to stopping bullying.

There are many resources available on the topic of bullying, including StopBullying.gov. A simple Internet search or visit to your local library will produce a wealth of more detailed information and advice if you need it.

B. GROOMING PROBLEMS

These include anything from an unkempt appearance to hygiene issues. Grooming problems occur for a variety of reasons. Perhaps no one has shown your mentee how to clean himself properly and take care of his skin and hair. Perhaps there is a health problem involved, the child is being neglected at home, or has a weight issue that results in grooming problems. Children from impoverished environments or children who are homeless commonly face grooming challenges related to cleanliness and access to proper clothing and food.

Your own grooming habits can provide a powerful example for your mentee; however, there may be times when you need to talk with her about grooming and personal hygiene. Of course, this is a topic that requires special sensitivity. Sometimes an indirect approach can work. You might introduce a book on the topic to read together or get a video on making the best of your appearance. There are websites that allow you to see how you would look if you changed certain aspects of your appearance, as well as websites on health issues specifically for kids. A good one is KidsHealth.org, which has sections for adults, kids, and teens, as well as educators. If you decide to talk to your mentee, consider your mentee's age, gender, and what you know about her or his circumstances to figure out the best approach. For example, as noted earlier, girls tend to be more sensitive about body image.

Some kids will respond to a respectful but direct approach, such as, "I have noticed that your clothes and face could be a lot cleaner. Can we talk about that?" Other kids may appreciate a humorous approach, such as, "I see you have your sloppy look on today." You can also talk about how to dress appropriately for activities you might be doing together, although you need to be sensitive to the fact that your mentee may not have appropriate clothes. Girls might respond to a "makeover" activity where you take turns styling each other's hair and makeup. During the course of this activity, you can talk about hygiene and cleanliness.

If you suspect that your mentee's family is not able to provide for basic grooming needs, talk to your program coordinator. A school nurse can also be quite helpful for advice on how to talk to your mentee. For example, he or she may be able to refer a young person to a doctor or other health care specialist who can treat teenage acne, a particularly embarrassing challenge for many young people, especially those without adequate health care. The school nurse may also be able to secure or make a referral to free sources for skin- and haircare products and so on.

C. OBESITY

According to 2010 data from the federal government (www.letsmove.gov), child obesity has tripled over the past 30 years, and nearly one-third of children in the United States are now considered to be either overweight or obese. The numbers are even higher in African American and Latino children, nearly 40 percent of whom are overweight or obese.

Not only does a weight problem put young people at greater risk for conditions like diabetes, heart disease, and asthma, it also makes them more likely to be overweight as adults. Further, overweight children are frequent targets for bullying, teasing, and social exclusion. The issue is so serious that it has attracted the attention of the medical community, schools, federal and state policymakers, and the White House.

At the most basic level, weight problems result from poor food choices and lack of physical activity, so this is where mentors can begin to influence their mentees. Lecturing your mentee about being more active or criticizing food choices won't work, but there is a lot you can do.

> Be a good role model for healthy behaviors when you are with your mentee. If you have a weight problem yourself, consider asking your mentee if he would like to create a mutual "biggest loser" game. Keep it fun; don't put pressure on your mentee, but use the game as an excuse to modify eating habits and level of physical activity. Set challenges for each other, such as who can go the longest between meals without having a snack or who can walk around the block the most times in a week. Keep track of weekly activities, and the next time you get together talk about how you've each met your challenges.

> If possible, incorporate more physical activities into your time

together. Talk about physical activities you both enjoy and ask your mentee what she would like to do with you when you get together. You might go for a walk instead of sitting while you talk, shoot some hoops, race each other, play with a Frisbee, dance together, or take short exercise breaks when you are doing more sedentary things. Avoid time-killing, snack-conducive sedentary activities like watching television together.

> If you have meals or snacks together, make them healthy, and talk about why they are healthy. Teach your mentee how to analyze food choices and read food labels.

> If your mentee's weight or a weight-induced disability would make physical exercise too difficult, consult with his family and your program coordinator.

Two websites that have good information for adults and young people on weight and other health issues are kidshealth.org and girlshealth.gov. Also, check out the First Lady's campaign *Let's Move* (www.letsmove.gov) to help your mentee "eat healthy" and "get active," as well as *Eat Well & Keep Moving* (hsph.harvard.edu/research/prc/projects/eat-well-keep-moving).

D. PARENTAL LOSS OF A JOB

The whole family is affected when a parent loses a job. Typically, we think about the parent's loss of income with all its attendant effects on housing, ability to provide for basic needs, money for college, and the like. Beyond this are issues like loss of health insurance, the parent's emotional state, increased stress levels, more arguments between parents (in a two-parent family), conflict between parents and children, and disruption to normal family routines. Single-parent families and families living at or near the poverty level will face even greater challenges, as will families that go through longer periods of unemployment.

Children often internalize the worries and stress their parents are exhibiting but may refrain from saying anything because they do not want to add to their parents' burdens. For example, your mentee might be concerned about things like becoming homeless or having to move, change schools, and lose friends—including you. She might worry that her parents will have to separate if one finds a job in a different location; or worry about how the loss of income will affect her: Will she get the new bike or computer she was promised? Will she be able to pay for college applications? What about college? She may also feel embarrassed and ashamed, find it difficult to concentrate in school, and have trouble sleeping.

Nonetheless, there are positives. Your mentee may get to spend more time with the unemployed parent. The family's efforts to economize can make your mentee feel more needed in the family by helping out with chores the family would have paid to have done in the past. Your mentee may also become more empathetic toward his peers who are in similar situations.

There are a number of things you can do to support your mentee:

> Encourage her to talk to you about what she is feeling, acknowledging that it may be a little harder for her to turn to her parents right now.

> Help him put his family's situation in context, noting that many families are affected by the ongoing recession and continuing high rate of unemployment.

> Encourage her to express some of the negative feelings she has, reassuring her that she is not being disloyal or selfish because she has these feelings.

> Talk about how other families are facing similar situations, and ask him what he would do to help the kids in those families. Ask whether any of these ideas could work in his own family, and help him act on them. Brainstorm with him about ways his family can have fun together without spending money.

> Help her come up with ideas to address immediate concerns such as how she can afford to go on the class field trip or to the school prom.

E. PARENT WITH A LONG-TERM MILITARY DEPLOYMENT

Your mentee's age will influence the reaction he has to a parent's deployment, but it is not uncommon for children of any age to exhibit anxiety and worrying, irritability and misdirected anger, disruptive behavior, attention seeking, trouble sleeping, trouble concentrating at school, a decline in school performance, a loss of interest in daily activities, and regression to an earlier developmental stage. Teens may act out through substance use and other risky behaviors. The reactions are similar to those found in children facing other loss situations such as divorce, with the added fear of losing their parent permanently. (See the discussion of divorce and separation later in this question.)

The signs of distress will probably begin before the parent is deployed as the child anticipates the loss of that parent and the changes in her family and home life. When the deployment begins, the family will go through an adjustment phase during which members create new family roles and routines. This process can offer your mentee various growth opportunities. She is likely to take on additional responsibility within the family, which can lead to increased self-esteem, maturity, and independence. She will probably have a closer relationship with her nondeployed parent and may receive additional social support from friends and relatives who live nearby. Many schools and communities have additional support services for military families and their children and make it a point to recognize and thank their military parent, which will increase your mentee's sense of family pride.

The coping ability of the nondeployed parent makes a major difference in whether the children handle the deployment well. Another factor is the extent to which they are able to communicate on a regular basis with their deployed parent. The military has made such communication a priority, so most deployed parents are able to use cell phones, e-mail, Skype, and other means to stay in touch.

You can be most helpful by offering emotional support, encouragement, and nonjudgmental understanding. Some mentees will want to talk about what's going on; others won't. In either case, you may need to adjust your mentoring style and activities to accommodate your mentee's emotional state and challenges. For example, your mentee is probably feeling that life has gotten pretty out of control, so give him more opportunities to make choices in your activities together. You may also find yourself coping with unexpected outbursts of anger or loss of interest in your usual activities. If so, allow him the freedom to express all his feelings, no matter how negative.

You will be an important source of stability and comfort in your mentee's life during this period, so you may find it helpful to do some Internet research on this subject to educate yourself about how children react to various aspects of a parent's deployment and how you can best help. A good place to start is the website for Operation Military Kids at www. operationmilitarykids.org/public/home.aspx, a collaborative effort of the U.S. military and community groups, such as Boys and Girls Clubs, 4-H, and schools. Links on their website will take you to your state for further information. Their downloadable booklet *Tackling Tough Topics: An Educator's Guide to Working with Military Kids* provides good information and helpful tips that are just as relevant to mentors as they are to teachers. It also lists a variety of additional supportive resources for military families.

It is important to be aware that the period after parents return from deployment may be more stressful than when they were gone. Injuries, pain, post-traumatic stress disorder, and reunification struggles between parents can make for an even more difficult period for your mentee. Problem behaviors your mentee exhibited in the early stages of deployment may resurface strongly; this should be your cue to encourage her to talk about what is going on and how she feels. Again, your best roles are to be a stable, caring, supportive presence in your mentee's life and to be the "safe" person she can talk to about her negative feelings, such as fear, anger, frustration, and depression.

F. APPLYING FOR FINANCIAL AID FOR COLLEGE

We touched on ways you can support your mentor's interest in and efforts to apply for any type of postsecondary education in Question 39c. Also note that some mentees have a parent or guardian who cannot or will not complete the financial portion of applications for college scholarships or aid. This is a tough problem for kids to face because parental inability or unwillingness is not considered sufficient reason or cause for what is called "a dependency status" override (an official declaration that a child's parents are relieved of the responsibility to help their children pay for college).

If your mentee finds himself in this situation, the first thing to do is urge him to talk with his guidance counselor about it (and go with him to the meeting if you can). Also, visit finaid.org/otheraid/parentsrefuse.phtml for a series of highly practical tips to help if a parent refuses to fill out financial application forms; if a parent is involved in a divorce and doesn't want to disclose information; if a parent has the financial wherewithal to contribute and won't; and so on.

G. PEER PRESSURE TO SMOKE, DRINK, OR USE DRUGS

After years of decline, drug use among young people is rising again. According to the National Institute on Drug Abuse, marijuana use in general and daily marijuana use have increased among U.S. students between grades 8 and 12. In 2010, almost 14 percent of 8th graders and 35 percent of 12th graders have used it. While alcohol use in general is declining, almost 14 percent of students in grade 8 and 41 percent of students in grade 12 reported using it in the month before the survey. Prescription and over-the-counter drug use also is increasing. The most frequently abused prescription drugs are the painkillers Vicodin and Oxycontin, and Adderall, commonly prescribed for ADHD. The most commonly abused over-the-counter drugs are cough and cold remedies. Ecstasy use is also on the rise. Cigarette use has leveled off after falling for several years (National Institute on Drug Abuse; drugabuse.gov/infofacts/HSYouthtrends.html).

Contrary to the popular belief that kids pressure other kids into trying tobacco, alcohol, or drugs, the reality is that peer pressure may be much more subtle and indirect. It is true that a friend or older sibling may directly offer drugs or alcohol, but it is also common for kids to start using to avoid feeling different or being left out of the social scene. Whether a young person decides to start using depends on many factors, including (a) parental and family influences, such as the family's patterns and history of use and addiction and what the young person's parents have communicated about use; (b) the young person's personal risk factors for use (see chapter 7 for information on risk factors); (c) the prevalence of use among the young person's peer group and close friends; (d) how easy it is to get alcohol or drugs; and (e) how much risk he or she perceives there is in using.

Attitudes toward drug use, especially marijuana use, have grown more lenient in recent years; this can lead adults to underestimate the harms of drug use by young people, and it can cause young people to view marijuana as harmless. There is also a lack of knowledge about how any drug, including alcohol, affects the vulnerable teen brain.

Research sponsored by the National Institute on Drug Abuse (drugabuse.gov) has identified the ways in which alcohol and drugs produce feelings of pleasure by affecting the brain's chemistry, actually changing the way the brain works. These changes can cause especially detrimental long-term effects in young people whose brains are still developing physically. A good overview of these issues is available at teenbrain.drugfree.org.

If you are mentoring a preteen or teenager, chances are your mentee will have some exposure to alcohol and drug use, although she may never bring up the subject. Most kids prefer to keep their drug use hidden from the adults in their lives, fearing their disapproval or limitations on their freedom. In fact, young people say their greatest motivation not to use alcohol or drugs is that they don't want to disappoint their parents. They will probably feel the same way about you.

Even though you may not suspect that your mentee is using tobacco, drugs, or alcohol, you may still want to bring up the topic. Your objective is to open the door for an ongoing dialogue, not just a one-time conversation. And the best way to keep the conversation going over time is to avoid lectures and focus on getting your mentee to be willing to talk about these issues. As always, your goal is to help your mentee learn critical thinking and problem-solving skills that he can use to avoid risky or harmful choices. Some ideas follow for how you can do that. (If you suspect your mentee is already using alcohol or drugs, see Question 50.)

An indirect approach usually works better than just coming out and asking, "Are you smoking, drinking, or using any drugs?" You can tell your mentee something you learned about the topic and ask her opinion. Or, you might encourage her to tell you what she did on the weekend and ask if there were any kids smoking, drinking, or doing drugs. Ask her if that happens often, and ask what she thinks about it. It helps if you really don't know much about such activities because then the mentee's role can be to help you learn. Other door openers are movies or television shows that show drug use frequently. You can ask what your mentee thinks about the choices the characters in the show make. It is best at this stage to listen without offering any advice, although you can casually say something like, "I sure hope you don't do that. I'd hate to see you get hurt or get into trouble." You want to keep her talking so that you can help develop her critical thinking skills and gradually influence her away from using.

Take time to educate yourself and use materials and websites you find as conversation starters. There are some great websites like the teen pages of kidshealth.org and teens.drugabuse.gov that you and your mentee can visit together. Don't concentrate on this topic for weeks at a time, but do introduce it as opportunities arise. As one great mentor we know— Richard Plepler—says, "find the right organic moment."

If you have used drugs yourself, you may be tempted to tell your mentee about your experiences in the belief that they will serve as a "warning." This is a risky strategy because your mentee looks up to you, and no matter what you say, he is likely to decide that if you did it, it can't be all that bad. Also, your mentee's family might have second thoughts about you as a mentor if they learn you are revealing such information. It is best to steer clear of the topic. If your mentee directly asks if you used drugs when you were younger, ask why he wants to know, and turn the topic back to what choices he is facing. If he is persistent in asking, you can say something like, "I'm mentoring you because I care about you and want you to have a good life. Our relationship is not about me, it is about you. I hope I learned some things growing up that can make your life better, and I really hope you won't do drugs." You may take a different approach with your own children if you have them, but as a mentor, you must always keep in mind the beliefs and values of your mentee's family. Also, feel free to share the bad experiences people you know had with drugs.

If your mentee shares that she is thinking about whether to try using tobacco, alcohol, or drugs, ask her to describe what is going on. When did she start thinking about this? Did something happen—for example, a friend started doing it—to make her want to try it, too? Together, brainstorm the reasons to do it and the reasons not to do it. Discuss the probable risks and the benefits. How might using affect any life goals your mentee has? Tell her directly that you would be concerned and disappointed if she decided to use drugs in any form because you know kids can really get messed up or get in trouble over it. Ask your mentee if she would like you to help her get more information on tobacco, alcohol, or drugs or help her figure out how to say no. Reinforce your belief in her good judgment and your hopes and dreams for her. Tell her that no matter what she decides, you will still care about her and will be there for her.

H. FAMILY PROBLEMS

Family problems can take three forms: problems between your mentee and his family, problems that cause stress in the family, and serious problems within the family that affect your mentee. Here are some ideas for how to handle each type of situation.

1. Problems your mentee has in relationship to family, including things like being upset with family rules or conflicts with parent(s) or siblings.

As a mentor, you can provide a safe opportunity for your mentee to vent and complain about what is going on at home. Especially when they reach their teens, most kids will be critical of their family and feel constrained by rules. Don't feel that you have to provide any answers or advice. Just let your mentee talk it through, and focus on helping her with problem solving if appropriate to the circumstances. You may think the parents are being unreasonable, but you should not communicate this to your mentee. You really don't know exactly what is happening, you may not be familiar with the family's culture and values, and you risk the family seeing you as an adversary if you take their child's side against them. Getting personally involved will compromise appropriate mentoring boundaries; your role is not to fix your mentee's life or family. The role of sympathetic listener and friend is something no one else is likely to offer your mentee. If you feel the situation is persistent or serious enough that another adult should intervene on behalf of your mentee, talk to your program coordinator.

2. Problems that cause stress in the family, such as parental fighting, financial worries, or challenges in dealing with a parent or sibling with a chronic health problem.

Follow the same approach of listening, sympathizing, and problem solving to help your mentee deal with the issue. You can help your mentee learn more about the situation through books or websites and use these learning experiences to encourage him to talk about his feelings and help him understand that he is not alone; other kids face these same challenges. It is also useful to help your mentee develop coping strategies to use in specific situations. For example, if your mentee lies awake every night listening to family members fighting, you can help him think of ways to block out the noise or perhaps even give him earplugs. You can educate yourself on stress-reduction strategies and share them with your mentee. For example, you might add going for a short walk or "relaxation breaks" to your sessions. And you can help your mentee think about other adults, perhaps at school or at their place of worship, to whom they can turn for help or advice. Your goal should be to strengthen your mentee's resilience and ability to respond to stressful situations within the family. Depending on your personal situation and the parameters of your mentoring program, you may also tell your mentee to call you when things feel difficult for them. Also, take a look at our answer to question 40 as well as the related questions in chapters 4 and 5 (e.g., Question 44).

3. Problems within the family that adversely affect your mentee, such as substance abuse and domestic violence.

In addition to listening, sympathizing, and problem solving, you may have to make a judgment about the potential physical or psychological harm to your mentee if there are serious family problems. Is the problem having a negative and persistent effect on her mood, coping skills, or academic performance? Is she showing signs of abuse, such as bruises or other injuries? Is she showing signs of depression? Is she using alcohol or drugs to "self-medicate"? Are her basic needs being neglected? If you answer yes to any of these questions or if you are just feeling really uncomfortable with the situation, you should consult your program coordinator as soon as possible. He or she will be able to take whatever action might be required to involve other helping resources. In addition, your coordinator can support you and help you better manage the situation. You will also find more specific information on family situations in chapters 5 and 6. For example, Question 45 tackles family violence; Question 62, substance abuse in the home.

I. PARENTAL DIVORCE OR SEPARATION FROM A PARTNER

Divorce has long been a fact of life in the United States, so it is not surprising that many children will experience their parents' divorce or separation. Some children will experience not just one, but two or more divorces or separations in the family. Divorce is distressing and painful for everyone involved. Some of the reactions children have to divorce or separation include the following:

> Profound feelings of loss and grief, even though they may have hated the fighting that preceded the breakup.

> A belief that they are at least partially responsible for the breakup.

> Feelings of anger, rejection, abandonment, and embarrassment.

> Worries and guilt about divided loyalties.

> A feeling that they have lost both parents because the custodial parent may now be less available to them.

> Inability to concentrate on schoolwork.

> Fear and apprehension about how the divorce will affect them financially, socially, and emotionally over the longer term.

> Psychosomatic symptoms, including headaches, loss of appetite, and stomachaches.

In addition to reactions common at any age, children may have age-specific reactions. Early elementary school kids may have a hard time understanding the permanence of the change in their lives and will find the whole situation confusing. They will often fantasize and believe that their parents will get back together. Children in later elementary school may feel more angry than confused. They may also have a sense of powerlessness, which can feed the anger. This anger can be directed toward one parent or the parent's partner if the child blames her or him for the separation, or it may be directed indiscriminately through acting-out behavior. Because one parent is gone, the young person may start to feel responsible for taking care of the remaining parent. Some psychologists believe that young people in this age group suffer the worst effects because they are old enough to grasp the situation and realize they are powerless to change it, yet not old enough to distance themselves by pursuing their own lives as teenagers may do.

Teenagers may express negative feelings of loss, grief, anger, and powerlessness through acting-out behavior, such as substance use or fighting. Their anger may be directed externally, resulting in aggressive, violent outbursts, or internally, leading to depression and possible suicide risk. They may also have a moral reaction to the divorce, judging their parents harshly. Because of their age, their custodial parent may turn to them for emotional support and help with family responsibilities.

As you can see from reading this information, young people can really benefit from having mentors as caring, stable adults in their lives—people who will just focus on their needs and allow them to share all their feelings no matter how negative. You can also provide your mentee with structure, predictability, and pleasant routines during a time when he feels overwhelmed and off balance. With good emotional support, most children will adapt to their new situation, and the majority of them will not suffer long-term negative consequences. Specific ideas include the following:

> Be especially careful not to break appointments. Keep a stable routine that your mentee can count on and look forward to.

> Listen, listen, listen. Encourage your mentee to talk about the divorce or separation, and help her articulate what she is feeling.

> Help your mentee understand that feelings of distress are normal and will get better with time. If you have experienced divorce or separation, you can talk about how you helped yourself heal.

> Reassure your mentee that he is not to blame for the divorce or separation.

> Be understanding about behavior changes you may see. Talk to your mentee about the behavior and what feelings may be prompting the behavior.

> Help your mentee develop ways to express anger.

> Help your mentee develop skills for coping when stress levels build up in the family.

> Don't be offended if your mentee cancels get-togethers. She may have additional family responsibilities that interfere. Talk to your mentee and your program coordinator about how to adapt your relationship if it is going to be an ongoing situation.

> Provide help with schoolwork if your mentee is having difficulty at school.

> Be patient. Even in the best of circumstances, it may take years for your mentee to adjust to a divorce.

You should be prepared for the possibility that your mentee's family situation may change in a way that you are no longer able to continue your relationship, at least in its present form. The family may have to move, or your mentee may have to start babysitting for younger siblings every day after school. In circumstances like these, work with your program coordinator to determine the best course of action, doing everything possible to maintain some level of contact.

J. DEATH OF SOMEONE THE MENTEE KNOWS

Your mentee's reaction to a death will depend on your mentee's age and how close the person was to him. The death of a parent, grandparent, teacher, or good friend is obviously going to have a deeper impact than the death of a distant relative or family friend. A sudden and unexpected death typically produces stronger reactions than a death that is due to a long-term illness.

Children's reactions to death vary depending on their age and ability to understand the concept of death. Being familiar with these differences will help you know what types of support your mentee needs. Her reactions also will be influenced by the family's cultural and religious beliefs. In some cultures and religious groups, grieving is expressed freely and openly, while in others it is kept private. Common reactions to death among kids include a period of numbness and disbelief, deep feelings of grief, fear and anxiety, anger, trouble sleeping, and emotional fragility. Some of the developmental differences in reaction to death include the following:

> Children younger than 8 or 9 are just beginning to see death as something that happens to everyone eventually and that could happen to them. They have a very limited understanding of what causes death (e.g., disease, accidents), and they may believe that their actions or behavior caused the death. They may be confused about whether their loved ones are coming back. They tend to focus on how the death is going to affect their life and worry about who is going to take care of them if the person they lost was a parent or guardian or teacher. They especially need reassurance and comfort.

> Children between the ages of 9 and 12 understand that death is inevitable and universal. They understand the varied causes of death, and they are interested in what happens after death. They may appear to become fixated on the idea of death as they struggle to understand its meaning in their lives, and they may worry about dying or losing other loved ones. Children in this age range can become upset about being left out of the adult discussion about the death and funeral plans; they are struggling to understand and want to be part of the larger family response to the death. In addition to comfort and reassurance, they need patient responses to their questions, which may be repeated over and over. It is helpful to understand your mentee's cultural and religious beliefs as you participate in these discussions with them.

> Teenagers have the abstract reasoning skills to understand that death is truly final. In fact, teens are often fascinated with the idea of death as evidenced by their love of movies and lyrics that feature death. When the person who died is close to them, they can have very strong emotional reactions ranging from grief to anger. Depending on their own vulnerabilities, they may question life in general, experience feelings of despair, and become depressed. Teens are more likely to turn to their peers for comfort and may even shut out family members and other adults. Their growing cognitive skills, independence, and peer group attachment can serve as protective "buffers" that allow them to come to grips with the death over time. You can support your teenage mentee by validating his feelings, helping him develop coping skills to deal with feelings of anger, and helping him find ways to memorialize his loved one.

Regardless of your mentee's age, you can help by providing emotional support and comfort, allowing her to grieve as long as she needs to, answering her questions to help her understand what has happened, providing reassurance that she will not always feel as bad as she does now, and helping her find ways to cope with the pain and anger. Follow her lead in what you talk about or information you provide. It's OK to say, "I don't know" to her questions, but offer to get more information. Your mentee may feel abandoned or lost in the shuffle following the death, so the stability and closeness of your relationship will be an important anchor during a period when the adults in the family may be focused on their own grief and the immediate family needs resulting from the death.

K. DATING AND RELATIONSHIP ISSUES

Be prepared. Children as young as 5 or 6 may talk about having a boyfriend or girlfriend, and it is not unusual now for children to be encouraged into relationships at ever younger ages.

DATA POINT
Tweens and Relationships

In 2006, a survey of tweens (11- to 14-year-olds), parents of tweens, and teens (15- to 18-year-olds) found that 37 percent of 11- and 12-year-olds say they have been "in a relationship." More than 25 percent of them said that oral sex and "going all the way" were part of relationships at this age, and about one-third of respondents in this age group said they knew other kids who had engaged in these behaviors. The study also found surprising levels of verbal and physical abuse in tween relationships, which was more likely to occur in relationships with early sexual activity. It found that parents underestimate the prevalence of these behaviors, especially with regard to their own children.

Source: National Teen Dating Helpline and Liz Claiborne Inc. (2006); loveisrespect.org /wp-content/uploads/2008/07/tru-tween-teen-study-feb-081.pdf.

Your mentee may begin to talk about having a boyfriend or girlfriend at a young age, and in the past you might have viewed this as an innocent rite of passage. Now you need to consider the risks of early sexual activity and sexually transmitted diseases, emotional or physical abuse in the relationship, and the possibility of multiple sexual partners before a child has even left middle school. Relationships themselves are also different. The traditional dating relationship, in which a couple goes out and does things together, is changing. Group dating is becoming more common, and couples may prefer to spend their time together at home where many parents allow them to entertain each other in their bedrooms. Kids today are also more open to homosexual and bisexual relationships. Bear in mind that *the majority of tweens and teens have not engaged in sexual activity.* Their concerns about dating and relationships may focus more on how to find a boyfriend or girlfriend, the dynamics of creating and sustaining a relationship, managing conflict, and ending a relationship.

All these shifts can present quite a challenge to a mentor. Because sexuality-related issues are so sensitive, it is helpful if your program coordinator raises this topic during the family orientation process to gain some sense of the topics they might consider off-limits in the mentoring relationship. Some parents and guardians will be OK with your having sexuality-related discussions with their child; others may feel strongly that this is their role, not yours. Of course, your mentee may want to talk to you about things he would not want to bring up in their family. This can place you in an awkward situation, so confer with your program coordinator about how to proceed.

As with other situations, what your mentee needs most from you is someone to listen nonjudgmentally, understand, provide support, and help with problem solving. Avoid asking questions about whether or not she is sexually active, but be prepared to respond if she brings up the topic by helping her clarify what is going on and engaging in problem solving as appropriate. For help in responding to the concerns of sexually active mentees, see Question 47 for information on safety issues in dating relationships.

L. BECOMING SEXUALLY ACTIVE . . . OR NOT

Depending on the level of trust and comfort in your relationship, your mentee may confide in you that he is trying to decide whether to become sexually active. Depending on your mentee's family's wishes, your own values and comfort level, and the boundaries you have created for your relationship, you may or may not want to have this conversation with your mentee. If you are mentoring a tween or teen, we recommend that you speak with your program coordinator about how to respond before the situation arises. If you do not want to have this conversation with your mentee, you can be prepared with ideas of other people he could talk to (the school nurse, health educator, a youth minister).

If you do decide to have the conversation, you can guide your mentee through a decision-making process:

> Help your mentee identify and understand the reasons why she wants to become sexually active. Is this something she initiated, or is she feeling pressured to do it? Does she feel like she needs to fit in with other kids who are doing it? Does she think losing her virginity is an important rite of passage at her age? Is having sex likely to make her relationship stronger, or will this be more like a "hookup" (a casual sexual encounter)? Posing these questions can provide an opportunity to talk about other ways of meeting emotional needs, gaining peer approval, or having a caring relationship.

> Help your mentee assess the risks and benefits of becoming sexually active. Some factors to consider include his family and religious values, the nature of the relationship with his potential partner, his emotional well-being, the risk of sexually transmitted diseases, and the risk of pregnancy. You can steer him toward websites or written materials with further information on how to protect against these risks.

> Help your mentee identify possible ways of handling the situation, and offer information on resources or services to get more information related to these options.

> Once she makes a decision, tell her you are there to support her, and encourage her to come to you for further help with these issues as appropriate.

Typically this is the sort of conversation you would keep confidential. The exception would be if your mentee's age and/or the age difference between your mentee and the proposed sexual partner falls within the parameters of your state's sexual abuse or sexual assault statutes. In such instances, you should report the situation to your program coordinator.

QUESTION 43. *What kinds of things should I keep just between my mentee and me?*

In general, what your mentee tells you should be kept private and confidential between you. This will be an important ingredient for building trust, especially with teenagers. There are certain situations that you will not be able to keep confidential, and you should make sure your mentee knows what these are in advance. It is important not to make promises of confidentiality that you cannot keep. Talking about these issues in the early stages of establishing your mutual boundaries and expectations will help protect the trusting relationship you are creating. You can talk with your mentee about how this is a special relationship between the two of you and explain that you will not be talking about them to their parents, teachers, or other adults unless there is a significant problem that threatens their health or wellbeing. It is helpful to be specific in describing these situations, which will include child abuse, suicide risk, risk of harm to another person, and serious illegal activity, such as sexual activity that falls under the state's sexual abuse or sexual assault statutes for underage young people.

If and when you feel it is necessary to break confidentiality, you should first discuss it with your program coordinator, who can advise you on how to handle it with your mentee and involve your mentee's family as needed. If you are mentoring a teenager, you can consider telling your mentee when you find it necessary to break confidentiality, explaining your concerns and your feeling that he needs help beyond what you can provide. You can discuss with your mentee the person(s) you want to tell, what you will tell them, and what you think will happen next. You also can offer to go with your mentee to talk to an appropriate helping professional if he is willing and the law allows him to seek such help independently of his parents.

DATA POINT
Mentoring Helps Young People Who Drop Out/Disconnect

Opportunity Road: The Promise and Challenge of America's Forgotten Youth reports on a survey aimed at understanding how young people between 16 and 24 become disconnected from school and work and how to help them reconnect. Seventy-three percent (73%) of those surveyed remain hopeful that they will be able to achieve their life goals. Further, 52% of those who said they have a great deal of support feel confident about their future; while only 37% who believed they were "on their own" felt the same. Young people identified successful peers (79%); college mentors (69%); parents or family (67%) and business mentors or community advocates (65%) as sources of support that would be meaningful to them.

Source: America's Promise Alliance, Civic Enterprises & Peter D. Hart Research Associates (2012).

QUESTIONS ABOUT ISSUES
THAT RARELY ARISE

We may need to solve problems not by removing the cause but by designing a way forward even if the cause stays in place.

EDWARD DE BONO, INTERNATIONAL SCHOLAR
AND PROPONENT OF LATERAL THINKING

In chapter 3, we talk about issues that commonly arise in mentoring relationships. In this chapter, we tackle situations that fall at the other end of the incidence spectrum. In fact, many mentors will never encounter the issues addressed here. Mentors who do typically are mentoring young people with or from troubled backgrounds, or teenagers hitting really rough patches. If your mentee falls into either of these categories, we strongly recommend that you seek out and participate in training geared to her specific needs. If you are engaged in a formal mentoring program, targeted, high-quality training should be readily available. If you are mentoring informally, take advantage of the range of resources for informal mentors that we review in chapter 2 (see especially Question 15).

Most mentors who work with young people who are troubled and who find themselves in problematic circumstances intentionally chose to do so. They have a special calling or feeling for this group of kids, sometimes derived from life experiences that are similar. Whatever your motivation is for doing this vital work, it is important that you remind yourself—frequently—that it is the mentee's family, not you, who carries the burden of responsibility for the issues in your mentee's life. Whether or not family members respond appropriately and adequately, you can play a crucial supporting role. Imagine your mentee facing these situations without your support. You can be sure that he occasionally does, too.

Finally, as you read our answers to questions that follow, bear in mind that the general principles guiding your response should be similar to those introduced in chapter 3. Stay calm, listen carefully to understand what your mentee is feeling, don't jump to giving advice, be honest about what you cannot handle alone and when you have to break confidentiality, explain why, and stress how much you care for your mentee. The more challenging the situation, the more vital it is that you exhibit the steadiness and steadfastness that is the essence of good mentoring.

QUESTION 44. *My mentee has a chronic health condition (such as diabetes, asthma, obesity). Do I need to make special provisions for that?*

A chronic health condition is one that lasts for several months or more and interferes with normal childhood activities. Unless you are in a specialized mentoring program for children with specific medical issues, it is likely that your mentee is able to function pretty normally most of the time with the health condition. You should discuss your mentee's condition and needs with your program coordinator who usually takes responsibility for involving the family, but if you are an informal mentor, you will likely be dealing with the family directly. Your program coordinator or the family should provide you with information about your mentee's health condition, as well as guidance on how to accommodate any special needs. Some possible accommodations you may have to make include the following:

> Understanding the extent to which pain or discomfort could limit your mentee's activities.

> Understanding the medications your mentee takes and the effects they may have.

> Modifying the types of things you do with your mentee, such as avoiding certain situations or building more physical activity into your time together.

> Being sufficiently knowledgeable about your mentee's health condition to be able to respond if a problem comes up, such as having to

administer an epinephrine injection for an allergic reaction to certain foods or insect stings.

> Avoiding foods that your mentee is allergic to or managing what your mentee eats to avoid a diabetic reaction.

You are likely to be more comfortable if you educate yourself about your mentee's health condition. Most physicians' offices have useful pamphlets and other reading material on common medical conditions. Most chronic health conditions also have associations that exist to provide information and support to those who have the conditions. For example, the Juvenile Diabetes Research Foundation (jdrf.org) has useful information for adults and kids. A simple Internet search of the health condition should produce information on other organizations. The website kidshealth.org also has good, jargon-free information on many of the health issues young people face, and it includes sections specifically for parents, kids, and teens.

Children who have chronic health conditions often feel different from their peers and may be excluded from some normal school and extracurricular activities. They also may become targets for bullies because of their differences. It is not unusual for them to occasionally feel lonely, rejected, excluded, inferior to other kids, and angry. A chronic health condition can be particularly difficult for teenagers. It may interfere with peer and dating relationships and the ability to participate in sports or other activities. It may also require disease management treatments young people find embarrassing, such as injecting themselves with insulin.

As a mentor, you can help develop your mentee's strengths and resilience, as well as provide emotional support. She will especially benefit from being able to talk to you about things she might not say to her parents. You can also help her develop coping skills to handle her emotions and to deal with situations that might come up, like bullying or being excluded from an activity. If she is socially isolated, you might want to consider helping her cultivate or strengthen a few "best friend" relationships by including her friends in some of your activities.

Because your mentee's life may be circumscribed by rules and limits related to his illness, he needs opportunities to break free now and then. You can empower your mentee by giving him choices whenever possible and letting him decide what you will do when you are together. You also can encourage him to do things that will give him a sense of control over his disease, such as becoming an advocate for research on his condition or acting in a peer support capacity. Join him in a walk or other campaign designed to raise money for research leading to a cure for his illness, encourage him to join an online support group for children with the illness, and so on.

QUESTION 45. *I'm concerned about my mentee's safety at home. Am I overreacting?*

The focus here and in the next two questions is on safety issues related to interpersonal violence, which can take the form of: a) domestic violence, or b) child abuse. In the past two decades, violence within families, schools, communities, and dating relationships has captured much media attention. While many programs and policies have been enacted to prevent and respond to violence, it still continues to affect young people in various settings. Many people are not aware of how often children are victimized by and exposed to violence. The Office of Juvenile Justice and Delinquency Prevention within the U.S. Department of Justice conducted a study in 2008 to assess the levels of exposure to violence in children under the age of 17. This study found that "more than 60 percent of the children surveyed were exposed to violence within the past year, either directly or indirectly (i.e., as a witness to a violent act; by learning of a violent act against a family member, neighbor or close friend; or from a threat against their home or school)."

It is important that you are able to recognize and respond to violence and problems associated with it, but you do not have to worry about acting alone. The response typically may include intervention from the police, the state child welfare agency, school counselors, community programs, and faith communities.

Clearly you cannot fix these problems, but developing a fuller understanding will provide you with perspective on what your mentee is facing (for more on this, see Question 58). You can then tailor your support to your mentee's needs. Also bear in mind that getting help early is important because prolonged exposure to violence and the persistent fear children feel can actually produce changes in the brain that have lifetime implications (Perry, 2001). Getting help early also reduces the likelihood of longer-term post-traumatic stress disorder.

> ### ⊡ DATA POINT
> ### Children and Violence
>
> Nearly one-half of the children and adolescents surveyed (46.3 percent) were assaulted at least once in the past year, and more than one in ten (10.2 percent) were injured in an assault; one in four (24.6 percent) were victims of robbery, vandalism, or theft; one in ten (10.2 percent) suffered from child maltreatment (including physical and emotional abuse, neglect, or a family abduction); and one in sixteen (6.1 percent) were victimized sexually. More than one in four (25.3 percent) witnessed a violent act, and nearly one in ten (9.8 percent) saw one family member assault another.
>
> Source: Finkelhor et al. (2008) for the U.S. Department of Justice.

A. DOMESTIC VIOLENCE

Where there is domestic violence, children live in perpetual fear, and the effects on them are similar to those observed in children who are the victims of child abuse. In fact, domestic violence and child abuse often go hand in hand. It is also important to note that violence is intergenerational: children who are exposed to violence, or who are victims of violence, are more likely to become bullies or engage in acts of violence and aggression. In part, this is attributable to the feelings of anger and powerlessness they experience—feelings they dare not express at home and that emerge in other settings, including school, community, and dating.

Some of the things you may observe in children who are affected by violence at home are quite similar to abuse warning signs and include high levels of anger and poor anger management skills; aggressive acting-out behavior, including bullying; anxiety and nervousness; depression; learning problems; avoidance of talking about their family; frequent illness and complaints of stomachaches and headaches; poor personal hygiene; a tendency to feel excessively guilty and responsible for things that go wrong; and, in younger children, a high level of clinginess. In addition to having these warning signs, teens may become suicidal, run away from home, use drugs, and engage in other self-harming behaviors. They also are more likely to be involved in dating relationships characterized by aggressive or violent behavior, either as victim or perpetrator.

B. CHILD ABUSE

Child abuse includes neglect of a child's basic needs, physical harm, sexual contact, and emotional mistreatment. Some of the warning signs of child abuse include injuries or bruises; behavioral or personality changes; learning, behavioral, and other problems at school; developmental delays or regressing to behavior more typical of a younger child and a generalized distrust of adults. Children may seem wary and "on alert," always looking over their shoulder waiting for something bad to happen. You may see evidence of poor hygiene and indications that their basic needs (food, clothing) are not being met. Teens may act out through substance abuse, running away, or sexual promiscuity; show signs of exhaustion, depression, and anxiety; and even attempt suicide.

In addition to showing the warning signs of abuse in general, children who are being sexually abused may be fearful of any physical contact with an adult and may show signs of physical discomfort in their genital area such as difficulty sitting, walking, or riding a bike. They may demonstrate a knowledge of sexual terms or bring up sexual topics in a way that is inconsistent with their stage of development. StopItNow.org has a useful list of age-appropriate sexual behaviors. Again, see Question 58 for information about the incidence of child abuse and how to recognize and prevent it.

WHAT YOU CAN DO ABOUT FAMILY SAFETY ISSUES

If you suspect child abuse, you must bring it to the attention of your program coordinator or the appropriate child welfare agency. You can find a current list of child abuse hotlines in various states at childwelfare.gov /pubs/reslist/rl_dsp.cfm?rs_id=5&rate_chno=11-11172. Initiate a conversation with your mentee if you are worried about what may be happening. Tell your mentee what you are observing and that you are concerned; indicate that you are there for her if she wants to talk about it. Your mentee may or may not be open with you about what is happening, especially if the situation involves abuse or family violence.

If your mentee does open up, remember that reporting suspicions of abuse to your program coordinator will involve breaking confidentiality. If you have a program coordinator, discuss how to handle this with your mentee. If your mentee is old enough, it would be ideal if you could convince him that he needs help and then persuade him to let you talk to someone else to begin the process of getting it. More typically, he will be afraid to have you tell anyone, and you will have to say that you are so concerned about his safety that you feel you have no choice but to tell someone. We hope you will have explained this ground rule to your mentee early in your relationship. You can talk with him about who you will tell and what is likely to happen next, assuring him that the professionals you contact will be there to help as well as protect him. If you want to avoid this conversation with your mentee, you can report your suspicions and not bring it up at all. Your mentee may never know it was you who made the report, and the chances are very high that you are not the only person noticing these warning signs.

As a mentor, you cannot change what is happening in your mentee's home, but you can compensate for things she may be experiencing. You can help strengthen her resilience and coping skills. And you can do the following things even if your mentee never confides in you:

> Be a reliable, trustworthy, gentle, nurturing, caring adult in his life.

> Listen and encourage her to talk about all her feelings, especially the ones that may make her feel ashamed.

> Assure (and reassure) him that he is not alone and you are there for him.

> Tell her that kids are not to blame if adults do harmful things to them.

> Answer his questions honestly, simply, and age appropriately.

> Model and talk about ways to cope with negative feelings, especially anger, frustration, and feelings of helplessness.

> Teach her coping skills to take care of herself in stressful or dangerous situations.

> Help him with schoolwork.

> Talk about gender roles to help her overcome acquired beliefs about women as victims and men as controllers in relationships.

> Expose him to positive images of relationships through books, magazine articles, television shows, and movies.

> Avoid negative activities, such as playing video games that glorify violence.

Be aware that an abuse report, by you or another caring adult, may result in your mentee being removed from the home and put in protective custody. This could include a placement in a facility or with a temporary foster family. If this happens, talk to your program coordinator or the relevant child welfare office to see if you can get the contact information for the child welfare social workers who are assigned to the case. You can request that they provide the opportunity for you to continue to see your mentee. If this is not possible, you may at least be able to make phone calls, communicate electronically, or write letters to your mentee to assure her that you have not forgotten her and that you still care for her. What happens next to your mentee will be out of your hands, but we hope the circumstances permit continued contact with you. Your program coordinator can play an important role in helping you negotiate the child welfare system.

QUESTION 46. *I am concerned about my mentee's safety at school or in the community. Should I weigh in?*

A. SAFETY AT SCHOOL

You may have concerns about your mentee's school because of its location in a dangerous neighborhood or because of the high levels of fighting, bullying, and other sorts of interpersonal violence among students. If you are mentoring in a school setting or interact with your mentee's school, you should mention your concerns to your program coordinator. You also can meet with the school principal to express your concerns. Many schools have a "school resource officer" with whom you can talk. This person is a local police officer assigned to the school to focus on school safety and violence prevention. Most schools now have antiviolence and antibullying policies and programs, although funding for these programs is often one of the first things eliminated in tough economic times.

If you feel your concerns are not being adequately addressed, you have a limited number of options. You can ask your program coordinator if you can meet with your mentee in a safer setting, and you can work with your mentee and school personnel on strategies to increase your mentee's sense of safety at school. You also can provide emotional and problem-solving support to help your mentee cope with situations that come up at school (see also Questions 42 and 48 for more information about bullying). And you can check out the National Center for Victims of Crime's Teen Victim Project for online material for teens and adults on community violence, gangs, dating violence, and other sources of victimization (ncvc.org/tvp /Main.aspx).

B. SAFETY IN THE COMMUNITY

According to the National Center for Posttraumatic Stress Disorder, a program of the U.S Department of Veterans Affairs, children who live in a poor, inner-city environment, are non-White, are in a gang, and use drugs or alcohol are more likely to be affected by community violence (ptsd .va.gov/public/pages/effects-community-violence-children.asp).

Children may be victims of violence, witnesses to violence, or both. Children who are victims of violence in the community might be robbed, beaten, bullied, or threatened. The experience of children who are witnesses may include seeing physical violence, such as domestic violence, assaults, beatings, muggings, or robberies. They also can be exposed to gang activity and even witness murder. The experiences of being both witnesses and victims can have long-term effects on children similar to those of living in a violent home or being a victim of abuse (see Question 45 on family safety issues). They may grow up thinking that no place is safe, even their own homes, where bullets could come through the window. For many of these children, school may feel like the safest haven they have. Children who have been victims or who have witnessed a serious act of violence, such as a killing, will be more traumatized than children simply living in these unsafe environments.

For more information on the effects of community violence on children, you can go to the website for the New York University Child Study Center: aboutourkids.org/articles/community_violence_effects_children. Some communities have organized systems involving police and social workers to respond to the needs of children who are exposed to violence, but most do not. As a result, children can be overlooked unless their behavior is troublesome enough to warrant attention from their family or school.

If your mentee is living in these circumstances, he will benefit from the same kinds of support we recommend for children who experience violence at home (see Question 45). You can become your mentee's advocate by working with your program coordinator, the family, and the school to find safe, out-of-school activities for him. Or, help him create a "safety action plan" and talk with your mentee about possible scenarios that might occur and help him think through in advance how he would handle them. This could include identifying places and areas to avoid, identifying safe places he can go if an incident occurs, knowing how to contact the police, and seeking adult support after an incident.

Children who live in unsafe communities may decide to carry weapons for protection. If you become aware that your mentee is doing this, you should strongly encourage finding other ways of feeling safe, and help her understand the consequences of carrying weapons, such as having a gun or knife turned against her or being expelled from school. You should report the weapon to your program coordinator.

Your mentee also may be attracted to gang membership for group identification or protection. Some signs of gang involvement include changes in friends, changes in clothing (such as wearing the same color combination all the time), gang symbols on clothing or possessions, tattoos, extra cash from unknown sources, carrying a weapon, and declining interest in school and family. Your relationship with your mentee is a powerful preventive influence against gang membership, but your mentee may be subject to other forces that are too hard to resist, such as the lure of easy money, threats of retaliation for not joining the gang, and a strong belief that being in a gang is the only way to be safe in the community.

If you suspect your mentee is tempted to become involved with a gang, talk to him about it, staying as nonjudgmental as possible and refraining from giving advice. Encourage him to talk in order to understand as much as you can about his motivations and his assessment of the risks and rewards of gang membership. Understanding his perspective will help you know how to approach helping him. In general, you want to be able to meet the needs a gang fills so that joining one will no longer be attractive. You can also consult your program coordinator about additional resources or help you can access to address this issue. If your mentee has already joined a gang, you should not try to deal with the situation alone. Gangs can be dangerous and unpredictable. You should inform your program coordinator, and he or she may elect to inform the local police. If you feel your personal safety is at risk, discuss with your program coordinator the feasibility of continuing the mentoring relationship.

QUESTION 47. *I am concerned about my mentee's safety in a dating relationship. What can I advise?*

The National Center for Victims of Crime defines dating violence as "controlling, abusive and aggressive behavior in a romantic relationship which may include physical violence, verbal abuse, sexual assault and emotional abuse." Such behavior occurs in both heterosexual and same-sex relationships. Additional information is available at ncvc.org (click on "Dating Violence Resource Center" in the "Resource Centers" menu). According to a 2006 study conducted by the National Teen Dating Abuse Hotline and the Liz Claiborne Foundation, one in five girls reports having been hit, slapped, or pushed by a dating partner. Highlights of the report are available at loveisrespect.org/is-this-abuse/dating-abuse-fast-facts. As a result of this study, the website LoveIsRespect.org and the National Teen Dating Abuse Helpline were created. Visit this website and that of the National Center for Victims of Crime (ncvc.org) to learn more about dating violence.

If there is a high degree of closeness and trust in your relationship, your mentee may bring up this topic, or you may observe changes, including signs of physical injuries. Your mentee may talk about her dating partner's behavior toward her. Some of the things to be on the alert for include a dating partner who is very jealous, wants to control your mentee's social life or her relationship with you, obsessively tracks her whereabouts, is verbally abusive, seems excessively needy, or insists on a level of sexual activity for which your mentee is not ready. In the early stages of a dating relationship, your mentee might interpret these as signs of love.

Your mentee also may show emotional and behavioral changes that could include frequently canceling your sessions; constantly checking his cell phone when with you (especially if you have set ground rules about not using it when you are together); irritability and anxiety; unexplained bruises or scratches, especially after the weekend; becoming secretive; and seeming worried and distracted.

If you suspect dating violence, it will be hard to approach the topic in a nonthreatening way. Most young people are embarrassed or ashamed of what is happening, and they may still be intensely loyal to their dating partners. Consequently, they are likely to be reluctant to or even strongly resist talking with you. Stress that you are there for your mentee, but do not press the issue. If you are fairly certain that something is going on, consult your program coordinator, who may want to inform the family. If you are seriously concerned about your mentee's safety, either your program coordinator or you should definitely involve the family. You also can familiarize yourself with helping resources in the community (such as the National Dating Abuse Helpline and your local domestic violence hotline) so that you are ready to offer help if and when your mentee decides to seek your help.

QUESTION 48. *My mentee is being bullied and doesn't want to go to school anymore. How can I help?*

This problem should be brought to the attention of your program coordinator, who will discuss it with your mentee's family. If you are mentoring informally, you can discuss the situation with your mentee's family directly. It will be the family's decision whether to pursue action to stop the bullying, and it is possible that they will not want to do so. If they do want to take action and if the bullying is occurring at school, it is reasonable to expect the school to play a role in solving the problem. If family members schedule a meeting with the school, they can decide whether to include you in the meeting. The goals of the meeting will be to discuss what is happening, decide what actions need to be taken, and make a plan to protect your mentee. Some states now require schools to have antibullying policies and programs. The website bullypolice.org maintains status reports on what each state is doing to address bullying.

If the bullying is occurring outside school, or if it is a case of cyberbullying (which occurs over the Internet, usually through social media sites), your mentee's family may choose to contact the local police. Even when the bullying is occurring out of school, your mentee may be afraid to see the bullies at school. If the bullying outside of school is by another student, the school may still have legal power to take action.

As the mentor, your role is to support your mentee in coping with the bullying (see Question 42a for more guidance on how to do this). In this situation, focus on helping your mentee develop skills, strategies, and a plan that includes how to avoid bullies, how to handle the situation if she does encounter bullies, how to engage bystanders in responding to bullies, and deciding which adults at the school she can tell when the bullying occurs. Don't forget to reinforce the importance of her education.

QUESTION 49. *My mentee is pregnant and has asked me for advice. Any guidelines here?*

This can be a delicate and sensitive situation depending on your relationship with your mentee and her family. Some parents and guardians may be incensed if you provide advice to their child on this topic, while others might appreciate your support and involvement as they try to help their child. The more you know about your mentee's cultural, religious, and family values, the more comfortable you will be in responding. If your mentee is younger than 18, you should consult your program coordinator before responding to the request for advice. If you would like to delay the discussion or seek your program coordinator's input, you can tell your mentee you need time to think about it before you can talk to her about options.

When you do talk to your mentee, as in other sensitive situations, you should take the approach of encouraging her to talk and explore options rather than plunging in with ready advice. Ask if she has told her family about the pregnancy, and ask about the family's response. You do not want to put yourself in the position of seeming to offer conflicting advice. You can ask if she has told the baby's father, and ask what his views are, as well.

The Resource Center for Adolescent Pregnancy Prevention, a program of ETR Associates Inc., provides "pregnancy options counseling" guidelines at etr.org/recapp for educators to help pregnant teens assess their options. The parent section of the website kidshealth.org also has useful information on how to respond to a pregnant teen.

When you talk to your mentee, keep these guidelines in mind:

> Keep calm so that your mentee will feel comfortable talking to you.

> Thank your mentee for trusting you enough to want to talk to you, and tell her how much you care about her.

> Encourage your mentee to talk about how she feels about the pregnancy, how her family feels, and how the baby's father feels.

> Ask your mentee what options she has considered. These might include keeping the baby and raising it, giving the baby to a family member to raise, adoption, or abortion. Ask which of these options her family and the baby's father support. Ask her which option she prefers.

> Your own values and religious views may make it difficult to continue the discussion if your mentee is considering abortion. It is OK to tell your mentee that this is not something you feel equipped to provide guidance on and to suggest who else she can talk to— a school nurse or local health clinic, for example.

> If you do continue the discussion, encourage your mentee to see her doctor or other health care provider before she makes a decision. If you are quickly able to find information on local helping resources for each of the options she is considering, you can give her this information.

> You can help your mentee think about ways to stay in school no matter what options she is considering.

After your mentee has made her decision, you can be an important source of support for her. You might find this challenging, however, if her choice is at odds with your own religious beliefs and values. If she decides to have an abortion and you are pro-life, you may choose to help her connect with another adult, such as a school nurse or counselor, to provide support on this issue. If she decides to have the baby, she will need significant levels of support to obtain appropriate medical care and stay in school. Your program coordinator also can maintain closer contact with her and help her connect with needed resources. Some school districts have programs specifically for teen mothers to provide them with the support they need to finish school. Note that if your mentee is the father, you can adapt this guidance to help support him.

QUESTION 50. *I think my mentee may have a drinking problem or may be using drugs. Should I bring this up?*

You can find out how many kids are using drugs, what drugs they are using, and tips for how to prevent alcohol and drug use by returning to Question 42g. If you want information on specific drugs and their effects, visit the drug information page on the website of the National Institute on Drug Abuse (NIDA) at drugabuse.gov/DrugPages/DrugsofAbuse.html.

Figuring out whether a young person has a drinking or drug problem, and knowing when and whether a professional needs to intervene, is tricky. Kids' natural inclination is to lie about or minimize the extent to which they drink or use drugs, but chances are that if you are seeing or hearing things that concern you, something is going on. People do not become drug addicts or alcoholics overnight. They go through fairly predictable stages during which there is an increase in the quantity of drugs or alcohol consumed accompanied by an increase in the frequency of using.

Nearly half of all kids will try one or more drugs by the time they graduate from high school according to the National Institute on Drug Abuse, which conducts an annual survey of youth drug use in the United States. A little more than 21 percent of young people have tried an illicit drug by grade 8; this number more than doubles by the time they are in grade 12 (nida.nih.gov/infofacts/hsyouthtrends.html).

When young people first try drugs or alcohol, typically at a middle school age, we say they are *experimenting* with drugs—trying a drug or drinking a few times to see whether they like it. Contrary to popular opinion, experimentation does not last for months or years. After a short period of time, young people have a pretty good idea of how they are affected by alcohol or other drugs, and they make a decision to continue using or not to use again.

If they decide to continue using, the young people move from experimentation to *casual or social use.* During this stage, they typically will use at parties or other get-togethers with their friends. According to the NIDA, close to 10 percent of U.S. 8th graders and 24 percent of 12th graders have used an illicit drug, and close to 14 percent of 8th graders and 41 percent of 12th graders have used alcohol in the past month.

One of the most troubling trends is the quantity of alcohol or drugs consumed. Kids today "drink to get drunk." This same NIDA survey found that 11 percent of 8th graders and 29 percent of 12th graders had consumed five or more drinks at a time within the prior two weeks. As you can see, the quantity used and frequency of use increase with age.

At some time during this stage, warning signs may start to appear, but the absence of warning signs does not mean an absence of risk. Some of the most common risks young people face include alcohol- or drug-related car accidents, unintended or unwanted sexual activity, and harmful effects from the types of drug used or quantity of alcohol consumed. Their use also may be starting to cause conflicts at home over missed curfews, coming home drunk, mood swings, and other issues. Further, the younger kids are when they start using and the more often they use, the more likely they are to have long-term effects in their brain and addiction problems as an adult.

It is hard to say exactly when use becomes *substance abuse*. It is a gradual process marked by increasing frequency of use, increasing quantities consumed, and the desire to try new and stronger drugs. The interest in stronger substances is due to tolerance, a process whereby the body needs ever higher doses of the drug (including alcohol) to feel the desired effects of getting high. There will be warning signs by this stage of use. It is a safe assumption that if you are observing warning signs, your mentee is not experimenting but is using on a more or less regular basis.

By the time someone is addicted, he is spending more and more energy getting and using alcohol or drugs, and there are significant negative effects in his life. In fact, *addiction* means that changes have taken place in a person's brain so that he needs his drug of choice just to feel normal. As a result, there is a compelling motivation to keep using no matter what the negative consequences.

Common warning signs of alcohol and drug use and abuse include the following:

Regular/Social Use Warning Signs

> Changing friends

> Lying or being secretive about activities

> Getting caught at school events using drugs or consuming alcohol

> Breaking curfew

> Showing mood swings, especially on the weekends

> Putting less effort into schoolwork

> Talking about getting high or "wasted"

> Taking prescription drugs from home

> Needing extra money

Abuse Warning Signs (In Addition to the Preceding Signs)

> Showing more extreme and more frequent mood swings and irritability

> Fighting more often with family members

> Responding when confronted about behavior by saying, "You don't trust me"

> Making significant changes in clothing or appearance

> Being found with drugs or paraphernalia at home or school (kids will almost always say they were holding it for someone else)

> Violating school drug policy, resulting in suspension or expulsion

> Having money (when money is missing at home) or an unexplained new source of money

> Losing interest in out-of-school activities

> Skipping classes or not going to school

> Showing physical signs of being under the influence, such as red or glassy eyes, slurred speech

> Having frequent respiratory infections, runny nose, chronic cough, and so on

If you observe any of these signs, bring them to the attention of your program coordinator or your mentee's family. Chances are your mentee's family or teachers are also seeing troubling behaviors but may not be aware of what is causing them. Families have a hard time responding to potential drug problems for a variety of reasons—they may not be knowledgeable about drug warning signs, they may be in denial about what they are seeing or there may be a family history of addiction issues. As a result, they don't take action until their child is in serious trouble at school or in the community. In most cases a professional assessment is needed to determine exactly what is going on and what help the young person needs.

Some general guidelines for talking to your mentee about your concerns are presented in the following list. Your goal should be to get her to talk to you in the hope that she will agree to accept help. It can really help if you first walk through with your program coordinator or other helping professional how you will approach your mentee. Of course, if you think there is an imminent risk of harm, talk to your program coordinator as soon as possible.

> Be prepared. Document the behaviors or personality changes that are concerning you.

> Understand the problem. Either through Internet research or talking to knowledgeable professionals, get a better understanding of what

drugs kids in your area are using and how different drugs affect the body and mind. Compare the warning signs you are observing to this list and other lists of warning signs. A good website about drugs that you can also share with your mentee is teens.drugabuse.gov. A similar site on underage drinking is thecoolspot.gov. The Mothers Against Drunk Driving (MADD) website is another good place to get more information on underage drinking: madd.org/underage-drinking.

> Think about what you hope to accomplish with the conversation. Are you hoping your mentee will agree to get help, or are you just looking for information to confirm or dispel your suspicions?

> Think about what your next steps will be if your mentee is willing to admit there is a problem or if he denies any problem. Whom would you want him to talk to as a next step (e.g., school nurse or counselor, addiction professional)? Check with that person about her or his willingness to see your mentee.

> Choose a time to talk when you can have a good conversation in a place where you won't be interrupted or possibly overheard.

> Share the behaviors you have observed and tell your mentee you are concerned about what is going on. Wait for her to respond.

> Tell your mentee that you are wondering whether he is using drugs or drinking excessively based on what you are seeing. Again, wait for a response, which most likely will be a denial. Try to avoid yes or no questions such as, "You're not using drugs, are you?"

> Ask your mentee about things she has done while under the influence that she regrets or that have embarrassed her.

> Ask him if he ever worries about his use.

> Ask her how much she knows about alcohol- or drug-related problems and the longer-term harm they can cause.

> If your mentee persistently denies any alcohol or drug involvement, ask if there is something else happening that might be causing the behaviors about which you've expressed a concern.

> If your mentee does open up, listen carefully and nonjudgmentally. Ask clarifying questions, especially about what drugs he is using, how often he is using, and how much he consumes each time he uses. Expect that he will minimize what is happening.

> Ask her if she would be willing to talk to someone else about what is happening.

> If he denies that there is any problem, reiterate your concern and how much you care for him. Stress that you are there for him no matter what is happening.

Continue to monitor your mentee's behavior, and bring your concerns to the attention of your program coordinator. Follow guidelines for breaking confidentiality if necessary. Periodically mention your concerns again to your mentee.

QUESTION 51. *My mentee has confided in me about not being certain about her or his sexual orientation. How should I respond to this confidence?*

While most young people know what their sexual orientation is, it is not uncommon for others to wonder about or experiment with their orientation during their teens. Your mentee will probably not share such information with you unless she really trusts you. Depending on your own values and religious beliefs, you may or may not be comfortable with what you hear. If you find that you are so uncomfortable you can't discuss the issue with your mentee, it is better to be up front and honest. You can tell her that you appreciate her trusting you with such an important thing in her life, and thank her for that trust. The discussion may just end there; perhaps your mentee only wants to let you know and is not looking for any guidance on the issue. If, however, she seems to want your perspectives or guidance, you can go on to say that you do not feel equipped to help her with this issue. Then, offer to help connect her with someone else she can talk to about it, such as a school counselor or health educator. School counselors have often had to deal with sexual orientation issues in the context of bullying, and schools in general are more equipped to respond to these issues than they were in the past. Follow up to see if your mentee has talked to anyone.

If you are willing to have your mentee talk to you about the subject, remind yourself that your role is to listen, understand his feelings, and provide "neutral" guidance to help your mentee figure out how he is going to handle the situation. You also can ask your mentee if any other kids suspect he is gay or if they taunt him about it. Stress the importance of talking to an adult at school or in other settings if such bullying is occurring (see Questions 42 and 48 for more information on bullying). You may want to further educate yourself on the topic by talking to a knowledgeable professional or by doing Internet research.

This is an issue you can keep confidential between you and your mentee, unless you feel your mentee is at risk in some way or seems depressed or is using drugs in response to the feelings she is having, for example. Gay teens have a higher rate of suicide than the general teen population, so be alert for suicide risk (see Question 52). If you have any concerns about your mentee's well-being, talk to your program coordinator.

QUESTION 52. *I think my mentee might be depressed, even considering suicide. What should I do?*

Depression and suicide are serious problems among young people. In studies over many years, suicide typically ranks as the third leading cause of death among U.S. teens. While girls make more suicide attempts, boys die more frequently from suicide. According to the Centers for Disease Control and Prevention (2009), "A nationwide survey of youth in grades 9–12 in public and private schools in the United States found that 15% of students reported seriously considering suicide, 11% reported creating a plan, and 7% report[ed] trying to take their own life in the 12 months preceding the survey. Each year, approximately 149,000 youth between the ages of 10 and 24 receive medical care for self-inflicted injuries at Emergency Departments across the U.S." (cdc.gov/violenceprevention/pub/youth_suicide.html).

You might encounter the issue of suicide with your mentee in three ways. You might observe warning signs that set off alarm bells, your mentee may directly say something to you, or your mentee may make a suicide attempt. While we will give you some guidance to recognize suicide warning signs and to have a direct conversation about suicide with your mentee if it seems necessary, we stress that this is not something you can handle on your own. In every case where you are concerned about the potential for suicide, you must seek help as soon as possible, even if it means risking your mentee's trust. It is better to risk losing your relationship than to risk losing your mentee. It is crucial that you act quickly because the urge to commit suicide can be overwhelming for short periods of time during which the person may act.

If you don't have or cannot reach a program coordinator or another helping professional quickly, seek guidance from the national suicide hotline or a local crisis center. The phone number for the National Suicide Prevention Lifeline is 800-273-8255. Their website also has a searchable database of crisis centers (suicidepreventionlifeline.org/CrisisCenters /Locator.aspx). Another resource is the Samaritans, a national suicide prevention program with local chapters that are often listed in the phone book. Additional information about youth suicide can be found on the website of the American Association of Suicidology at suicidology.org/web /guest/stats-and-tools.

RECOGNIZING AND RESPONDING TO WARNING SIGNS OF SUICIDE

Some young people appear to be at greater risk for suicide than others. Among these are young people who have made a prior suicide attempt or experienced the suicide of a friend, parent, or other close family member. Other higher-risk groups include young people who have a mental illness, including depression (which may or may not be diagnosed); lesbian, gay, bisexual, or transgender (LGBT) youth; and young people who are abusing alcohol or other drugs.

Suicide warning signs are often divided into two categories: "high risk of suicide" warning signs, which indicate that a suicide attempt could be imminent, and "general risk of suicide" warning signs, which indicate that the young person may be considering suicide. It is important to note that you may not ever see the high-risk signs, although someone else in your mentee's life may see them. This is why it is so important to get help immediately whenever you see *any* warning signs so that all the relevant information can be put together.

HIGH RISK OF SUICIDE WARNING SIGNS

The following list is not all-inclusive, but it does indicate some of the more common behaviors you might observe:

> Having a specific suicide plan, including an imminent time frame and plans to use a method to which they have access.

> Acquiring the means to kill oneself, especially having access to a gun.

> Giving away possessions and making final arrangements, such as saying good-bye to people or posting good-bye messages on social media sites.

> Talking in ways that indicate that his life is hopeless, that he feels helpless to make it any better, that he is alone—no one else can help him either—and expressing that he is in such intolerable pain that he just can't take it anymore.

GENERAL SUICIDE WARNING SIGNS

This list also is not all-inclusive, but it does point out some of the more common things you are likely to observe:

> Talking or writing about wanting to commit suicide (as opposed to talking or writing about the idea of suicide more conceptually).

> Sudden or unexpected changes in behavior, including declining school performance and increasing disciplinary problems.

> Loss of interest in normal activities.

> Neglect of personal appearance.

> Avoiding friends and family—and you.

> Increasing use of alcohol and other drugs to escape negative feelings.

> Depression, which can often be seen as sadness in girls and expressions of anger in boys; however, it is important to note that this is a generalization and may not apply to your mentee.

> Overreaction to criticism or failure and a high degree of self-criticism.

> Significant or persistent change in eating or sleeping patterns.

> Persistent physical complaints, especially headaches and stomach problems in spite of medical care.

> Increase in risk-taking behavior.

> Self-inflicted wounds. While cutting oneself is not always evidence of potential suicide, it is still serious behavior that should be addressed by a mental health professional.

> Pessimism about her future.

> Difficulty adjusting to a loss, such as breaking up with a boyfriend or girlfriend or parents' divorce.

If you observe any of these warning signs within a short period of time or consistently over a longer period, or if you just have a "bad feeling about things," trust your instincts. It is not common to wonder whether someone might be suicidal, so the fact that the idea occurs to you probably means something is going on that needs to be evaluated by a professional. You should take action by talking to your program coordinator or your mentee's family if you are mentoring informally. Talk to a suicide prevention professional before you act. This might well be the most serious situation a mentor encounters and is one you cannot handle on your own. If you do not have a program coordinator and you are the one contacting the family, you can start by telling them what you have observed and telling them how concerned you are. Try to engage the parents or guardians as your partners in figuring out what is going on by asking if they have observed any unusual or troubling behaviors in their child in recent weeks. You can say that you are not sure what is going on but that some of the signs you are seeing could indicate that the young person is at risk of suicide.

It helps to write down everything you can remember observing before you have this conversation so you can be as specific as possible. It also can be very helpful to have a list of suicide warning signs with you so that you can make comparisons between the list and what you have been seeing.

Be prepared. It is not unusual for families to minimize the seriousness of what you are telling them; they often assume that these warning signs are just typical adolescent mood swings. This reaction could be due to the fact that what you are telling them is so frightening that they may go into a mild state of shock and have trouble processing the information. You may find that you have to be somewhat assertive in conveying your concern about the possibility of suicide. It also helps if you can provide your mentee's family with some options for next steps. You could ask if they know anyone they can talk to about the issue, a member of the clergy in their faith, a family doctor, or a school counselor. If they resist these suggestions, you can give them the number for a suicide hotline and suggest that they consult someone there about the information and get that person's advice on what to do next. One approach to take if you are meeting with resistance is to say that something seems to be going on, and although you and they are not sure what, taking their child to a professional can at least rule out the issue of suicide. "Better safe than sorry," you can advise. At some point, you will have to leave it in their hands, but tell them that you are willing to help in any way you can, and ask if they would like you to talk to your mentee about your concerns.

We recommend that you follow up with the family to see how things are going, to see if they have talked to anyone, and to offer your support. Do not be surprised if they have not taken any action. If that is the case, tell them what you are continuing to see and express your concern. You are walking a fine line between protecting your mentee and overstepping your role, and you also risk their perception that you are meddling in their family affairs. At some point you may just have to back off altogether so that they do not want to terminate your relationship with their child.

An additional step you can take is to talk to a professional at your mentee's school to alert that person to what you see so he or she also can be tuned in to possible warning signs and have a counselor meet with your mentee to assess what is happening. If you are comfortable doing so, talk with your mentee yourself, sharing what you are observing and saying how concerned you are. Keep your program coordinator informed about the situation.

TALKING TO YOUR MENTEE ABOUT SUICIDE

As we noted at the beginning of this question, your mentee may initiate a conversation about suicide by saying something to you like, "Sometimes I really feel like hurting myself" or "My life really sucks, I don't know why I'm alive" or "I don't see how I can go on" or "What's the point of living?" or "Who cares whether I'm alive or dead?" When you hear such comments, don't assume your mentee is feeling bad for the moment. Respond as we have outlined in the following bulleted list.

If you want to bring up the topic after you have informed your mentee's family and your program coordinator about the warning signs you are seeing, follow your program coordinator's guidance in deciding whether to have this conversation.

If you do have a conversation, initiated either by your mentee or by you, find a place where you can have uninterrupted privacy and allow enough time for a serious conversation. If your mentee brings it up just as your session is ending, extend the session if you can, or tell him you want to see him again as soon as possible to talk about what he just said. Your goal is to gather the information you need to help you decide what to do next, not to give advice or solve your mentee's problem. It is important to remain clear about the difference.

As stressed elsewhere, the best approach to helping your mentee is to listen far more than you talk and to convey to your mentee how much you care for her. This is especially true in potential suicide situations because it is important to understand your mentee's emotional state and possible suicide plans as you plan what do next.

> Encourage your mentee to talk about his feelings regarding his life at this point in time. As your mentee talks about what is going on, ask questions that get at the underlying feelings he has about what is going on. Keep the focus on the here and now rather than the past. Doing so will help you assess what feelings he has and determine how persistent and strong these feelings are.

> Listen for feelings of unbearable pain, inability to tolerate more pain, helplessness, hopelessness, and feeling alone. The more intensely your mentee expresses such feelings, the more serious the situation.

> Help your mentee focus on what she would like to change to feel better. Ask what would make her feel better or make the situation more bearable. This will help you assess how hopeless she feels.

> Explore what he thinks he can do to change things. You also can ask what he did when faced with similar situations in the past. How did he cope with such bad feelings? What made a difference then? Did he think about or attempt suicide then? This will help you assess how helpless he feels and whether he is at increased risk due to a prior attempt.

> Ask who she thinks could help her with her problems. If she says you, indicate that you are very willing to help but that you don't think you can do so alone. Tell your mentee you would like it if you can both talk to another trusted adult. Ask about other adults she trusts who might be more knowledgeable about how to help her, and suggest some if she has no ideas. This will help you assess how alone she feels and how willing she is to accept help.

> If possible, agree on a next step of talking to someone, preferably a mental health professional.

> If your mentee does not believe anyone can help, ask him if he has thought about suicide as a way out. Your heart will probably be in your throat when you do this. You may be worried that you are planting the idea—you're not. You are opening a door to allow your mentee to get help. You should be specific in phrasing the question, for example, "Have you considered suicide?" or, "Have you thought about killing yourself?" Asking a vague question like, "You're not thinking about hurting yourself, are you?" will not allow you to assess how serious the situation is.

> If your mentee answers no, tell her how glad you are and continue to make a plan for getting help by talking to a professional.

> If your mentee answers yes, the next step is to ask him if he has planned how he will do it, what method he will use, and when he will do it. Try to assess how imminent the risk is. An imminent risk situation would involve a concrete plan and time frame; your mentee might say, for example, "I thought I would use my dad's gun this weekend," or, "I thought I would hang myself when my parents are away from the house." A lower risk, but still very serious situation, might produce a response like, "I'm not sure, maybe I'll take some pills."

> If your mentee does have a specific plan and time frame, explore whether or not she has access to the method she plans to use. You might ask, "Where does your dad keep his gun? Can you get it easily?" or, "What exactly would you use to hang yourself?"

> If you feel that your mentee has a serious intent to commit suicide in the near future and has a plan to do so, you must inform the family as soon as possible, even to the extent of going home with your mentee and waiting for his parents. Your mentee may resist this, insisting that he is OK. Tell him you will believe this once he has talked to someone else who knows more about this than you do. Assure him that you are there for him and will help in any way you can.

> If you think the risk is less imminent, you should inform your mentee that you have to tell your program coordinator and her family about your concerns. Again, expect resistance or minimizing what she has just told you. She may even get angry with you for not keeping this to yourself. This can be very painful for you, and the best approach is to keep telling her that you care too much for her to walk away from the situation, that you could never live with yourself if anything happened and you had not told someone. Assure her that you will be there for her no matter what and that you will be happy to go with her if she is willing to talk to someone about her problems.

All this information may seem overwhelming and frightening. This is why it is so important for you to have a program coordinator or other helping professional who can either talk to your mentee or, at the least, support and advise you. You also can seek advice from the National Suicide Prevention Lifeline (800-273- 8255) or local crisis center.

We also hope your mentee's family will seek a professional evaluation to determine their child's suicide risk and recommend appropriate counseling or treatment. Unfortunately, many families do not follow through on counseling recommendations, so it is possible the issue will not be dealt with until a crisis occurs. It is also possible that the additional support you and others provide to your mentee may help him get through this difficult period. Continue to monitor warning signs, and continue to bring them to the attention of your program coordinator.

Plan to continue to support your mentee by encouraging her to talk about her feelings and her problems, and guide her in finding ways to cope. Review the information in chapter 7 to stimulate thinking about ways you can help your mentee build a strong social support system and become more resilient. Three things that have been demonstrated to help are physical activity, finding a volunteer project to help others, and engaging in social activities. It could be helpful to continue to encourage your mentee to talk to another helping professional. A mentor is without doubt a help, but a professional mental health expert (psychologist, psychiatrist, or social worker) almost always has a pivotal role in helping a young person not only want to live but learn to live.

QUESTION 53. *My mentee has been arrested. How can I help?*

Your mentee's family or your program coordinator may call to let you know about the arrest. It is possible your mentee will be the one to make the call. The first thing to do is to get more information about what happened and what is going to happen next. Has your mentee actually been placed under arrest or just taken to a police station? What was the offense? How serious an offense was it? Will your mentee be eligible for a diversion program? Will he have to go before a judge? Are there programs to help with problems your mentee might have, like substance abuse or anger management?

You can offer your support to the family and ask what they would like you to do, if anything. Don't be surprised if they are very angry with their child. This is one of those situations where you have to stay in the background unless the family asks you to be part of the response to the situation. You likely can attend a court hearing if there is one. In fact, your mentee's legal counsel may want to demonstrate to the judge that there is an ongoing support system for your mentee by pointing out that you are there.

States and towns differ in how they respond to illegal activity by young people with the action taken being at least partially dependent on the offender's age. Your local police department can probably provide information and guidance to you, depending on your mentee's age. You might need parental permission to be involved after an arrest has occurred. Some of the possible outcomes include the following:

> Your mentee's parents might be called, talked to by the police, and asked to take their child home.

> Your mentee might be referred by the police to a local juvenile diversion program where she will most likely be ordered to perform community service or make some form of restitution.

> Your mentee might be sent to a juvenile justice detention center.

> Your mentee might have a court hearing before a judge. The judge usually has a fair amount of latitude and can take steps like assigning your mentee to a community program, imposing a fine, placing him on probation, sending him to a juvenile justice facility, ordering drug treatment, putting him in a program for anger management or driving under the influence, or ordering some other action—depending on the offense and whether your mentee has a record of prior arrests.

When you see your mentee, you can encourage her to talk about what happened. Try to listen nonjudgmentally; your goal should be to help her process what went on and learn from it. Ask questions that will encourage your mentee to understand what she could have done differently and how she can avoid getting into trouble in the future. Brainstorm what strengths she has that she could have used to avoid whatever she did that was illegal. You may want to tell her you are disappointed but still optimistic, and stress your willingness to help her avoid ever getting in trouble like this again.

QUESTION 54. *My mentee has been put in a juvenile detention facility. What do I do now?*

If your mentee is under the age of 16, any records related to an arrest or subsequent actions by the legal system may be confidential. Your program coordinator or your mentee's family may be able to provide you with information about what is happening. With the permission and support of your mentee's family, you can talk to someone in the facility about options for continuing your mentoring relationship, if feasible given the location. If you cannot continue meeting with your mentee on a regular basis, you may be able to see him during visiting hours. You also can explore options for telephone or e-mail contact. Try to find out how long it is likely to be before your mentee returns home, especially if you are not able to continue seeing him in the facility.

We hope you will be able to maintain some type of regular contact, because your mentee will really be in need of your support after release. Some juvenile justice systems have now incorporated mentoring into programs because they recognize that a mentor can help with the transition back into the community and help reduce recidivism. Your mentee may return to hanging out with old friends and thereby be faced with the same situations that got her into trouble. As her mentor, you can help her develop strategies to avoid these situations, which typically involve drug use or dealing, gang involvement, or anger management issues. You can talk about being strong enough not to be influenced by others. Your mentee also will need help in identifying other activities and friends to replace those that led to the arrest. It is helpful to work on concrete short-term goals (like avoiding parties where drugs are available) as well as long-term goals (example: what she hopes to do with her life and plans to get there). Another role you can play is to be her advocate in seeking additional services that are needed to address substance abuse, mental health, academic issues, and other problems.

QUESTION 55. *My mentee's family has lost their housing and is now living in a homeless shelter. Can we stay connected?*

We hope your mentee is in a shelter that is close enough for you to continue your relationship. Your support during this challenging time will be crucial. Express ongoing respect and concern, not pity. Your mentee is probably very worried about his parents and the future of his whole family. It can be a time of very high anxiety, made worse by the fact that the family may not have any answers regarding what will happen next.

If you have a program coordinator, he or she may be able to get more information about your mentee's family situation. If not, you can talk directly to the family if you have a relationship with them. Some of the things you may want to know are whether your mentee will be able to attend school and whether the family has a plan for leaving the shelter for alternative housing or will have to stay there for the indefinite future. You can ask whether there are specific things the family would like you to do to support their child.

Assuming you are able to continue your relationship, you will be better equipped to support your mentee if you educate yourself about homelessness and how it affects young people. The staff at the shelter will probably be more than willing to talk with you about their experiences and what they have learned. Federal law requires that every state have a plan and system for educating homeless children, so your state education department is a good place for more information. Another source of information is the website of the National Association for the Education of Homeless Children and Youth (naehcy.org). There and elsewhere you will not be surprised to learn that your mentee will face numerous challenges, including the following:

> Loss of her home, possessions, and even pets.

> Stress of living in a shelter: coping with loss of privacy, cramped space, and potential for conflicts with other residents.

> Possibility of multiple moves and of having to switch schools with each move, which can lead to nonattendance.

> Possibility of having to live with other family members in cramped conditions.

> Embarrassment and fear that his friends at school will find out he is living in a shelter.

> Increased stress and conflict in the family.

These circumstances may all be difficult for your mentee to cope with, so the more you can encourage her to talk about how she is feeling, the better. You also can be responsive to basic needs that are going unmet. Check to see if your mentee has supplies to do homework, books to read, and basic grooming supplies. Provide them if your program's budget or your personal budget allows.

QUESTION 56. *I think my mentee and I have differences (regarding culture, gender, and/or race) that can't be bridged. Is it time to walk away from this relationship?*

Discuss this issue with your program coordinator as soon as possible. Please also refer to Questions 37 and 38. We strongly encourage you to do everything possible to avoid terminating your relationship. Your program coordinator may suggest that you attend a training session, read some information, or try some new activities in your mentoring sessions that will help you better understand your mentee's background, as well as help your mentee understand yours. It is possible that neither of you knows how to build a bridge of understanding to connect your backgrounds. With guidance from your program coordinator, you may discover that you and your mentee are able to take a few small steps that will begin to increase mutual respect and understanding. If, in spite of this effort, you still feel that that the relationship cannot be salvaged, talk to your program coordinator about how best to end it (see also Question 36 on terminating relationships).

5

QUESTIONS ABOUT
SPECIAL CIRCUMSTANCES
SOME MENTEES FACE

"You are not your circumstances."
TEACHER AND MENTOR NELSON BROWN TO 11-YEAR-OLD KRISTIE ZAPPIE

We said at the outset that we do not like the term "at-risk youth," but clearly there are too many American children who routinely find themselves in circumstances that place them at risk for developmental delays and other problems that can have long-term consequences. That jeopardy may come from the environments in which the adults in their lives place them—in homes marked by violence or drug abuse, or in schools or neighborhoods where the community allows such problems to prevail. The risk could be the result of a parent's status as an undocumented immigrant or as one of the growing number of Americans living without access to adequate health care. Or it may be a result of a parent's absence altogether, due to incarceration or lack of either the financial or emotional means to provide care.

The questions in this chapter address issues raised by mentors whose mentees' lives are affected—or disrupted—in these ways. The answers aim to provide advice, as well as information, that can help put risk factors in context. The answers also set the stage for a full discussion of Developmental Assets, which can provide an effective antidote and are outlined in chapter 7. As you read them, bear in mind the crucial insight that teacher and mentor Nelson Brown conveyed to 11-year-old Kristie Zappie. "You are not your circumstances, Kristie. You are smart, you work really hard, and you have a future. A good one, too." Mr. Brown was absolutely right about

Kristie, whom we have come to know and appreciate as a close colleague and friend. You will be equally right to convey the same kind of message if your mentee lives with difficult circumstances, too.

QUESTION 57. *My mentee is in foster care. What does that mean?*

To begin, we urge you set aside any preconceived notions you have about children in foster care. Our experience is that the popular image of fostered children is a negative one: a generalized impression that kids both enter and emerge from the experience damaged in meaningful and perhaps irreparable ways. In fact, children in foster care are at heightened risk for behavioral and educational difficulties (Smith, 2011). For example, 65 percent of 18-year-olds who "age out" of foster care programs do not complete high school (Harden, 2004). Yet, it is equally true that high-quality foster care, quick and safe transitions to a permanent living arrangement, and a host of other factors (e.g., strong ties with extended family, informal support systems, and personal resilience) can and do produce a different set of outcomes.

Even more meaningful to a mentor is that you are or will be working with one child, not a statistic or an aggregation of either empirical evidence or communal impressions. And both foster children themselves and a growing body of research suggest that mentors, especially for children who are older and/or are in longer-term placements, can play a key role (Annie E. Casey Foundation, 2008; Ahrens, DuBois, Richardson, Fan & Lozano, 2008). One proponent, U.S. Senator Mary Landrieu, sponsor of the Foster Care Mentoring Act of 2011, says this: "Mentoring relationships can play an enormous role in helping foster youth reach their academic and personal potential . . . and can [help foster youth] learn to thrive when someone gives the energy and time to show that they care."

The basic facts about foster care are these: A child is placed in foster care when a child protective services agency and the court determine that is it not safe for the child to live at home. The cause for such action is maltreatment or risk of it, stemming from neglect or physical or sexual abuse. The U.S. Census Bureau estimates that there were 424,000 children in foster care placements in 2009, a decline of 25 percent from the peak 10 years earlier (U.S. Census Bureau, 2010). The nature of placements varies and includes the homes of relatives (in an arrangement called kinship care) or nonrelative adults who volunteer to serve as foster parents;

group homes or institutions (including mental health treatment centers or orphanages—there are still a few); and pre-adoptive homes. The length of time a child stays in foster care (or a single foster care placement) varies, too: the average is 33 months, although the stay is often longer if the child or teen has developmental or behavioral issues, is part of a large sibling group, or is a member of an ethnic or racial minority (American Academy of Pediatricians, 2011). A little more than half of children in care are reunited with their birth parent(s). The Foster Care Alliance estimates that 12 million adults were in foster care.

Because children who have been in foster care for any length of time are, without doubt, at additional developmental risk, you will be in a better spot if you are mentoring a child through a formal program. A number of mentoring programs have developed a special interest in this population of young people, starting with the pioneering efforts of former first lady of the state of New York, Matilda Raffa Cuomo, founder of Mentoring USA. In a formal program, you'll have access to specialized resources and support. Nonetheless, if an opportunity to informally mentor a fostered child presents itself, don't instantly shy away. The outcomes for kids in foster care who don't get additional support of many kinds—including mentoring—are troubling. No doubt you are needed, and a strong network of personal support and good online resources (aecf.org/KnowledgeCenter .aspx) may make you a very good mentor, especially if you think there is more than a reasonable chance that you can be a *reliable* source of friendship and guidance. Kids in foster care or who have been fostered typically have had more than their fair share of unreliable adults in their lives. They don't need another one.

⊡ DATA POINT
Aging Out of Foster Care

Many youth who "age out" of foster care instead of returning home face tough challenges to making a successful transition to adulthood. Only 48 percent had graduated from high school at the time of discharge, and only 54 percent had graduated between two and four years following discharge. As adults, children who spent long periods in multiple foster care placements were more likely to face unemployment, homelessness, and incarceration, as well as experience early pregnancy. Support (including mentoring) can be crucial.

Sources: Casey Family Programs (2001); Child Trends (2011); Courtney and Pillavin (1998); Reilly (2003) and Spencer Collins, Ward & Smashnaya (2010).

QUESTION 58. *My program coordinator told me my mentee has been the victim of abuse (physical or sexual). How common is this and what might signal to me that it is happening again?*

First of all, review Question 45 if you suspect your mentee is currently being abused. Otherwise, note that reports released by local governments and national monitoring agencies all estimate that 3 million children in the United States are reported abused or neglected each year. This horrifying statistic includes four forms of abuse—physical abuse, sexual abuse, emotional/psychological abuse, and neglect—all described by the American Academy of Pediatrics in the Highlight that follows.

If you suspect any form of abuse, you must inform your program coordinator or the relevant child protective services in your state immediately. You can find a current list of child abuse hotlines in various states at www.childwelfare.gov. (Look under "State Related Organizations Lists" on the home page.) If your program coordinator has alerted you (or if you become aware that the child you are mentoring has been the victim of abuse or neglect of any sort) he or she will or should provide you with additional counsel, support, and perhaps training. All will be geared to helping you understand three things: what your mentee has experienced, how you should respond if your mentee brings up the subject . . . or not, and the role a close relationship with a caring adult can play in increasing a child's resiliency and blunting some of the impact. Your support as a mentor is not a substitute, however, for the services of qualified mental health and other professionals that abused children typically need. If you or your program coordinator believes that your mentee needs but is not getting this level of help, depend on your coordinator to locate and make the proper referrals.

Alternatively, if you are in a formal mentoring program and your program coordinator doesn't make the offer of additional support, *ask* for and insist on getting guidance. And if you are mentoring informally and find that your mentee has been or is being abused, be equally dogged in learning about the issue and, if the abuse is ongoing, seek professional help on how to intervene and do so quickly. Abuse and neglect can have serious short-term and long-term consequences. Three children die each day in the United States from abuse and neglect. Children who have been severely mistreated may become depressed or suicidal, withdrawn, or violent. As they get older, they may turn to alcohol and drugs, or simply take the not irrational step of running away.

HIGHLIGHT
Information to Recognize and Prevent Child Abuse

The following information is to assist health care providers, family, and the community to recognize child abuse and neglect and prevent it from happening.

• *Physical abuse* is when a child is hit, slapped, beaten, burned, or otherwise physically harmed. Like other forms of abuse, physical abuse usually continues for a long time.

• *Sexual abuse* is when a child engages in a sexual situation with an adult or older child. Sometimes this means direct sexual contact, such as intercourse, other genital contact, or touching. But it can also mean that the child is made to watch sexual acts, look at adult genitals, look at pornography, or be part of the production of pornography. Children many times are not forced into the sexual situation, but rather are persuaded, bribed, tricked, or coerced.

• *Emotional/psychological abuse* is when a child is regularly threatened, yelled at, humiliated, ignored, blamed, or otherwise emotionally mistreated. For example, making fun of a child, calling a child names, and always finding fault are forms of emotional/psychological abuse.

• *Neglect* is when a child's basic needs are not met. These needs include nutritious food, adequate shelter, clothing, cleanliness, emotional support, love and affection, education, safety, and medical and dental care.

Source: The American Academy of Pediatrics (2011). Reprinted with permission.

Because child abuse can have such far-reaching consequences, it is also important that mentors be mindful of the symptoms of child abuse so that they can play a part in ensuring that their mentees are either living in or finding a safe environment. The symptoms of abuse and ways to take effective action are covered in Question 45. The American Academy of Pediatrics is an excellent source of information on the nature and extent of child abuse in the United States. One straightforward and easily accessible review of the subject is the academy's clearly titled report *What to Know about Child Abuse* (downloadable at healthychildren.org). It is a good place to start your search for what you will want and need to know. In fact, consider the site an invaluable resource for easy-to-access information about all kinds of child health matters.

QUESTION 59. *My mentee's family recently immigrated to the United States. What can I do to be mindful of that, but not excessively so?*

This is an especially important question because the United States is becoming an increasingly diverse society. As both immigration and the number of children born to immigrant parents have increased, so too have the number of mentoring programs that target or serve the children of immigrants. You may be mentoring in a program that serves a specific population of immigrant children, or you may have been paired with an immigrant child within the larger context of a general mentoring program. No matter what form your mentoring takes, you will find that although both immigrants and their children face special challenges and risks, they also have powerful assets to help them adapt to and become part of their new home in America. In *Mentoring Immigrant and Refugee Youth,* MENTOR (2009) highlights a few of them.

CHALLENGES AND RISKS

> Separation from family members, including periods of separation from one or both of their parents and siblings

> Adjusting to a new culture, language, and living conditions, including a strong possibility that they will live in poverty

> Recovering from traumatic experiences as a result of leaving their homeland and/or traumatic experiences related to genocide, war, torture, and death of family members or friends

> Renegotiating family norms, rules, and parent-child roles as the family and children adapt to the American culture and language

> Difficulties in adjusting to school for a variety of reasons, including limited English proficiency (both in parents and children), possibly less well-educated parents, inadequate or interrupted schooling in their country of origin, attendance at lower-performing, segregated schools, and attendance problems resulting from the child's role as an interpreter or child care provider for the family

> Coping with negative racial, religious, or culture-based stereotyping and discrimination, which may also include bullying by other children

ASSETS AND STRENGTHS

> Strong family ties and family value systems that create a sense of belonging and support

> Interdependent immigrant communities that foster mutual support and problem solving

> Flexibility in adapting to change and resilience in acquiring new leadership, problem-solving, and negotiating skills

> The ability to speak two (and sometimes more than two) languages

> Family and community belief in education as the key to success in the United States

As a mentor you can play a pivotal role in helping immigrant children embrace their new life and capitalize on the assets they bring to it. But do your homework. Learn about your mentee's ethnic and cultural identity and country of origin. If you are in a formal mentoring program, you can expect to receive training and support to help you better understand your mentee's culture and issues related to the immigrant experience. If such training and information are not available, look for them elsewhere. Good places to start are the many faith-based communities that are actively involved in supporting recent immigrants and refugees, along with periodic training seminars offered by local Mentoring Partnerships. One easily accessible online resource is a toolkit built on MENTOR's *Mentoring Immigrant and Refugee Youth* (available at mentoring.org/downloads /mentoring_1197.pdf). Also, take a look at Question 37, and remember that special credit goes to those who read the strong chapter on immigrant youth in DuBois and Karcher's *Handbook of Youth Mentoring* (2005).

Take every opportunity to engage your mentee. Ask him to teach you about the country where his parents were born or offer to learn about the country together if he isn't very familiar with his country of origin. It will make for a fascinating learning experience for both of you.

Meanwhile, bear in mind that most experts believe it is important to do the following:

> Encourage your mentee to maintain the cultural, religious, and family values of her country of origin while simultaneously helping her adapt to U.S. culture.

> Encourage your mentee to respect his family rules and values, which he may resist in his effort to assimilate.

> Support your mentee in her efforts to do well in school and encourage her to stay in school, since children of immigrants drop out at alarmingly high rates (see Question 39).

> Be on the alert for behaviors that might indicate your mentee is having a hard time coping, such as depression, drug use, inability to manage anger and aggression, or involvement with gangs.

Mentors of immigrant children are in a unique position to recognize unmet needs and serve as advocates and intermediaries who can see that such needs are addressed. In addition, if conflicts or difficulties emerge at school or in the community, you can work with your program coordinator to support your mentee and his family as they try to resolve such issues. However, we urge you to think about how involved you want to be in your mentee's life. You can set limits, but it is important to do so early on in your relationship so that you don't build expectations that can't or won't be met. If you are in a formal mentoring program, discuss the likely extent of your commitment with your program coordinator and also revisit Questions 21, 31, and 32. If you are mentoring informally, talk about these concerns with someone in your personal network.

An additional issue for you to consider in mentoring a child from an immigrant family is the nature of your relationship with your mentee's family. If you are mentoring in a community-based program where you are expected to have some contact with the family, you may feel challenged by language and cultural differences. Your mentoring program should provide you with support, including facilitating language translation and helping you better understand your mentee's culture.

QUESTION 60. *I think my mentee's family is in the United States illegally. What are my obligations?*

You are under no obligation to take action if you suspect that your mentee's parent(s) may have entered the country illegally. People are classified as undocumented immigrants if they have entered the United States illegally or have stayed past their visa expiration date. It is not unusual for one parent to be in the country legally while the other has entered illegally. As a mentor, you are unlikely to know the immigration status of your mentee's parent(s) unless one or both of them are apprehended by the immigration authorities. It is also important to note that if your mentee

> ### DATA POINTS
> ### Children of Immigrants
>
> The Population Reference Bureau reports that between 1990 and 2007, the number of children in immigrant families nearly doubled, from 8.3 million to 16.5 million, while the number of children in U.S.-born families increased by only 3 percent. Children of immigrants account for 22 percent of all children and are the fastest-growing segment of the U.S. population under 18. By 2020, one in three children is projected to live in an immigrant family.
>
> Source: Mather (2009).
>
> In 2009, the number of immigrant children rose to 17.4 million, or nearly one in four of all U.S. children.
>
> Source: Child Trends (2011).
>
> Among the 50 states, California (47 percent), Nevada (32 percent), New York (32 percent), Texas (30 percent), and New Jersey (30 percent) have the highest proportions of immigrant children. With the exception of Nevada, these are historically gateway states that still serve as entry points for many immigrant groups.
>
> Source: Annie E. Casey Foundation (2007).

was born in the United States, he or she is an American citizen, even if the parents entered the country illegally.

If your mentee's parent(s) are apprehended for being in the country illegally, they may be detained and deported by U.S. Immigration and Customs Enforcement (which is part of the U.S. Department of Homeland Security). If the children also are in the country illegally, they, too, are likely to be deported. The status of children who are legal citizens in these cases has been the subject of much controversy, however. There have been cases in which the children were left totally on their own when their parent(s) were taken away by the authorities. More efforts are now being made to involve local child welfare authorities when the parents are taken into custody or deported.

If your mentee's parent(s) are apprehended by immigration authorities, you may hear about it directly from your mentee, your program coordinator, or your mentee's school. If there is no family member to care for your mentee while the parents are in detention, your mentee may be placed in a temporary foster home or other juvenile facility. It should still be possible for you to meet, or at least talk. You should be in a better position to deal

> ### DATA POINT
> ### Children of Immigrants and Citizenship
>
> The Urban Institute reports that most children of immigrants are U.S. citizens. In 2007, 87 percent of these children were citizens. Almost all citizen children of immigrants are citizens by birth (97 percent), while the rest are citizens by naturalization.
>
> Source: Fortuny and Chaudry (2009).

with this eventuality if you are mentoring through a formal program, since you can turn to your program coordinator to support you in your efforts to make contact. We also suggest you review Question 53.

This is an obvious point but it is worth emphasizing: your mentee will face many additional challenges if one or both of her parents has been detained or deported. If your mentee is a U.S. citizen with the option and support system to stay in the country, she is likely to feel very conflicted about whether to go back with her parent(s) or stay and finish her education. Few mentors have faced similar situations, and many feel overwhelmed and inclined to end the mentoring relationship. Please stay with it. Even if minimal, maintaining consistent contact with your mentee will be important to her. Also bear in mind that your program coordinator should be able to identify local legal aid or immigration services that can provide guidance about how you can best support your mentee. These agencies also offer services that can support your mentee and her family, and a good program coordinator will make referrals for the mentee and her family. A list of some national service organizations is available in MENTOR's *Mentoring Immigrant and Refugee Youth: A Toolkit for Program Coordinators* (mentoring.org/downloads/mentoring_1197.pdf).

QUESTION 61. *My mentee has a parent in prison. Should I ignore this or bring it up with my mentee?*

Although the United States has less than 5 percent of the world's population, it has almost a quarter of the world's prisoners (Liptak, 2008; U.S. Census Bureau, 2011). That translates into well over 2 million prisoners held in federal or state correctional facilities or local jails. According to the National Resource Center on Children and Families of the Incarcerated,

> ### DATA POINT
> **Prisoners in the United States**
>
> In 1990, there were 773,919 prisoners under the jurisdiction of U.S. federal or state correctional authorities and 3,201,641 adults on probation or parole. In 2008, the corresponding numbers were 1,609,606 in state or federal prisons and 5,099,086 on probation or parole.
>
> Source: U.S. Census Bureau (2011).

this further translates into two remarkable statistics: nearly 2 million children currently have a parent in prison, and nearly 10 million more have a parent who is under the supervision of the criminal justice system via probation or parole.

You may learn about your mentee's status in one of several ways. You may be volunteering for a program that explicitly reaches out to this population of children. A prime example is the Amachi Program, which serves children of prisoners by linking "people of faith with children of promise." Alternatively, you may learn about your mentee's parent's status through your program coordinator. Or, more jarringly, your mentee's parent could be incarcerated sometime during the course of an ongoing mentoring relationship. No matter how you learn about the situation, it is best not to introduce the subject into your conversations with your mentee unless he indicates an interest in discussing it or offers another clear signal that he is comfortable addressing the subject. Remember, take your lead from your mentee; he will talk when he is ready (for more on this, please revisit Question 24).

It is important to recognize that children of incarcerated parents typically face major life changes when their parents go to prison. These changes are even more pronounced if their mother is imprisoned (check out *Childern on the Outside* at nicic.gov/Library). Consider that:

> Depending on the circumstances of the arrest (for example, if the police forcibly entered your mentee's home and arrested a parent during a drug raid), your mentee may have post-traumatic stress disorder.

> If your mentee's other parent is not available or able to be their primary caregiver, your mentee may have to live with a relative (often a grandparent) or may be placed in foster care (see also Question 57).

Moreover, your mentee's living situation may change multiple times during the parent's incarceration. Such dislocation can cause profound feelings of loss—of her parent; of her former home, neighborhood, and school; and of her friends. Your mentee's reaction to these changes will be similar to those of a child whose parents are divorcing or whose parent is being deployed in the military. Question 42e can provide guidance on how to help your mentee cope. See also Question 35 for ideas about how to continue your relationship in some form. Your continued presence as a stable caring adult in your mentee's life will be more important than ever.

> Your mentee's life is likely to be more chaotic because of changes in his caregiver situations, the challenges facing his caregiver in taking care of him, financial difficulties, and the logistics of visiting his incarcerated parent. This may result in last-minute shifts in meeting times with your mentee or meetings that are entirely forgotten.

> If there are changes in caregiver arrangements, your program coordinator may need to obtain permission from the new caregiver for the mentoring relationship to continue.

> Your mentee may feel ashamed about the parent's incarceration and may not want to talk about it, especially in the early stages of the incarceration or of your relationship. Assure your mentee that she can confidentially talk to you about anything, but do not force the conversation. In the meantime, continue to engage her in fun activities and provide support to help her face the many challenges resulting from the situation.

> Your mentee may exhibit increased anger and frustration following the incarceration and following any visits (or canceled visits) to the parent. In addition to being angry that his parent engaged in illegal activities leading to the arrest, your mentee may be angry because he feels his parent has abandoned him. He is likely to have strongly conflicting feelings: anger toward his parent coupled with a longing to reunite with him or her, along with anger at "the system" because the parent was taken away. Encouraging your mentee to talk about whatever feelings he may have, and working with him on anger management and problem-solving skills, will give you a positive focus for your time together as well as help your mentee cope with the situation. You can also support your mentee's efforts to maintain a

relationship with his parent. Help him write a letter or take and send pictures or do artwork for his parent.

> While your role is not to replace your mentee's parent, you can be sensitive to ways you can provide added support to your mentee— doing something special for her birthday, providing additional help with schoolwork, and helping her maintain contact with old friends, to name a few possibilities.

Clearly, working with children who find themselves in this circumstance calls for more than an average level of sensitivity and care. Their constantly shifting environment will test your patience and your flexibility. Remind yourself that it is even harder on your mentee and that his need for the presence of another caring adult is acute.

Another potentially disruptive circumstance you may encounter is a parent's release from prison. Even when eagerly anticipated, release can plunge a family into new or even greater chaos. Roles and responsibilities shift in much the same way they do when a deployed parent returns home or an alcoholic parent goes through treatment. The returning parent is likely facing a myriad of reentry challenges, including not having or not being able to get a job; resisting the temptation to start using alcohol or drugs again; trying to live up to the family's expectations; or coping with her or his own feelings about her or his life or with trauma resulting from the incarceration itself. If the returning parent was abusive in the past, your mentee may dread the parent's return, react with anger, and attempt to be away from home as much as possible. Your mentee may also get into fights, start using alcohol or drugs, exhibit signs of depression, or engage in various risky behaviors.

Please revisit the questions in chapters 3 and 4 for help in tackling some of these situations. Again, remember that your continuing role as a consistent caring adult in your mentee's life will be very important during the reentry phase. Seek help from your program coordinator to respond to any issues that arise or seek their advice on the best ways to handle your mentee's feelings and behaviors. Whether you are mentoring formally or informally, check out the resources of the National Resource Center on Children and Families of the Incarcerated at fcnetwork.org. The center has a wide array of materials that will be helpful, including a list of programs in each state that serve this population.

QUESTION 62. *I've learned that my mentee has a parent who is an active substance abuser. Do I have an obligation to act on that knowledge?*

You may have learned about this situation through your mentee, your program coordinator, or your mentee's family. Your mentee is only likely to tell you if there is a strong feeling of trust in your relationship, since her instinct is to protect her family (and sometimes herself) by hiding or lying about a parent's problem. Thank her for trusting you, and tell her she can talk to you about how she feels or just vent about what is going on. Stress that you will keep anything she tells you confidential. If your mentee's family tells you, you should ask them if they have also told the program coordinator. If so, engage your program coordinator in thinking through how best to support your mentee. If, instead, your program coordinator tells you, you can ask for further information: How long has this been going on? What help, if any, has the family been receiving? Are there behavioral or emotional issues your mentee is likely to have? What specific approaches to conversations does your program coordinator suggest?

Since parental substance abuse is likely to have significant effects on your mentee's life, you will want to learn more about it. Two good sources of information are the websites of the Center on Addiction and the Family (COAF) at coaf.org/organization/orgmain.htm and the National Association for Children of Alcoholics (NACoA) at nacoa.net/aboutnacoa.htm. The NACoA website also has a section just for kids that is suitable for children 10 years old and up.

What you will learn from these organizations is that parental addiction has a major disruptive influence on the family. There are likely to be higher levels of dysfunctional behavior and communication, fighting, domestic violence, and divorce. The family dynamics during the stage when they are adjusting to the substance abuse are similar to those of a family with a deployed parent (see Question 42e). Roles and responsibilities are "reassigned," and children often have to assume adult responsibilities to compensate for the inadequacies of the addicted parent. Parenting skills are compromised and family life is often unpredictable. Children also quickly learn that they cannot trust the addicted parent, who may say or do things or make promises while under the influence that they never remember. Lying becomes a way of life as the family strives to keep the addiction hidden and cope with feelings of shame. The family also lives with a constant sense of fear of something bad happening to the addicted

DATA POINTS:
Substance Abuse in U.S. Families

More than 1 in 10 children in the United States under the age of 18 were living with a substance-dependent or substance-abusing parent.

Over 8.3 million children (11.9 percent) lived with at least one parent who was dependent on or abused alcohol or an illicit drug during the past year.

Of those children living with a substance-abusing parent, 7.3 million (10.3 percent) lived with a parent who was dependent upon or abused alcohol and 2.1 million (3 percent) lived with a parent who was dependent upon or abused illicit drugs.

Among children residing in single-parent households, living with a substance-dependent or substance-abusing parent was more likely in a father-only household (16.1 percent) than in a mother-only household (8.4 percent).

Source: Office of Applied Studies, Substance Abuse and Mental Health Services Administration, U.S. Department of Health and Human Services (2009).

parent, such as a car accident, arrest, or loss of a job. There is a pervasive sense of fear and anxiety related to the unpredictable behavior of the addicted parent, as well. You should also be alert to the possibility of child abuse, including sexual abuse. Such offenses often occur when a parent is under the influence of alcohol or other drugs (see Questions 45 and 58 for more information on family safety and child abuse issues).

According to the Center on Addiction and the Family, some of the effects on children who are growing up in a substance-abusing family include the following:

> Disruption of normal development, increasing the likelihood of social, emotional, physical, or mental health problems

> Higher likelihood of witnessing family violence

> Higher incidence of problems such as anxiety, depression, suicide attempts, substance abuse, and eating disorders

> Increased likelihood of academic and behavioral problems at school, although the oldest child in the family is often a highly successful overachiever

> Tendency to blame themselves or feel responsible for the addicted parent's behavior

> Tendency to become socially isolated to prevent others from finding out about the addicted parent

Some of the things you can do to support your mentee include:

> Reassuring your mentee that he is not to blame for his parent's substance abuse.

> Encouraging your mentee to talk about how she is feeling and listen to her nonjudgmenally as she speaks.

> Helping your mentee understand that his feelings are normal and will get better as he talks about things.

> Being sensitive to behavioral or mood changes that may signal some change for the worse in the situation.

> Monitoring your mentee for signs of child abuse (again, see Questions 45 and 58), substance abuse (Question 50), depression, and an inclination toward suicide (Question 52).

> Focusing on being a stable, predictable, trustworthy adult, and— very important—keeping a stable routine to which your mentee can look forward.

> Helping your mentee develop ways to express anger and frustration.

> Helping your mentee develop coping skills to take care of herself, such as listening to loud music to drown out sounds of fighting, having someone to call when her intoxicated parent arrives to pick her up from a party, getting homework done at school, and so on.

Finally, remember that many children of addicted parents have a very limited social life. They may avoid bringing friends home or going out in public with their parent(s). As noted earlier, they may shy away from making friends because they fear that their parent's problems will be exposed or in a mistaken belief that they must protect their parent from either prosecution or ridicule. They may even find that other young people have been "warned off" by parents who don't want their children to befriend kids from troubled families. If you sense that these considerations apply to your mentee, make a special effort not only to be a good friend to your mentee but also to look for opportunities to help him expand his social life and the social settings in which he is comfortable. The lack of a social life is one void mentors are ideally suited to help fill.

QUESTION 63. *The life my mentee describes leads me to believe that he or she lives in extreme poverty. Can I do anything more than worry about this?*

Your concern about the poverty that affects your mentee's life is well founded. Mohandas Gandhi called poverty the "worst form of violence." Today, the U.S. government reports that 15.5 million children suffer from this form of violence, 3.8 million more than in 2000. These are the children who live in families with incomes below the federal poverty level, which is set at $22,350 a year for a family of four (Federal Interagency Forum on Child and Family Statistics, 2011). Overall, the official child poverty rate—which is one of the United States' official measures of economic hardship—increased 18 percent between 2000 and 2009. This translates into 2.4 million children living below the federal poverty line. Furthermore, many experts agree that official poverty measures tell only part of the story. Research consistently shows that families need an income of about twice the federal poverty level (or $44,700) to make ends meet. Using this gauge, 31 million of the nation's children (or 42 percent) live in low-income families (National Center for Children in Poverty, 2011).

What are the possible consequences for your mentee and other children living in poor families? Very troubling. According to the National Center for Children in Poverty, hardships affecting poor children (which include food insecurity, lack of safe housing and neighborhoods, lack of access to schools operating with adequate rigor and resources, lack of adequate medical and dental care, and extreme economic vulnerability) make poverty the greatest threat to child well-being. Compared with their peers, children raised in poverty, especially young children, are more likely to have cognitive, behavioral, and social or emotional problems. They are disproportionately exposed to a wide range of risk factors, from environmental toxins to maternal depression and trauma and abuse. They are at increased risk of a broad range of negative outcomes that extend beyond childhood into adulthood, including those enumerated by Child Trends and other respected researchers (Duncan & Brooks-Gunn, 1997; Moore, Redd, Burkhauser, Mbwana & Collins, 2009):

> Negative academic outcomes, including lower reading scores and greater likelihood of dropping out

> Greater likelihood of being on the wrong side of the technology divide

> Reduced working memory, which is associated with chronic stress

> Greater incidence of negative behaviors: disobedience, impulsiveness, difficulty getting along with peers, and aggression

> Fewer positive behaviors: positive peer relations and compliance with such things as school rules

> Higher rate of teen childbearing

> Lower self-esteem and greater likelihood of feeling anxious, unhappy, and dependent

> Substandard nutritional status, producing problems associated with low weight-for-age, stunted growth, and obesity

> Greater number of accidents and injuries

> Much greater likelihood of being a poor adult, an effect with a racial differential (33 percent of African American children who were poor during childhood remained poor at ages 25–27, compared to 7 percent of poor White children)

> Greater likelihood of failing to fully capitalize on talents and realize potential

> Greater likelihood for low productivity and low earnings

> Greater likelihood of posing economic costs to the country through reduced productivity and output, the cost of crime, and increased health expenditures

Clearly a mentor is not expected to compensate fully for the serious and wide-ranging challenges that can confront poor children. But mentors can and do play a role in helping their mentees compensate for current deprivations or the consequences of past ones. And it is especially important for mentors to bear three things in mind when they are working with children who are growing up in poverty. First, your expectations for what they can accomplish should not be lowered. At the same time, it is important to do what you can to provide—or, more likely, help them secure—the extra help they are likely to need to achieve their potential (for example, extra tutoring or academic coaching, more opportunities for exposure to cultural institutions and events, and more help in gaining access to the online world). Second, mentors are not Santa Claus (see Question 33), and you are not expected to give your mentees money or to buy them things that they don't have. However, if you have the resources and the mentoring program you are participating in doesn't have rules against it, there

> ⊞ DATA POINT
> ### Rates of Child Poverty
>
> The percentage of children living in poverty and extreme poverty (less than 50 percent of the U.S. federal poverty level) has increased since 2000. Moreover, official rates of poverty are highest for young children: 24 percent of children younger than 6 live in poor families while 19 percent of children ages 6 and up do. Rates of poverty vary tremendously across the states. For example, the rate of child poverty is 10 percent in New Hampshire and 30 percent in Mississippi.
>
> Source: White, Chau, and Aratani (2011).
>
> Among all children living in the United States in 2009, the poverty rate was three times higher for Black children and nearly three times higher for Latino children when compared with rates among White, non-Latino children. In 2009, 36 percent of Black children, 33 percent of Latino children, and 12 percent of White, non-Hispanic children lived in poverty.
>
> Source: Federal Interagency Forum on Child and Family Statistics (2011).
>
> The country's economic challenges have not left children unaffected. The recent recession has wiped out many of the economic gains for children that occurred in the late 1990s. In 2009, 31 percent of U.S. children lived in families with no full-time working parent. In 2010, nearly 8 million children lived with at least one parent who was unemployed and actively looking for work, double the number in 2007. Also troubling are data about the number of children affected by the combined drop in housing prices and the foreclosure crisis.
>
> Source: Annie E. Casey Foundation (2011).

is no harm in providing your mentee with what may seem like everyday essentials to you, but may be luxuries to your mentee. This could embrace such things as a nice meal out to their very own books to a computer or other school- or education-related equipment.

Finally, young people who are old enough to be aware that they live in comparative poverty are likely to have strong feelings about it—ranging from embarrassment, to resentment, to a driving need to succeed. If your mentee refers either directly or indirectly to his status, it's best to deal with the issue straightforwardly and especially important that you neither deny nor sugarcoat the facts. However, it is equally important that you find every opportunity to reinforce the idea that poverty is surmountable and to offer information about how either you or people you know have, in fact, overcome it. Hope in a positive future is one key to achieving that future, and a good mentor is a strong and consistent purveyor of this important attribute.

QUESTION 64. *My mentee has a parent or family member who has a chronic or life-threatening illness. What should I know about this?*

(If your *mentee* has a chronic health condition, such as asthma, diabetes, or obesity, please see Question 44.) Mentees can be affected by a wide range of chronic and life-threatening diseases (such as diabetes, HIV/AIDS, cancer, arthritis, substance abuse, and multiple sclerosis) in immediate family members as well as in members of their extended family such as grandparents. According to the Robert Wood Johnson Foundation, nearly one in two Americans (or 133 million) has a chronic medical condition, the most common being high blood pressure, arthritis, respiratory disease, and high cholesterol. For most people, a chronic medical condition does not impair normal activity. But for those with serious chronic diseases, like severe mental illness or Parkinson's disease, the effects on patients and their families can range from disruptive to devastating (Robert Wood Johnson & Partnership for Solutions, 2004).

The effects on your mentee will depend on how serious and debilitating the illness is, whether it is life-threatening, which family member is ill, and your mentee's age. How your mentee reacts will also depend on what she has been told about the illness. Some families will tell their children exactly what is going on; others try to spare them the worry and anxiety by telling them very little. Unfortunately, this latter strategy can leave children even more anxious as they overhear conversations and try to piece together what is happening, often imagining a worse scenario than what exists. Problems such as substance abuse are frequently treated as family secrets, and children are cautioned not to talk about what is going on at home. (See Question 62 for more information on substance abuse in the family.)

If the family member has been ill since the beginning of your mentoring relationship, your program coordinator should have briefed you on how best to support your mentee. If the illness developed during the course of your relationship, you may notice personality and behavioral changes in your mentee. Contact your program coordinator for guidance. Children of the chronically ill can face tremendous pressure at home. A parent's illness may generate unwelcome lifestyle changes that force a child to give up cherished activities or place stress upon the family budget as bills for treatment or medications mount. Children may be called upon to play a part in caring for an ill parent or face special challenges because their parent is unable to care for them in the same way a healthy parent might. They can harbor fears about their parent's and their own well-being, and they can feel overwhelmed by added responsibilities assigned to them. According to researchers who examined the effects of having a parent with a chronic disease (Sieh, Meijer, Oort, Visser-Meily & Van der Leij, 2010), this circumstance can affect a child's academic performance, emotional life, and behavior in the following ways:

> Children may react to the stress associated with parental illness by isolating themselves, feeling guilty, and worrying about changes in parental health.

> Children can be forced to restrict daily activities or feel that they must restrict them.

> A fear of negative outcomes or death of a parent may result in such complaints as headaches, cramps, and weakened immune system response.

> Children of single mothers who are ill appear to be at increased risk for aggression or delinquency.

> Children may gain a sense of fulfillment or accomplishment by caring for their parent.

If you are mentoring a young person with a chronically ill parent, you can be especially helpful to him in three practical ways. You can let him vent by providing a safe space for him to express any fears or frustrations he be experiencing. You can introduce him to age-appropriate online resources that can help him understand more about the nature of the parent's illnesss and things that both he and the parent can do to cope. Check out the National Institutes of Health's MedlinePlus for useful and easy-to-access material (nlm.nih.gov/medlineplus/copingwithchronicillness) and kidshealth.org. Finally, you can figure out how best to lighten your mentee's load by figuring out where he needs help and then delivering it. Is he neglecting his schoolwork in favor of caring for a parent? Spend at least part of your time together in a place where he can concentrate on catching up. Does he just need some fun in his life? If so, find ways to integrate activities you know your mentee will enjoy and may not otherwise have the opportunity to do, like going to a movie or a restaurant or taking a short daytrip to a place he has always wanted to visit. Chronic illness is very likely to produce chronic stress; mentors can play an important part in their mentees' lives by simply helping them to get a needed break.

A good resource for children facing family health issues, particularly cancer, is the Children's Treehouse Foundation (childrenstreehousefdn .org). It maintains a list a list of support groups for children by state. Finally, see Question 42J for information on how to help your mentee if the family member's illness is terminal.

QUESTION 65. *My mentee's parents don't seem to value education. Should I address this issue?*

This is surely something that should concern you . . . and all mentors. The 21st-century economy is unlikely to welcome young people who are not well prepared academically. And research suggests that a consistent predictor of a child's academic achievement is parental expectations for the child's educational attainment. This holds true across income groups. Furthermore, according to Child Trends, parental expectations for academic achievement outweigh other measures of parental involvement, such as attending school events, with educational outcomes (Child Trends, 2010). In addition, the following should be noted:

> Parental expectations directly affect the amount of parent-child communication about school.

> Parental expectations affect a child's own aspirations and expectations.

> Families with high educational aspirations for their children tend to provide more out-of-school learning opportunities for them.

> Students who reported that their parents expected them to attend college had better attendance and more positive attitudes toward school.

If you are a mentor who learns that your mentee's parents have low expectations for what she can achieve academically—either in the long or the short term—plan to play a role in countering that influence. See

> ### DATA POINT
> ### Parental Expectations and Academic Achievement
>
> A great majority of parents expect their children to graduate from high school and complete at least some postsecondary education. Overall, parents have higher academic expectations for girls than for boys (74 percent expected their daughters to get a bachelor's degree or higher, while 66 percent expected their sons to do so). The proportion of parents with the greatest expectations for attainment (a bachelor's degree or more) is highest among Asian/Pacific Islanders (89 percent), followed by Whites (72 percent), Latinos (67 percent), and Blacks (62 percent). Finally, only half of low-income parents (those with annual incomes of $25,000 or less) expect their children to obtain a bachelor's degree, while 80 percent of those with incomes of $75,000 held that expectation.
>
> Source: Child Trends (2010).

Question 39 for tips to help your mentee do better at school and offer all the encouragement you can to your mentee regarding both her current schoolwork and what you think she can achieve in the future. And try to find opportunities to, quite literally, see other kids whose circumstances resemble hers who are doing well in school or achieving success in some type of postsecondary educational institution. For example, many former mentees have told us that one of the most important things their mentors did for them was take them to visit specialized vocational training schools (for electronics or the visual arts) or college campuses. Simply seeing or meeting students who looked like them in these settings suggested possibilities they hadn't considered. If you are mentoring an older child, explore whether her own or her parents' expectations of her for advanced education reflect a belief that financial barriers stand in the way. They are likely to be absolutely right about the reality of financial barriers, but your job is to help your mentee see that they are not necessarily insurmountable. Then do all you can to help her figure out how she could get the aid she needs to attain the kind of education that will give her a real shot at realizing her potential and succeeding (also see Question 39A–C).

QUESTION 66. *I meet my mentee in his school, and it is appalling—so unrelentingly bad that I don't think my mentee should be going there. What can I do?*

One of the most distressing things for children, parents, and mentors alike is to see their ambitions for a good education thwarted by low-quality schools and schooling. The past 20 years have brought increasing attention to the quality of U.S. schools, along with a series of new approaches to assessing school performance. The No Child Left Behind Act of 2001, for example, mandates that the U.S. Department of Education determine annually how every public school and school district are performing. It does so by using a measure called Adequate Yearly Progress (note, however, that this measure is currently being reassessed). Another tactic used to determine how schools throughout the country are performing is to identify which schools produce a disproportionate number of dropouts. These schools, which have become known as "dropout factories," are high schools that see 60 percent or less of their students graduate each year. In 2009, 1,634 U.S. schools were identified as dropout factories (Balfanz, Bridgeland, Fox & Moore, 2011), while the number of students who had the misfortune of attending these schools numbered 2.1 million.

If you are concerned about the school your mentee is attending, a good first step is to find out whether the school is ranked as a low-performing school by the U.S. Department of Education (visit ed.gov and search for low-performing schools in your state) or Great Schools (www.greatschools .org). If your mentee is a high school student, see if he is attending one of the nation's dropout factories by visiting the website of the Everyone Graduates Center of Johns Hopkins University (every1graduates.org).

What happens if your concerns are confirmed and your mentee is enrolled in a school that should be embarrassed to call itself an institution of learning? You can follow the advice outlined in Questions 39 and 46. Also, remember that students who attend struggling schools often qualify for free tutoring through the No Child Left Behind Act. Check out tutorsforkids.org/families to learn what you can do to ensure that your mentee gets the tutoring to which he is entitled. You can learn more about the state of U.S. schools and find ways to support efforts to improve their quality. Two good places to find out how to translate your interest into action are the Alliance for Excellent Education (all4ed.org) or America's Promise Alliance (americaspromise.org). Clearly, despite progress, this is an area in which considerable work remains to be done.

DATAPOINTS
America's Dropout Factories

Twelve percent of U.S. schools produce 50 percent of the nation's high school dropouts.

Source: U.S. Department of Education (2010).

There were 112 fewer dropout factories in 2009 than in 2008, while 183,701 fewer students attended dropout factories during the same period. Six states (California, Connecticut, North Carolina, South Carolina, and Tennessee) had a reduction of at least 10 dropout factories in one year. Utah is the only state without a dropout factory, while Florida and South Carolina have the highest percentage of such schools.

Source: Balfanz et al. (2011).

There are costs for dropping out for individuals, for communities, and for the nation. The average high school dropout makes 27 percent less income than the average high school graduate. Over a lifetime, this adds up to over a quarter million dollars in reduced personal capital. The lower wages of dropouts mean that $36 billion dollars in state and local funding is lost each year. Lower annual earnings of dropouts cost the federal government an estimated $158 billion or more in lost revenue each year. And each young person who drops out and enters a life marked by drug use and crime costs the nation between $1.7 and $2.3 million in crime control and health expenditures. A 1 percent reduction in dropout rates would reduce the number of crimes by 100,000 annually.

Source: Melville (2006).

QUESTION 67. *My mentee's family has fallen on the wrong side of the "digital divide." What resources can I bring to the situation?*

In low-income urban neighborhoods, 84 percent of children live in households that do not have access to the Internet. The problem is even worse in low-income rural areas. This means that, unless they can catch up, many children will be blocked from the enormous opportunities to work, learn, and play that are open to children who possess "21st-century literacy skills."

Check out Question 39a for specific ideas about what you can do to help your mentee assess where she stands with respect to Internet use and skills that should be the norm for children her age. Then work with

DATA POINT
Children and the Internet

Children who are already at a disadvantage are the least likely to have access to new technology. Minority children, children living in poor families, particularly those living in high-poverty neighborhoods, are the least likely to have computers at home or access to the Internet. Schools close some of the gap, but significant disparities remain even after access in schools is taken into account. Data also demonstrate that schools have experienced a tremendous increase in Internet access, growing from only 35 percent of K–12 Schools in 1994 to 98 percent in 2000.

Source: Annie E. Casey Foundation (2002).

her to build the skills she needs. One good resource is Common Sense Media. See especially *Zero to Eight: Children's Media Use in America* (2011, downloadable at commonsensemedia.org). Whether you are mentoring in a program that takes place in a school or in the community, spend time learning about Internet access at your mentee's school. Also, look beyond Internet access. While access is the first obstacle to overcome, training and parental involvement are also seen as important boosts to help kids make the most of any access they have. We believe many mentors, especially those who are skilled in this area or want to learn about it along with their mentees, can also offer a boost. In fact, helping a child begin to get up to speed in this important area is an ideal role for modern mentors. This is one barrier that need not be insurmountable for children living in disadvantaged circumstances. Seize the day.

PART II

Resources for Strong Mentors

6

ESSENTIAL GUIDEPOSTS

*The only thing more painful than learning from experience
is not learning from experience.*
ARCHIBALD MACLEISH, POET, WRITER, LIBRARIAN OF CONGRESS

There are some things that *every* mentor should be aware of—essential guideposts that will help you be a more confident mentor, as well as help ensure that the young person you are mentoring has a worthwhile experience. In our view, there are two absolute essentials: *Elements of Effective Practice for Mentoring,* third edition (hereafter, the *Elements*) and "First Do No Harm: Ethical Principles for Youth Mentoring Relationships" (*Ethical Principles*).

We introduce each one in the section that follows. We have also provided excerpts of the most relevant portions of each publication, as well as complete information on how to access them online.

Clearly, we think this material is important. And while we are not suggesting that you commit it to memory, we do think you should be familiar with each resource. Take a quick look at all of it the first time you read this section of *The Mentor's Field Guide,* and be mindful that it is available here for future reference. Believe us, you'll benefit from doing so.

ELEMENTS OF EFFECTIVE PRACTICE FOR MENTORING

The third edition of *Elements of Effective Practice for Mentoring* (MENTOR, 2009) offers standards for mentoring programs to apply when they are establishing or assessing themselves. First published in 1990, the *Elements* is used by most of the formal mentoring programs operating in the United States to build or protect the quality of their programming. Its pervasiveness is the product of many factors, including the level of respect for the research on which the elements are based; the inclusiveness of the process by which they have been developed; and even the color of the publication's cover. It's red, and that seems to help make it memorable. In fact, the first phone call we had with a young member of President Barack Obama's transition team went something like this: "We want to talk to you about the standards in that red booklet. They're good." And, notably, those were almost exactly the words a member of President George W. Bush's team had spoken six years earlier.

Despite its quality and memorable look, even if you are an experienced mentor it is possible that you will not be familiar with the *Elements*. That is largely because it wasn't written with mentors in mind. Instead, the principal audience is program coordinators, the frontline mentoring professionals we mention so frequently throughout this book. So although you may have heard a reference to or seen a copy of the *Elements* at a mentor training session, you probably considered it something for the mentoring program staff. And you are right. But when viewed from a certain perspective, the *Elements* can help mentors, too.

If you are involved in a formal mentoring program, the standards contained in the *Elements* can help you determine whether the kind of mentoring experience you're engaged in is, in fact, worth your time and effort—likewise, if you are planning to join a formal mentoring program. If your mentoring experience is an informal one, the standards can help you examine how to find substitutes for some of the supports available to mentors in formal arrangements, and that's vital. As we discussed in chapter 2, mentoring is most effective (and, some would say, only effective) when certain conditions prevail. Absent such things as mentor training, thoughtful matching of mentor-mentee pairs, an explicit process for helping set expectations, and ongoing support for mentors throughout the experience, mentoring frequently fails to achieve its potential. The *Elements* addresses each of these areas and can, therefore, be used as the basis for your own quality control checklist. Items for the checklist can be drawn from the standards and benchmarks included in the excerpts from the *Elements* that appear below. We also have provided questions we think it would be beneficial for you to ask yourself, or pose to those who are running the mentoring program in which you are or hope to be involved.

And don't be shy about doing the latter. The answers you get will make a difference for you and for the young people who inspired you to become a mentor in the first place.

EXCERPTS FROM *ELEMENTS OF EFFECTIVE PRACTICE FOR MENTORING*

The following material is reprinted with the permission of MENTOR: The National Mentoring Partnership. The complete document also can be downloaded at www.mentoring.org/program_resources/elements_and _toolkits. What we have included here is a list of the six operational standards recommended for use by mentoring programs, as well as benchmarks that can be used to test whether the standard is being upheld. Each set of standards and benchmarks is followed by questions you can use to determine whether the mentoring program you are involved in (or thinking about being involved in) follows the practices that encourage the development of strong and satisfying mentoring relationships for you and your mentee.

Standard 1: Recruitment

Standard: Recruit appropriate mentors and mentees by realistically describing the program's aims and expected outcomes.

Benchmarks:

> Mentor Recruitment—Program engages in recruitment strategies that realistically portray the benefits, practices and challenges of mentoring in the program.

Questions a Mentor Should Ask about Recruitment:

> When I was recruited, were the benefits, practices, and challenges of mentoring introduced and/or discussed?

> Was there a way for me to ask questions about anything that was said that particularly interested or concerned me?

> Was a written statement outlining mentor eligibility requirements mentioned? Was a copy made available to me?

Standard 2: Screening

Standard: Screen prospective mentors to determine whether they have the time, commitment and personal qualities to be an effective mentor.

Benchmarks:

> Mentor completes an application.

> Mentor agrees to a one (calendar or school) year commitment for the mentoring relationship.

> Mentor agrees to participate in face-to-face meetings with his or her mentee that average one time per week and one hour per meeting over the course of a calendar or school year. This benchmark may be addressed differently as long as there is evidence to support that the variation is associated with positive outcomes for mentees (e.g., combining in-person meetings with online communication or telephone calls; meeting almost exclusively online; meeting less frequently than once a week, with each meeting lasting an hour or more, on average). As a general rule, programs should aim to either meet this benchmark or provide a clear rationale for doing otherwise.

> Program conducts at least one face-to-face interview with mentor.

> Program conducts a reference check (personal and/or professional) on mentor.

> Program conducts a comprehensive criminal background check on adult mentor, including searching a national criminal records database along with sex offender and child abuse registries.

Questions a Mentor Should Ask about Screening:

> Does the program I'm involved in (or planning to be) seem serious about the screening process?

> Did they ask me to fill out an application?

> Did they specify and ask for a certain commitment of time in the application?

> Did I have a face-to-face interview?

> Was permission sought to do a background check on me?

> Did the proposed background check include a review of national criminal records databases, including sex offender and child abuse registries?

Standard 3: Training

Standard: Train prospective mentors in the basic knowledge and skills needed to build an effective mentoring relationship.

Benchmarks:

> Program provides a minimum of two hours of pre-match, in-person training.

> Mentor training includes the following topics, at a minimum:
> a. Program rules.
> b. Mentors' goals and expectations for the mentor/mentee relationship.
> c. Mentors' obligations and appropriate roles.
> d. Relationship development and maintenance.
> e. Ethical issues that may arise related to the mentoring relationship.
> f. Effective closure of the mentoring relationship.
> g. Sources of assistance available to support mentors.

Questions a Mentor Should Ask about Training for Mentors:

> Was I offered and/or required to participate in training for mentors?

> If I participated in the training, did those offering it strike me as knowledgeable?

> Was I encouraged to ask questions, and were my questions addressed when I raised them?

> Did the training cover all or at least most of the topics mentioned in the preceding benchmark?

Standard 4: Matching

Standard: Match mentors and mentees along dimensions likely to increase the odds that mentoring relationships will endure.

Benchmarks:

> Program considers its aims, as well as the characteristics of the mentor and mentee (e.g., interests, proximity, availability, age, gender, race, ethnicity, personality and expressed preferences of mentor and mentee) when making matches.

> Program arranges and documents an initial meeting between the mentor and mentee.

Questions a Mentor Should Ask about Mentor/Mentee Matching:

> Did the matching seem well planned and considered "a process"?

> Was I asked about my interests, whether I had a preference for working with a child in a certain age grouping (say a middle schooler versus an adolescent in high school)?

> Was I told that mentees involved in the program were also given the chance to express their interests and asked whether they had a preference for a particular type of mentor?

Standard 5: Monitoring and Support

Standard: Monitor mentoring relationship milestones and support mentors with ongoing advice, problem-solving support and training opportunities for the duration of the relationship.

Benchmarks:

> Program contacts the mentor and mentee at a minimum frequency of twice per month for the first month of the match and monthly thereafter.

> Program documents information about each mentor/mentee contact, including, at minimum, date, length and nature of the contact.

> Program provides mentor with access to at least two types of resources (e.g., expert advice from program staff or others; publications; Web-based resources; experienced mentors; available social service referrals) to help mentors negotiate challenges in the mentoring relationship as they arise.

> Program follows evidence-based protocol to elicit more in-depth assessment from the mentor and mentee about the relationship and uses scientifically tested relationship assessment tools.

> Program provides one or more opportunities per year for post-match mentor training.

Questions a Mentor Should Ask about Monitoring and Support for Mentors:

> First and foremost, is there a program coordinator or staff person I can contact; and, if so, was I given a phone number or e-mail address I can use to make contact?

> Does the program coordinator check in with me regularly (or promise to do so)?

> Does anyone keep a record of my contacts with my mentee?

> Did my mentoring program provide me with useful support materials in the form of publications; people (beyond the program coordinator who could provide help or feedback); or online resources (e.g., the mentor library on www.mentoring.org)?

> Does (or did) the program discuss using a research-backed instrument to assess various dimensions of my relationship with my mentee? Have I actually used it? Has my mentee? Is there any training available to me after the first, pre-match training takes place? Does it interest me, and/or is it provided at a time or via a vehicle that makes participation doable for me?

Standard 6: Closure

Standard: Facilitate bringing the match to closure in a way that affirms the contributions of both the mentor and the mentee and offers both individuals the opportunity to assess the experience.

Benchmarks:

> Program has procedure to manage anticipated closures, including a system for a mentor or mentee rematch.

> Program has a procedure to manage unanticipated match closures, including a system for a mentor or mentee rematch.

> Program conducts and documents an exit interview with mentor and mentee.

Questions a Mentor Should Ask about the Close of a Mentoring Relationship:

> Does the mentoring program have a plan for what happens at the end of a mentoring program year to mark progress and/or transitions?

> Does that plan strike me as sensible, appealing, something that I will actually participate in?

> Does the plan provide me (and my mentee) with ways to provide feedback on the experience?

> Was I given information about what would happen if, for some reason (say a change in job assignment, a family illness, or a move to another community), I had to end my mentoring commitment earlier than planned?

> Would my mentee be matched with another mentor?

ETHICAL PRINCIPLES FOR MENTORING

In 2009, a highly regarded team composed of Jean Rhodes, Belle Liang, and Renée Spencer introduced a set of ethical principles to guide youth mentoring relationships. Combining their expertise in clinical and community psychology and social work with their long-standing interest in the risks and rewards that attend youth mentoring, Rhodes, Liang, and Spencer sought to highlight the ethical dilemmas that can emerge from this relationship-based form of service. They had two additional objectives. First, they wanted to remind mentors of a point we have made repeatedly throughout this book and will make again here. Because a personal relationship lies at the heart of mentoring, disappointments and misunderstandings that arise may distress or even wound a mentee to a degree that other less personal interventions do not. Second, rather than simply highlighting this well-known challenge, Rhodes and her colleagues wanted to confront it head-on by providing mentors with a set of ethical principles that they can use as they work to build meaningful relationships with the young people they care about. The resulting publication's title begins with a telling phrase: "First Do No Harm: Ethical Principles for Youth Mentoring Relationships" (2009).

Unlike the *Elements,* Rhodes and her colleagues wrote the ethical principles with mentors explicitly in mind. You may find, however, that that they don't read that way in their original form. What we have provided instead is an abridged version, which was created by Rhodes for MENTOR (2011) and reproduced here with permission. Before urging you to take a careful look, let us note that the principles were based on the American Psychological Association's Ethical Principles of Psychologists and Code of Conduct (2002), ethical codes that have been developed to guide volunteers in a variety of community settings; current research; and their authors' collective experience with mentoring practices and practitioners.

Excerpts from "First Do No Harm: Ethical Principles for Youth Mentoring Relationships"

Five guiding principles for ethical behavior in youth mentoring relationships:

1. Promote the welfare and safety of the young person.

> Mentors should work to benefit their mentees. Although this idea may seem straightforward, there are often competing ideas about what might be good for the young person—ideas that are rooted in differing values, cultures, and worldviews. Promoting the welfare of a young person will, in many cases, require that mentors build rapport not only with their mentees but also with the mentees' primary caregivers so that they may develop an understanding of the family's belief systems and expectations for the child.

> A mentor also has the ethical obligation to do no harm. This encompasses the more extreme forms of harmful behavior, such as sexual harassment, abuse, and exploitation. Most programs have careful background checks and screening procedures in place, such as SafetyNET, and the incidence of such occurrences is minimal. For the most part, all but a small fraction of volunteers do not intend to deliberately harm their young charges. Nonetheless, if volunteers lack skills, knowledge, or caution, difficulties can and often do arise. Training and supervision can help volunteers recognize the boundaries and limits of their expertise and seek assistance from program staff when needed.

2. Be trustworthy and responsible.

> For volunteer mentors, this involves being aware of one's responsibilities for meeting frequency and match duration, as stipulated by the program. This type of consistency and reliability, which has been associated with more positive outcomes for youth participants (Rhodes & DuBois, 2006), serves as a cornerstone for trust in the relationship. Trust, in turn, is considered a key component of effective mentoring relationships (Sipe, 1996). Mentees have reported that honesty, keeping promises, and relationship longevity underlie trust (Liang, Spencer, Brogan & Corral, 2008).

3. Act with integrity.

> This related principle highlights the obligation of mentors to be thoughtful and forthright about the commitments (i.e., time, financial) to the relationship and to avoid setting up false expectations. Mentors should be reminded about the importance of their obligations to their mentees, as well as the meaning that is placed on plans and events; even minor disappointments and tardiness can accumulate in ways that erode trust and closeness. Mentors are expected to bear the greater responsibility for finding ways to effectively and consistently communicate with their mentees, to honor plans and commitments, and to seek guidance and consultation from mentoring program staff should they find that they are unable to do so.

> Mentors also should conduct themselves with integrity in their mentees' schools, homes, and communities by being respectful of customs and regularities and by not acting in ways that leave programs having to run interference.

> Finally, although there are always exceptions, mentors should be wary of entering into financial arrangements with mentees or their families. Although it might seem harmless for a mentor to cover one month's electricity bill, particularly when rationalized in terms of helping the mentee, this may have the unintended effect of establishing expectations of further (and perhaps greater) assistance.

4. Promote justice for young people.

> This principle calls for mentors to exercise good judgment and to take precautions to ensure that the potential biases inherent in their own backgrounds do not lead to prejudicial treatment of their mentees. The standards of the APA Ethics Code (2002) stipulate that psychologists do not engage in unfair discrimination based on age, gender, gender identity, race, ethnicity, culture, national origin, religion, sexual orientation, disability, socioeconomic status, or any basis proscribed by law (p. 5), and the same holds true for mentors. Mentors may not intentionally, or even consciously, engage in unfair treatment. However, the reality is that the largest proportion of volunteer mentors are White, middle-class students and professionals whereas mentees tend to be more economically and ethnically diverse (MENTOR, 2006).

> Mentoring programs have an obligation to provide training in cultural and gender sensitivity to raise volunteers' awareness of their own biases and blind spots. Unfortunately, programs often assume that once a mentoring relationship has been formed, the strength of the bond will work to prevent or lessen potential misunderstandings and miscommunications that may arise as a result of differences in cultural values and backgrounds.

> The sparse research does lend some provisional support to the assumption that a strong bond can offset cultural differences. A national study of mentoring relationships formed through Big Brothers Big Sisters (Grossman & Rhodes, 2002) found that although cross-race matches terminated slightly more often than did same-race matches, this was not the case among those pairs who were matched primarily on the basis of similar interests. Nevertheless, unacknowledged prejudices can subtly affect interpersonal relationships (Cohen & Steele, 2002).

> Promoting justice can also extend beyond the one-to-one relationship with a mentee. By bringing more-privileged adults into the lives of less-privileged young people, mentoring has the potential to promote widespread social change. Mentors' close personal connections with vulnerable youth afford them the opportunity to develop a firsthand understanding of the challenges faced by young people today, which can inspire mentors as well as mentees to redress social ills and advocate for social change that could improve the health and well-being of all young people living in these kinds of circumstances.

5. Respect the young person's rights and dignity.

> Except in extreme situations (e.g., abuse, neglect, and endangerment), volunteers should seek to understand and respect the decisions and lifestyle of a young person and his or her family. Respect for self-determination involves behaving in ways that enable rather than interfere with mentees' and their families' abilities to exercise their own reasoning and judgment. Mentors should seek to understand their mentees' personal goals, desires, and values and not undermine their capacities to make their own decisions.

> Issues of confidentiality, which abound in mentoring relationships, have been given insufficient attention. Young people and parents

often disclose deeply personal information to volunteers, sometimes with specific injunctions against sharing it with the other. And having a place to share private thoughts and feelings is an aspect of mentor relationships that young people have identified as being particularly meaningful to them (Spencer, Jordan & Sazama, 2004). These adults can serve as important sounding boards, particularly for young people who are exploring their identities and may experience new forms of conflicts in their relationships with their parents (Allen, Moore & Kuperminc, 1998). Training regarding issues of confidentiality should be provided, and decisions about such matters should be made in consultation with mentoring program staff.

UNDERSTANDING WHAT YOUNG PEOPLE NEED AND WHEN THEY NEED IT

In a nation rich in economic assets, there should be a parallel focus on being a nation rich in Developmental Assets.

PETER L. BENSON, *ALL KIDS ARE OUR KIDS*

In this chapter, we provide the basics on how young people develop and what support they need from adults in their lives as they do. We also focus on the concept of "Developmental Assets," an important framework developed by Search Institute that describes the factors in children's lives that help them grow into healthy, well-balanced adults. We also include information to help you understand the various risks young people face as they grow up, along with the factors that exacerbate those risks.

All mentors have a unique opportunity to help their mentees negotiate and learn from the various life stages, opportunities, and challenges they encounter as they mature. So think of yourself as your mentee's "life coach." And plan to be an effective one by learning about the issues your mentee is likely to face at different ages, what his capabilities and strengths are likely to be at 6 or 11 or 16, what supports are routinely available, and what impediments are typically present.

A PRIMER ON STAGES OF DEVELOPMENT

Children go through fairly predictable stages in their physical, emotional, social, and intellectual development; however, it is important always to keep in mind that each child is a unique person who will develop at her or his own pace. Young people's life circumstances also will influence their development, either positively or negatively. For example, most people are now aware of how poverty may negatively affect a child's development through inadequate health care, lack of supports for learning, and unsafe neighborhoods. Many of these issues were addressed in earlier chapters of this book.

Understanding the stages of development a young person goes through will help you (a) understand your mentee's needs; (b) understand your mentee's behavior; (c) be realistic in expectations of your mentee and the mentoring relationship; (d) be better prepared in deciding how to approach the mentoring relationship, including appropriate boundaries; (e) be on target in thinking about what kinds of activities or discussions might interest your mentee; and (f) be better equipped to handle sensitive issues that may come up.

Pages 173–178 describe three stages of development that are commonly used: ages 6 through 8, 9 through 12, and 13 through 18. We must stress, however, that development is a gradual and continuous process; there are no definitive beginnings or endings to these categories, and chronological age is not the only factor defining development. These stages are used to provide a general framework for describing what goes on for many children within these age groupings. There are significant changes between the beginning and ending of each stage, with the stages usually overlapping.

We have described the major areas of development that you will be most aware of and that will have most relevance for your mentoring relationship:

> *Physical development* describes what your mentee is capable of doing physically, what changes her body is going through, and what the behavioral implications are for her stage of physical development.

> *Social and emotional development* describes how your mentee is interacting with the people and the world around him and the emotions he may be experiencing.

> *Mental development* describes your mentee's cognitive or intellectual abilities—how she processes information about the world, what she is capable of understanding or learning, and how she thinks about things, for example.

Ages 6–8, early elementary school

Physical Development

> Mastering more varied physical skills, with large-muscle skills stronger than small-muscle skills.

> Like to be physically active.

> Starting to enjoy using new physical skills by participating in sports.

> Like to challenge themselves in learning new physical skills.

Social and Emotional Development

> Moving from self-centeredness to greater ability to share and interact with others.

> Want approval from adults in their lives.

> Girls and boys begin to play separately.

> Like to play games, sometimes making up their own games.

> May fight with friends but make up quickly.

> Bullying behavior begins to appear.

> Primarily dependent on parents/ adults for sense of security.

> Just beginning to understand finality of death.

Mental Development

> Have short attention spans, which increase with age.

> Thinking is concrete, relying on their own senses.

> Becoming more curious about the world around them.

> Like projects to work on but may not care about finishing them.

> Learning to read can be either a source of great pleasure or frustration.

> For the most part, they enjoy school and learning unless there are developmental impediments to learning.

> Beginning to master use of computers and other electronic devices to play games.

Implications for Mentors

> Mentees will respond better to doing things together than to "just talking." Talking should be a byproduct of activities.

> Keep activities short, and switch activities when needed to maintain mentees' interest. Don't insist on finishing things like a game or book.

> Use simple and concrete language and concepts when talking to mentees.

> Relate what you are talking about to things in mentees' immediate world so they have a frame of reference to understand what you mean.

> Build in opportunities for physical activities, or take breaks for some physical activity (even if just stretching or tossing a ball) during your mentoring sessions.

> Play games that will challenge mentees' thinking abilities.

> Encourage mentees to explore new ways of looking at the world and people through reading and observations.

> Positively reinforce mentees' good qualities and new skill development.

> Encourage mentees to like school and reading by doing activities to reinforce learning.

> Talk with mentees about bullying, asking if they ever see it taking place.

Ages 9–12, middle grades

Physical Development

> Body changes are slow at beginning of this stage but accelerate with approach or arrival of puberty.

> Puberty brings significant physical and emotional changes, including feeling "out of control" of their body and out of sync with their peers if they are developing more quickly.

> Physical coordination continues to improve with greater small-muscle development.

> Eye problems may appear as vision problems or eyestrain from using electronic media.

> Still a strong tendency to be physically active; can be harder to transition to quiet activities.

> Enjoy sports if participation is encouraged.

Social and Emotional Development

> Growing sense of independence from parents/ adults but still want parent/adult approval.

> Growing sense of connection to peers, with friendship groups forming and re-forming.

> Depend on both parent/adult and peer approval.

> Bullying behavior strongly influenced by peer groups.

> Social bullying emerges, particularly through the use of exclusion, especially by girls.

> Growing sense of self-consciousness and need for peer approval.

> Concerned about what others think of them.

> Feelings can be easily hurt.

> Crushes may emerge.

Mental Development

> Abstract thinking emerges but still tends toward "black and white" thinking.

> Develop strong interests and curiosities.

> Enjoy learning for the sake of learning.

> Like to solve problems.

> Become interested in setting goals and making plans to achieve them.

> Growing awareness of the larger world around them and its risks and problems; more attention paid to news media.

> Moral thinking emerges with strong sense of right and wrong, fair and unfair.

> Growing ability to understand someone else's point of view and feelings.

> Hero worship of music, sports, TV, movie, and video game characters.

Implications for Mentors

> Let mentees' interests guide your choice of activities.

> Talk to mentees in simple, concrete language, and introduce abstract concepts with increasing frequency as they get older.

> Engage mentees in problem-solving games and activities, and talk about how they are solving the problems.

> Ask mentees for opinions on what is happening in the world, at school, or in their peer group.

> Use open-ended questions to encourage mentees to talk about their life, school, likes, dislikes, frustrations, and challenges.

> Begin to talk with mentees about issues like bullying, drugs, and developmental changes associated with puberty. Start by asking what they see going on in their world and what they think about it.

> Help your mentee develop skills and strategies to solve problems and cope with challenges.

> Help your mentee develop a strong sense of empathy and concern for others; do activities that will benefit others.

> Positively reinforce new skills and achievements.

Ages 13–18, adolescence

Physical Development

> Major physical changes with onset of puberty; adult height achieved by midteens.

> Being out of sync physically with peers can be cause for anxiety.

> Concerns about body image.

> Growing physical strength, coordination and abilities.

> Brain development still incomplete and highly vulnerable to long-term effects of alcohol and drug use.

> Sexual activity begins.

Social and Emotional Development

> Growing independence and pulling away from parent/adult influences.

> Becoming more critical of parents and other adults, rejecting their views and values.

> Hyperaware of appearance and self-conscious about anything that makes them stand out from peers; feeling of being on stage.

> Susceptible to praise and recognition, even though they may act like they don't care.

> Want to feel autonomous and be trusted and validated for their decisions.

> Searching for intimacy in relationships.

> Redefining relationship with family.

> May experience emotional ups and downs and mood swings; these are exacerbated by alcohol and drug use.

> Mental illness such as depression and bipolar disorder may emerge during teens.

> Learning to cover up and mask insecurities.

Mental Development

> Growth of abstract thinking and reasoning.

> Believe they have the cognitive ability to manage their life without parental or adult advice.

> Developing internal values and beliefs.

> Like to set goals and work toward them.

> Thinking more about their future and life choices.

> Strong problem-solving skills emerging.

> Growing ability to understand their world and its problems and challenges.

> Strong feelings and beliefs about social, national, and international issues emerge.

> May be quite idealistic and interested in helping others, solving social problems.

> Ready to accept increasing levels of responsibility and accountability.

> Able to understand that their actions have consequences.

Implications for Mentors

> Continue all the above approaches.

> Encourage mentees to have a bigger role in defining your relationship and activities while maintaining appropriate structure and boundaries.

> Talk to mentees as you would to a friend, seeking and respecting their opinions.

> Encourage mentees to turn to you for emotional support and guidance in solving problems and life challenges.

> Be prepared to handle sensitive issues and problems mentees may face, such as drugs, sex, bullying, and depression.

> Listen, don't lecture.

> Support mentees in learning from their mistakes.

> Encourage mentees to set post–high school goals and plans, and support them to achieve them.

> Be an advocate for mentees, especially when helping them set and work on goals.

> Be a good role model for what you want your mentee to be.

> Be willing to learn from your mentee.

PRINCIPLES OF POSITIVE YOUTH DEVELOPMENT: HELPING YOUNG PEOPLE THRIVE AND SUCCEED

The concept of "positive youth development" has evolved out of research on resilience—the ability of some children to thrive under adverse life conditions; out of research on what conditions or "protective factors" help young people succeed in life; and out of the experiences of those who work with young people. The concept also was a response to the prevailing view of young people by those who only saw problems and risks in their lives. You are probably familiar with the term "at-risk youth." Under this concept, too many young people were being defined by their challenges and limitations, not their capabilities and strengths, whereas mentoring is really about helping young people develop positively. An excellent overview of positive youth development principles can be found in the document *A Mentor's Guide to Youth Development,* available from Education Northwest (educationnorthwest.org).

THE POWER OF DEVELOPMENTAL ASSETS

The principles of positive youth development are at the core of the work of Search Institute in Minneapolis. The institute has conducted and reviewed extensive research studies to identify which factors are most important in helping young people thrive and succeed. This research led to the identification of 40 Developmental Assets, which are positive experiences, relationships, opportunities, and personal qualities that young people need to grow up healthy, caring, and responsible. The framework of Developmental Assets steps back to look at the whole—to pull many pieces together into a comprehensive vision of what young people need to thrive.

Search Institute's research shows that the more assets young people have, the less likely they are to engage in risky behaviors. In addition, these common themes about the importance of assets have emerged from numerous findings:

> Assets promote academic success.

> Assets divert youth from risky behaviors and increase civic engagement.

> Assets give young people the strengths they need to make positive choices in life.

> Across the United States—in big cities and small towns—more than half of young people surveyed now report experiencing 20 or fewer of the 40 Developmental Assets.

THE FRAMEWORK OF 40 DEVELOPMENTAL ASSETS®
FOR ADOLESCENTS

Search Institute has identified the following building blocks of healthy development that help young people grow up healthy, caring, and responsible.

EXTERNAL ASSETS

Support
1. **Family Support**—Family life provides high levels of love and support.
2. **Positive Family Communication**—Young person and her or his parent(s) communicate positively, and young person is willing to seek advice and counsel from parent(s).
3. **Other Adult Relationships**—Young person receives support from three or more nonparent adults.
4. **Caring Neighborhood**—Young person experiences caring neighbors.
5. **Caring School Climate**—School provides a caring, encouraging environment.
6. **Parent Involvement in Schooling**—Parent(s) are actively involved in helping young person succeed in school.

Empowerment
7. **Community Values Youth**—Young person perceives that adults in the community value youth.
8. **Youth as Resources**—Young people are given useful roles in the community.
9 **Service to Others**—Young person serves in the community one hour or more per week.
10. **Safety**—Young person feels safe at home, at school, and in the neighborhood.

Boundaries and Expectations
11. **Family Boundaries**—Family has clear rules and consequences and monitors the young person's whereabouts.

12. **School Boundaries**—School provides clear rules and consequences.
13. **Neighborhood Boundaries**—Neighbors take responsibility for monitoring young people's behavior.
14. **Adult Role Models**—Parent(s) and other adults model positive, responsible behavior.
15. **Positive Peer Influence**—Young person's best friends model responsible behavior.
16. **High Expectations**—Both parent(s) and teachers encourage the young person to do well.

Constructive Use of Time
17. **Creative Activities**—Young person spends three or more hours per week in lessons or practice in music, theater, or other arts.
18. **Youth Programs**—Young person spends three or more hours per week in sports, clubs, or organizations at school and/or in the community.
19. **Religious Community**—Young person spends one or more hours per week in activities in a religious institution.
20. **Time at Home**—Young person is out with friends "with nothing special to do" two or fewer nights per week.

INTERNAL ASSETS

Commitment to Learning
21. **Achievement Motivation**—Young person is motivated to do well in school.
22. **School Engagement**—Young person is actively engaged in learning.
23. **Homework**—Young person reports doing at least one hour of homework every school day.
24. **Bonding to School**—Young person cares about her or his school.
25. **Reading for Pleasure**—Young person reads for pleasure three or more hours per week.

Positive Values

26. **Caring**—Young person places high value on helping other people.
27. **Equality and Social Justice**—Young person places high value on promoting equality and reducing hunger and poverty.
28. **Integrity**—Young person acts on convictions and stands up for her or his beliefs.
29. **Honesty**—Young person "tells the truth even when it is not easy."
30. **Responsibility**—Young person accepts and takes personal responsibility.
31. **Restraint**—Young person believes it is important not to be sexually active or to use alcohol or other drugs.

Social Competencies

32. **Planning and Decision Making**—Young person knows how to plan ahead and make choices.
33. **Interpersonal Competence**—Young person has empathy, sensitivity, and friendship skills.
34. **Cultural Competence**—Young person has knowledge of and comfort with people of different cultural/racial/ethnic backgrounds.
35. **Resistance Skills**—Young person can resist negative peer pressure and dangerous situations.
36. **Peaceful Conflict Resolution**—Young person seeks to resolve conflict nonviolently.

Positive Identity

37. **Personal Power**—Young person feels he or she has control over "things that happen to me."
38. **Self-Esteem**—Young person reports having a high self-esteem.
39. **Sense of Purpose**—Young person reports that "my life has a purpose."
40. **Positive View of Personal Future**—Young person is optimistic about her or his personal future.

AN ASSET CHECKLIST

Many people find it helpful to use a simple checklist to reflect on the assets young people experience. This checklist simplifies the asset list to help prompt conversation in families, organizations, and communities. ***Note:*** *This checklist is not intended nor appropriate as a scientific or accurate measurement of Developmental Assets.*

- ☐ 1. I receive high levels of love and support from family members.
- ☐ 2. I can go to my parent(s) or guardian(s) for advice and support and have frequent, in-depth conversations with them.
- ☐ 3. I know some nonparent adults I can go to for advice and support.
- ☐ 4. My neighbors encourage and support me.
- ☐ 5. My school provides a caring, encouraging environment.
- ☐ 6. My parent(s) or guardian(s) help me succeed in school.
- ☐ 7. I feel valued by adults in my community.
- ☐ 8. I am given useful roles in my community.
- ☐ 9. I serve in the community one hour or more each week.
- ☐ 10. I feel safe at home, at school, and in the neighborhood.
- ☐ 11. My family sets standards for appropriate conduct and monitors my whereabouts.
- ☐ 12. My school has clear rules and consequences for behavior.
- ☐ 13. Neighbors take responsibility for monitoring my behavior.
- ☐ 14. Parent(s) and other adults model positive, responsible behavior.
- ☐ 15. My best friends model responsible behavior.
- ☐ 16. My parent(s)/guardian(s) and teachers encourage me to do well.
- ☐ 17. I spend three hours or more each week in lessons or practice in music, theater, or other arts.

☐ 18. I spend three hours or more each week in school or community sports, clubs, or organizations.

☐ 19. I spend one hour or more each week in religious services or participating in spiritual activities.

☐ 20. I go out with friends with nothing special to do two or fewer nights each week.

☐ 21. I want to do well in school.

☐ 22. I am actively engaged in learning.

☐ 23. I do an hour or more of homework each school day.

☐ 24. I care about my school.

☐ 25. I read for pleasure three or more hours each week.

☐ 26. I believe it is really important to help other people.

☐ 27. I want to help promote equality and reduce world poverty and hunger.

☐ 28. I can stand up for what I believe.

☐ 29. I tell the truth even when it's not easy.

☐ 30. I can accept and take personal responsibility.

☐ 31. I believe it is important not to be sexually active or to use alcohol or other drugs.

☐ 32. I am good at planning ahead and making decisions.

☐ 33. I am good at making and keeping friends.

☐ 34. I know and am comfortable with people of different cultural/racial/ethnic backgrounds.

☐ 35. I can resist negative peer pressure and dangerous situations.

☐ 36. I try to resolve conflict nonviolently.

☐ 37. I believe I have control over many things that happen to me.

☐ 38. I feel good about myself.

☐ 39. I believe my life has a purpose.

☐ 40. I am optimistic about my future.

INCORPORATING THE DEVELOPMENTAL ASSETS INTO YOUR MENTORING RELATIONSHIP

As you can see, the framework of Developmental Assets is directly applicable to your mentoring relationship. There are many ways to make use of the information; we include several in the following list. Search Institute's website also has numerous useful resources and publications with more information about the 40 assets and how to use them (www.search-institute .org).

> You can use the assets to help you focus your and your mentee's goals for the mentoring relationship.

> You can use the assets to think about activities and conversations with your mentee.

> You can use the assets to think about areas where your mentee might need additional support or where you might be an advocate for your mentee.

> You can fill out the "Asset Checklist" as an activity with your mentee (best for mentees over the age of 9) and use it as a launching point for conversations.

> You can use the assets when having discussions with your program coordinator or your mentee's family regarding your mentee's needs and how you might help.

> You can ask to discuss the concept of Developmental Assets at a mentor training session or mentor support group meeting.

> You can use the assets to identify areas of greatest need when your mentee is facing a personal crisis or serious problem.

RESEARCH ON RISK FACTORS FOR VARIOUS PROBLEMS

As we noted earlier, the youth-serving world has moved away from the concept of risk factors, replacing it with the more positive and actionable concepts of assets, strengths, capabilities, opportunities, and competencies. We recognize, however, that many mentors also find it useful to think about the risks their mentees face as a way to prioritize areas to pay attention to and to discuss their mentees' situations with other helping professionals. This concept of risk and protective factors was based on the work of Hawkins and Catalano (1992) and was used for many years by the federal government in discussing prevention approaches and strategies.

We have included a chart summarizing their work. People find the chart helpful because it shows how young people are not just at risk for a single problem but rather how these risk factors in young people's lives can place them in jeopardy of developing multiple problems. The chart is from the document *Delinquency Prevention Works, OJJDP Program Summary*, published by the Office of Juvenile Justice and Delinquency Prevention in the U.S. Department of Justice in November 1995.

The chart is described as follows: "Based on Hawkins and Catalano's work (1995), [this information] summarizes 30 years of research on risk factors for co-occurring problem behaviors, including delinquency. A dot (●) indicates that empirical research clearly supports the presence of a risk factor increasing the chances an adolescent will exhibit a particular problem behavior. The lack of a dot indicates that the item is under study and that a definitive answer is not yet known (Hawkins and Catalano, 1992)."

RISK FACTORS FOR HEALTH AND BEHAVIOR PROBLEMS

Adolescent Problem Behaviors

Risk Factor	Substance Abuse	Delinquency	Teenage Pregnancy	School Dropout	Violence
Community					
Availability of Drugs	●				
Availability of Firearms		●			●
Community Laws and Norms Favorable Toward Drug Use, Firearms, and Crime	●	●			●
Media Portrayals of Violence					●
Transitions and Mobility	●	●		●	
Low Neighborhood Attachment and Community Organization	●	●			●
Extreme Economic Deprivation	●	●	●	●	●
Family					
Family History of the Problem Behavior	●	●	●	●	
Family Management Problems	●	●	●	●	●
Family Conflict	●	●	●	●	●
Favorable Parental Attitudes and Involvement in the Problem Behavior	●	●			●
School					
Early and Persistent Antisocial Behavior	●	●	●	●	●
Academic Failure Beginning in Elementary School	●	●	●	●	●
Lack of Commitment to School	●	●	●	●	
Individual/Peer					
Rebelliousness	●	●		●	
Friends Who Engage in the Problem Behavior	●	●	●	●	●
Favorable Attitudes Toward the Problem Behavior	●	●	●	●	
Early Initiation of the Problem Behavior	●	●	●	●	●
Constitutional Factors	●	●			●

Source: Catalano and Hawkins, Risk Focused Prevention. Using the Social Development Strategy. 1995. Seattle: Developmental Research and Programs, Inc.

8

FINDING ADDITIONAL HELP

When you need help, the worst mistake you can make
is not to ask for it . . . and pdq, too.

TINA FEY, ACTOR, COMEDIAN, AND WRITER

In this chapter we want to reinforce for those of you who are mentoring through formal programs—or intend to be—that there are ongoing sources of support that you can and should depend upon. We also want to remind adults who are mentoring informally that you don't have to go it alone. There are a growing number of resources available to mentors in formal programs that you can tap into as well, and we hope you will.

We also have a request: give us your feedback on *The Mentor's Field Guide*. We would warmly welcome your thoughts on two areas. First, feedback in the form of questions you wished we had covered. Second, we'd like to hear about any experiences you have had that address questions we raised here. For example, during the course of your relationship with your mentee, did you learn something that would strengthen the answers to questions easy (What are some of the things that my mentee and I can do together?) or hard (I think my mentee may be being physically or sexually abused. What should I do?). Wisdom derived from your accumulated experiences, good or bad, is genuinely invaluable.

ONGOING SUPPORT

If you read most or even just a few sections of the *Field Guide*, you know that we believe the availability of ongoing support for mentors is essential.

So your job is to assemble a support network. If you are a part of a strong mentoring program, that job is an easy one. As discussed in Question 14, you can depend on your program coordinator and other program staff for backup. Building a support network is more difficult if you are mentoring informally or if you are mentoring in a program where no program coordinator has explicitly been made available to you or if the assigned coordinator is unavailable, inexperienced, or just inept. No matter which scenario applies, there are resources available beyond those offered by skilled program coordinators.

Clearly, we think the *Field Guide* is one resource to which you can always turn when you need a second opinion, a referral, or even just a reminder of the fundamentals of strong mentoring. Other top-flight resources fall into three categories: people to talk to (or e-mail, text, or tweet); organizations to turn to for general information about mentoring, as well as—and even more important—specialized resources that address specific types of mentoring, mentees, or settings in which mentoring is provided; and books to read. Resources in each category are noted below, along with contact information that is as current as possible as of this printing. We have also noted whether the resources are likely to be available to those mentoring in formal programs and/or those mentoring informally.

PEOPLE TO TALK TO

We are convinced that having someone to whom you can pose questions, lay out a tough issue, or share a triumph is and will always be vital to strong mentoring. In addition to a program coordinator whom those who are mentoring through formal programs can and should rely upon, people to whom you can turn include other mentoring professionals, experienced mentors, and others in your personal network (including other young people) whose experiences apply and whose opinions you trust.

Mentoring professionals: Many youth development organizations, as well as those dedicated exclusively to mentoring, have professionals on staff to respond to questions and offer reliable advice. But their resources are stretched more than ever in the currently difficult economic times, which means that if you contact them you are likely to enter a long queue. So the best place to turn first is MENTOR and its network of Mentoring Partnerships.

If you are lucky enough to live in a community that has a state or local Mentoring Partnership, advice is only an e-mail, call, or visit away (for the location of Mentoring Partnerships and contact information, see the list that follows or visit mentoring.org/about_mentor/mentoring _partnerships). Also, there is an excellent online mentoring forum from Education Northwest, within the National Mentoring Center website (mentoringforums.educationnorthwest.org), where you can ask questions and find useful advice from mentoring professionals and other mentors.

Experienced mentors: If you are mentoring in a formal mentoring program, you will undoubtedly meet other mentors. The trick is to identify mentors in your program who have had previous mentoring experience and are willing to be a sounding board for you. As discussed in Question 12, those mentoring in a formal program very likely were required to participate in training sessions along with other mentors and encouraged to get to know those in their group. Consequently, training sessions (in-person training and some online training systems) represent another opportunity to discover who not only is an experienced hand but also is someone from whom you would be comfortable seeking advice. So it would be ideal to leave these sessions with a phone number or e-mail address of one or more experienced mentors willing to take your call, text, or e-mail. And, as we noted in Question 13, helping you connect with other mentors is a primary job of your program coordinator. If you don't encounter an experienced mentor in the natural course of things, ask your coordinator to help you connect. And bear in mind that program coordinators are likely to be or have been mentors themselves and can offer the voice of experience as well. Finally, opportunities to connect with experienced mentors online are now mainly limited to connections made through the auspices of the formal mentoring program in which you are participating. But that's changing as mentoring programs and mentoring support organizations become more adept at providing online opportunities to "Ask a Mentor" and to interact with other mentors (witness the mentoring forums mentioned above).

Another productive approach can be pursued through your own personal network (actual or virtual).

The website for MENTOR: The National Mentoring Partnership (mentoring.org) has a wide range of useful information, including links to state Mentoring Partnerships and resource materials, webinars (online seminars), research summaries, and downloadable materials. If there is a Mentoring Partnership in your state, we recommend that you visit their website to see what resource materials and mentor trainings they offer.

Your Personal Networks: Many of you will know people in your personal network who have either been mentors or are employed in a youth field or simply live a life that makes them strong sounding boards on a wide variety of youth development issues. This might be someone in your family, a best friend, a colleague, or a spiritual leader to whom you often and comfortably turn for advice. If you are a new mentor, let that person know you are mentoring, see if he or she has any advice to share before you get started, and sound the alert that you hope you can call upon that person if you need help. If you are further along in your mentoring experience and have arrived at a place where you want to test ideas or try to resolve an issue, engage this person again. You have relied on this individual in the past, and his or her advice, or simple willingness to listen, is likely to be valuable once again.

If no one person immediately comes to mind, there are two other routes to follow. First, simply think carefully about who in your network of family, friends, or acquaintances you *think* would be good sounding boards and, in essence, give them a test drive. Tell them you are mentoring or planning to mentor and wonder if they would be willing to lend an ear as you move through your mentoring experience. Second—or simultaneously—use whatever social media you use to find out who in your Facebook, Twitter, LinkedIn, and other communities have been mentors, believe they have sound advice to offer, and are willing to be a resource for you. Of course, you could simply do this on an ad hoc basis as issues arise, but it is likely that identifying one or two people to depend upon will strengthen your mentoring in two ways. It will make you a more confident mentor, and it accords respect to the time and presumed talents of those you have recruited to help you. Being someone's sounding board is rarely a burden-free experience, so it is wise to signal that you are grateful for the willingness to help.

Finally, don't forget the young people (or younger people) who are part of your network. Sharing an issue (with appropriate consideration for confidentiality) with someone who is the same age as your mentee can provide a perspective that is difficult to duplicate. So take advantage of the counsel of any young people to whom you have easy access. And bear in mind that it is not just the class presidents, school valedictorians, or star athletes (or those destined to be) who make good sounding boards. Young people you know who have dealt with tough issues and found their way to positive resolutions can frequently be ideal resources, and many will be pleased to be asked to help.

ORGANIZATIONS THAT CAN HELP

Listed here are outstanding public agencies (including a few that might seem unlikely resources, e.g., the U.S. Department of Defense) and non-profit organizations that have much to offer new and experienced mentors. They can provide (1) general information about mentoring, (2) specialized information about mentoring, and (3) general information about youth development. As noted, all are accessible on the Web, by phone, or both. None use text messaging as of this writing.

State and Local Mentoring Partnerships

Please note that not every state has a state mentoring partnership. An up-to-date list is also available on the MENTOR website (www.mentoring.org). We have provided both a phone number and website when available.

Arizona: Mentoring Partnership of Arizona: 520-881-3300; volunteersoaz.org

Connecticut: Governor's Prevention Partnership: 860-523-8042; preventionworksct.org

Delaware: Delaware Mentoring Council: delawarementoring.org

Florida: Mentor Center of Palm Beach County; 561-374-7517; cscpbc.org/mentoring

Georgia: Georgia Mentoring Partnership: 478-474-1850; georgiamentoring.org

Illinois: Illinois Mentoring Partnership (in development): www.mentoring.org

Indiana: Indiana Mentoring Partnership: 317-396-2737; iyi.org/indiana-mentoring-partnership.aspx

Kansas: Kansas Mentors: 785-296-8447; kansasmentors.kansas.gov

Maine: Maine Mentoring Partnership: 207-620-7180; jmg.org /programs/maine-mentoring-partnership

Massachusetts: Mass Mentoring Partnership: 617-695-2431; massmentors.org

Michigan: Mentor Michigan: 517-335-4295; michigan.gov/mentormichigan

Minnesota: Mentoring Partnership of Minnesota: 612-370-9162; mpmn.org

New York: The Mentoring Partnership of Long Island: 631-761-7800; mentorkids.org; The Mentoring Partnership of New York: 212-953-0945; mentoring.org/newyork

North Carolina: North Carolina Mentoring Partnership: 919-215-1193; ncmentoring.net

Ohio: The Mentoring Center of Central Ohio: 614-839-2447; mentoringcenterco.org

Oregon: Oregon Mentors: 503-517-8990; oregonmentors.org

Pennsylvania: The Mentoring Partnership of Southwestern Pennsylvania: 412-281-2535; mentoringpittsburgh.org; United Way of Southeastern PA's Campaign for Mentoring: 215-665-2476: uwsepa.org

Rhode Island: Rhode Island Mentoring Partnership: 401-732-7700; mentorri.org

Tennessee: Memphis Mentoring Partnership/Grizzlies Charitable Foundation: 901-205-1253; teamupmemphis.org

Vermont: Mobius: The Mentoring Movement: 802-658-1888; mobiusmentors.org

Virginia: Fairfax Partnership for Youth: 703-324-5703; fairfaxyouth.org; Virginia Mentoring Partnership: 804-828-1536; vamentoring.org

Washington: Washington State Mentors: 425-416-2032; wamentors.org

National Organizations

America's Promise Alliance: 202-657-0600; americaspromise.org

Big Brothers Big Sisters of America: 215-567-7000; bbbs.org

The Center for Evidence-Based Mentoring (an alliance between the University of Massachusetts, Boston, and MENTOR: The National Mentoring Partnership): 617-287-6350; umbmentoring.org

City Year: 617-927-2500; cityyear.org

College Success Foundation: 877-655-4097; collegesuccessfoundation.org

Communities in Schools: 800-CIS4KIDS; communitiesinschools.org

Corporation for National and Community Service: 202-606-5000; nationalservice.gov

Education Northwest's National Mentoring Center: 800-547-6339; educationnorthwest.org

Experience Corps: 202-434-4600; experiencecorps.com

Fathers Incorporated: fathersincorporated.com

4-H: 202-401-4114; 4-h.org

Great Schools: 415-977-0700; greatschools.org

iMentor: 212-461-4330; imentor.org

Institute of Applied Research in Youth Development: 617-627-5558; ase.tufts.edu/iaryd

Intergenerational Center at Temple University: 215-204-6970; templeigc.org

MENTOR: The National Mentoring Partnership: 703-224-2200; mentoring.org

Mentoring USA: 212-400-8294; mentoringusa.org

National Dropout Prevention Center: 864-656-2599; www.dropoutprevention.org

100 Black Men of America: 404-688-5100; 100blackmen.org

Points of Light Institute/Hands On Network: 404-979-2900; 1-800-volunteer.org

Portland State Center for Interdisciplinary Mentoring Research: pdx.edu/mentoring-research

Public/Private Ventures: 215-557-4400; ppv.org

Search Institute: 800-888-7828; search-institute.org

United Way Worldwide: 703-836-7100 or 703-836-7112; liveunited.org

U.S. Department of Agriculture: 202-720-2791; usda.gov

U.S. Department of Defense: 703-571-3343; defense.gov

U.S. Department of Health and Human Services: 877-696-6775; www.hhs.gov

U.S. Department of Justice: 202-514-2000; justice.gov

READER FEEDBACK

We hope readers will share their reactions with us; we will be especially grateful to receive two kinds of feedback. Please share any questions that you think should have been covered in the *Field Guide*, but weren't. Please also share advice related to any of the questions that appear in the *Field Guide*. For example, do you have a new, different, better approach to dealing with an uncommunicative young person (Question 24) or striking just the right balance with regard to being supportive (Questions 23 and 34)? You can reach us via Search Institute, The Banks Building, 615 First Avenue, NE, Suite 125, Minneapolis, MN 55413. Many thanks!

ACKNOWLEDGMENTS

It is with great pleasure that we acknowledge and thank a long list of exceptional (and exceptionally generous) people for sharing their findings and their insight on what it takes to be a mentor worthy of the assignment. We looked to them for research and both real-life expertise and professional expertise and those that we depended upon most are noted below. To these colleagues, and in some instances professional heroes and dear friends, we offer our gratitude and our thanks. They not only informed the contents of *The Mentor's Field Guide*, they made the work of writing it a joy.

Research
The research of the nation's leading mentoring scholars—starting with that of Jean Rhodes, research director and influential founder of the UMASS/MENTOR Center for Evidence-Based Mentoring—constitutes a foundational resource. Rhodes's work, the authoritative research of David DuBois, Jean Grossman, Mary Agnes Hamilton, Stephen Hamilton, Michael Karcher, Janis Kuperschmidt, Belle Liang, Renée Spencer, Thomas Keller of the Portland State Center for Interdisciplinary Mentoring Research and Summer Institute on Youth Mentoring, and dedicated teams of researchers associated with Big Brothers Big Sisters of America, Education Northwest and Public/Private Ventures, inform a great many of our answers to mentors' questions. Also vital is the work of leading thinkers associated with the field of positive youth development, including Richard Lerner of Tufts University's distinguished Institute for Applied Research in Youth Development and the late Peter Benson and the practical-minded analysts he led at Search Institute.

Real-Life Expertise
This group includes mentors Barbara Canter, Hamp Coley, Marian Heard, Karen Darley, Susan Kanelidis, Stephen Manza, Robin Melvin, Thomas Mendell, Richard Plepler, Marilyn Pritchett, Suzanne Spero, and James Waller; as well as mentees Felton Booker, Leticia Rodriguez, and Mark

Prince; and those who have been both a mentor and a mentee, like Ean Garrett. They contributed the kind of wisdom that can only come from *doing* and then reflecting on what was done and how the action was received.

Professional Expertise

For professional *expertise*, or what is sometimes called practice wisdom, we relied on two principal sources. First is the expertise of the exceptionally dedicated and able human service professionals drawn from MENTOR and the network of local Mentoring Partnerships, many of whom also were mentoring program coordinators at some time during their careers. This group includes David Shapiro, Tonya Wiley, Ellen Christman, Libra Johnson, Kate Schineller and Linda Stewart and their colleagues at MENTOR, along with leaders of Mentoring Partnerships located throughout the country. Among those in the latter group, we especially want to thank Carolyn Becic, Jean Lahage Cohen and colleagues Bruce Beckwith and Franca Floro, Colleen Fedor, Joellen Gonder-Spacek, Linda Harrill, James Kooler, Andrew Mecca, Marilyn Pritchett, Jennifer Smith-Slaybough and Larry Wright. The second source of expert advice: leaders drawn from many parts of the human service field. It was to Gina Aldisert, Lisa Aramony, Shay Bilchik, Barbara Canter, David Eisner, Marian Heard, Irv Katz, Nina Sazer O'Donnell, Jean Rhodes, Jennifer Smith, and Sheila Plank who we turned frequently for insight, counsel, and friendship. And they were *always* there to deliver it.

Editorial guidance was provided by three exceptionally smart and very kind professionals: Karl Anderson, Kate Brielmaier, and Mary Byers. Each brought great dedication, patience, and skill to the task, and *The Mentor's Field Guide* is a far better book than it would have been without their direction and doggedness.

Finally, we thank Harris Wofford—the first person who thought this book was a good idea and who encouraged us to pursue it.

REFERENCES

Ahrens, K. R., DuBois, D. L., Richardson, L. P., Fan, M. Y., & Lazano, P. (2008). Youth in foster care with adult mentors during adolescence have improved adult outcomes. *Pediatrics,* 121 (2), e246–e252.

Allen, J. P., Moore, C., & Kuperminc, G. (1998). Attachment and adolescent psychosocial functioning. *Child Development, 69,* 1406–1419.

American Academy of Pediatricians. (2011). *Children's health topics: Child abuse and neglect.* Retrieved from www.aap.org/healthtopics/childabuse.cfm.

American Psychological Association. (2002). *Ethical principles of psychologists and code of conduct.* Washington, DC: Author.

Annie E. Casey Foundation. (2002). *Kids Count data snapshot. Connecting kids to technology: Challenges and opportunities.* Baltimore: Author.

Annie E. Casey Foundation. (2007, March). *Kids Count data snapshot: One out of five U.S. children is living in an immigrant family.* Baltimore: Author.

Annie E. Casey Foundation. (2011). *Kids Count data book.* Baltimore: Author.

Balfanz, R., Bridgeland, J., Fox, J., & Moore, L. (2011). *Building a grad nation: Progress and challenge in ending the high school dropout epidemic, 2010–2011 annual update.* A report by Civic Enterprises, Everyone Graduates Center at Johns Hopkins University, America's Promise Alliance, and the Alliance for Excellent Education.

Benson, P. L. (2006). *All kids are our kids: What communities must do to raise caring and responsible children and adolescents* (2nd ed.). San Francisco: Jossey-Bass.

Benson, P. L., Scales, P. C., Hamilton, S. F., & Semsa, A., Jr. (2006). Positive youth development: Theory, research, and applications. In R. M. Lerner (Ed.), *Theoretical models of human development*: Vol. 1, *Handbook of Child Psychology* (6th ed., 894–941). Hoboken, NJ: John Wiley & Sons.

Bogat, G. A., & Liang, B. (2005). Gender in mentoring relationships. In D. DuBois & M. Karcher (Eds.), *Handbook of Youth Mentoring* (205–217). Thousand Oaks, CA: Sage.

Casey Family Programs. (2001). *It's my life: Summary of a framework for youth transitioning from foster care to successful adulthood.* Seattle, Washington. Available at www.casey.org/Resources/Publications/directory/subject/IML.htm

Cavell, T., DuBois, D., Karcher, M., & Rhodes, J. (February 2009). *Strengthening mentoring opportunities for at-risk youth* [policy brief]. Available at www
.nwrel.org/mentoring/pdf/mentoring_policy_brief.pdf

Centers for Disease Control and Prevention, National Center for Injury Prevention and Control. (2009). *Suicide prevention, youth suicide.* Retrieved from www .cdc.gov/violenceprevention/pub/youth_suicide.html.

Child Trends (2010). *Parental expectations for the children's academic achievement.* Washington, DC: Author. Retrieved from www.childtrendsdatabank.org /alphalist?q-node/366.

Child Trends. (2011). *Foster care: Child Trends data bank.* Washington, DC: Author. Retrieved from www.childtrendsdatabank.org?q=node/199.

Cohen, G. L., & Steel, C. M. (2002). A barrier of mistrust: How negative stereotypes affect cross-race mentoring. In J. Aronson (Ed.), *Improving academic achievement: Impact of psychological factors on education* (303–327). San Diego: Academic Press.

Corporation for National and Community Service. (2006a). *Mentoring in America: A Summary of new research.* Washington, DC: Author.

Corporation for National and Community Service. (2006b). *Volunteers Mentoring Youth: Implications for Closing the Mentoring Gap.* Washington, DC: Author.

Corporation for National and Community Service. (2010). *Volunteering in America 2010.* Washington, DC: Author.

Courtney, M. E., & Pillavin, I. (1998). *Foster youth's transitions to adulthood: Outcomes 12–18 months after leaving out-of-home care.* Madison: School of Social Work, University of Wisconsin.

DuBois, D. L., Holloway, B. E., Valentine, J. C., & Cooper, H. (2002). Effectiveness of mentoring programs for youth: A meta-analytic review. *American Journal of Community Psychology, 30*(2), 157–197.

DuBois, D. L., & Karcher, M. J. (Eds.). (2005). *Handbook of youth mentoring.* Thousand Oaks, CA: Sage.

DuBois, D. L., & Neville, H. A. (1997). Youth mentoring: Investigation of relationship characteristics and perceived benefits. *Journal of Community Psychology, 25,* 227–234.

DuBois, D. L., Portillo, N., Rhodes, J. E., Silverthorn, N., & Valentine, J.C. (2011). How effective are mentoring programs for youth? A systematic assessment of the evidence. *Psychological Science in the Public Interest, 2*(2), 57–91.

DuBois, D. L., & Silverthorn, N. (2005). Natural mentoring relationships and adolescent health: Evidence from a national study. *American Journal of Community Psychology, 95*(3), 518–524.

Duncan, G. J., & Brooks Gunn, J. (Eds.). (1997). *Consequences of growing up poor.* New York: Russell Sage Foundation.

Federal Interagency Forum on Child and Family Statistics. (2011). *America's children: Key national indicators of well-being, 2011.* Washington, DC. Retrieved from www.childstats.gov/pdf/ac2011/ac_11.pdf.

Finkelhor, D., Turner, H., Ormrod, R., Hamby, S., & Kracke, K. (2009). *Children's exposure to violence: A comprehensive national survey.* Retrieved from U.S. Department of Justice Office of Juvenile Justice and Delinquency Prevention website: www.ncjrs.gov/pdffiles1/ojjdp/227744.pdf.

Fortuny, K., & Chaudry, A. (2009). *Children of immigrants: Immigration trends/fact sheet No. 1.* Washington, DC: Urban Institute.

Grossman, J. B., & Rhodes, J. E. (2002). The test of time: Predictors and effects of duration in youth mentoring programs. *American Journal of Community Psychology, 30,* 199–219.

Hamilton, S. F., & Hamilton, M. L. (2010). Building mentoring relationships. *New Directions for Youth Development, 126,* 141–144.

Harden, B. J. (2004). Safety and stability for foster children: A developmental perspective. *Future of Children,* 14(2), 30–47

Hawkins, J. D., & Catalano, R. F. (1992). *Communities that care: Action for drug abuse prevention.* San Francisco: Jossey-Bass.

Hawkins, J. D., & Catalano, R. F. (1995). *Risk-focused prevention using the social development strategy.* Seattle: Developmental Resources and Programs.

Hawkins, J. D., Catalano, R. F., & Miller, J. Y. (1992). Risk and protective factors for alcohol and other drug problems in adolescence and early adulthood: Implications for substance abuse prevention. *Psychological Bulletin, 112*(1), 64–105.

Herrera, C., Grossman, J. B., Kaugh, T. J., Feldman, A. F., McMaken, J., & Jucovy, L. Z. (2007). *Making a difference in schools: The Big Brothers Big Sisters school-based mentoring program.* Philadelphia: Public/Private Ventures.

Jekielek, S. M., Moore, K. A., Hair, E. C., & Scarupa, H. J. (2002). *Mentoring: A promising strategy for youth development.* Washington, DC: Child Trends.

Jenson, J. (2005). Research for knowledge and practice: Carrying on the tradition. *Social Work Research, 29*(1), 1–3.

Karcher, M. J. (2005). The effects of developmental mentoring and high school mentors' attendance on their mentees' self-esteem, behavior and connectedness. *Psychology in the Schools, 42,* 65–77.

Karcher, M. J. (2010, November 17). *The TEAM framework: Using TEAM to identify, train and support mentors.* Paper presented at the Fifth Annual Michigan's Premier Mentoring Conference, East Lansing.

Karcher, M.J., Davidson, A.J., Rhodes, J.E., & Herrera, C. (2010). Pygmalion in the program: The role of teenage peer mentors' attitudes in shaping their mentees' outcomes. *Applied Developmental Science, 14,* 212–227.

Karcher, M. J., Herrera, C., & Hansen, K. (2010). "I dunno, what do you wanna do?": Testing a framework to guide mentor training and activity selection. *New Directions for Youth Development, 126,* 51–69.

Keller, T. E., & Pryce, J. M. (2009). *Different roles and different results: Mentors who have stronger relationships and better outcomes in school-based mentoring.* Manuscript in preparation.

Keller, T. E., & Pryce, J. M. (2010). Mutual but unequal: Mentoring as a hybrid of familiar relationship roles. In M. J. Karcher & M. J. Nakkula (Eds.), *Play, Talk, Learn: Promising Practices in Youth Mentoring. New Directions for Youth Development: Theory, Practice, Research* (Summer), 33–50.

Landrieu introduces Foster Care Mentoring Act. Retrieved from Landrieu.senate .gov/mediacenter/pressreleases.

Larose, S., Tarabulsky, G., & Cyrene, D. (2005). Perceived autonomy and relatedness as moderating the impact of teacher-student mentoring relationships on student academic adjustment. *Journal of Primary Prevention, 26,* 111–128.

Lerner, R. M. (2008). *The good teen: Rescuing adolescents from the myths of the storm and stress years.* New York: Crown.

Lerner, R. M., Brittain, A. S., & Fay, K. (2007). Mentoring: A key resource for promoting positive youth development. *Research in Action, 1,* 3–15.

Let's Move: America's move to raise a generation of healthier kids. *Learn the Facts.* Retrieved from www.letsmove.gov/learn-facts/epidemic-childhood-obesity.

Levinson, D. J. (with Darrow, D., Klein, E. B., Levinson, M. H., & McKee, B.). (1978). *The seasons of a man's life.* New York: Knopf.

Liang, B., Spencer, R., Brogan, D., & Corral, M. (2008). Mentoring relationships from early adolescence through emerging adulthood: A qualitative analysis. *Journal of Vocational Behavior, 72,* 168–182.

Liang, B., Tracy, A., Kauh, T., Taylor, C., & Williams, L. (2006). Mentoring Asian and Euro-American college women. *Journal of Multicultural Counseling and Development, 34,* 143–154.

Liptak, A. (2008). U.S. prison population dwarfs that of other nations. *International Herald Tribune,* April 23.

Mather, M. (2009). *Reports on America: Children in immigrant families chart new path.* Washington, DC: Population Reference Bureau.

McEwan, H. (2000). On making things difficult for learners. In L. Stone (ed.), *Philosophy of education 2000: A publication of the Philosophy of Education Society.* Champaign, IL: Philosophy of Education Society.

McLearn, K. T., Colasanto, D., & Schoen, C. (1998). *Mentoring makes a difference: Findings from the Commonwealth Fund 1998 survey of adults mentoring young people.* New York: Commonwealth Fund.

Mecca, A. M. (2008). *Lifeplan: Tools every teenager needs to thrive not merely survive.* Marin County, CA: California Mentor Foundation.

Melville, K. (2006). *The school dropout crisis: Why one-third of all high school students don't graduate and what your community can do about it.* Richmond, VA: The University of Richmond Pew Partnership for Civic Change.

MENTOR. (2002). *Mentoring in America 2002: National poll sponsored by the AOL Time Warner Foundation.* Alexandria, VA: Author.

MENTOR. (2003). *Elements of effective practice* (2nd ed.). Alexandria, VA: Author.

MENTOR. (2006). *Mentoring in America 2005: A snapshot of the current state of mentoring.* Alexandria, VA: Author.

MENTOR. (2009). *Elements of Effective Practice* (3rd ed.) Alexandria, VA: Author.

MENTOR. (2009). *Mentoring immigrant and refugee youth.* Alexandria, VA: Author.

MENTOR. (2011). *Report to Congress on the SafetyNET Criminal Background Check Project.* Alexandria, VA: Author.

Merriam, S. (1983). Mentors and proteges: A critical review of the literature. *Adult Education Quarterly, 33,* 161–173.

Millenky, M., Bloom, D., & Dillon, C. (2010). *Making the transition: Interim results of the National Guard ChalleNGe Evaluation.* New York: MDRC.

Millenky, M., Bloom, D., Muller-Ravett, S., & Broadus, J. (2011). *Staying on course: Three-year results of the National Guard Youth ChalleNGe Evaluation.* New York: MDRC.

Moore, K., Redd, Z., Burkhauser, M., Mbwana, K., & Collins, A. (2009). *Children in poverty: Trends, consequences, and policy options* [research brief]. Washington, DC: Child Trends.

National Center for Victims of Crime, Dating Violence Resource Center. (2007). *Teen dating violence fact sheet.* Retrieved from www.ncvc.org/ncvc/main.aspx ?dbID=DB_DatingViolenceResourceCenter101.

National Dating Abuse Hotline. (2007–2011). *Is this abuse? Dating abuse fast facts.* Retrieved from www.loveisrespect.org/is-this-abuse/dating-abuse-fast-facts.

National Institutes of Health, National Institute on Drug Abuse. (2010). *NIDA InfoFacts: High school and youth trends.* Retrieved from www.drugabuse.gov /infofacts/HSYouthtrends.html.

Nutley, S., Walter, I., & Davies, S. (2003). From knowing to doing: A framework for understanding the evidence to practice agenda. *Evaluation, 9*(2), 125–148.

Office of Applied Studies, Substance Abuse and Mental Health Administration (2009). *The national survey on drug use and health: Children living with substance-dependent or substance-abusing parents: 2002–2007.* Washington, DC: SAMSHA. Retrieved from oas.samhsa.gov.

Parra, G. R., DuBois, D. L., Neville, H. A., & Pugh-Lilly, A. O. (2002). Mentoring relationships for youth: Investigation of a process-oriented model. *Journal of Community Psychology, 30,* 376–388.

Partnership at Drug-Free.Org. *A parent's guide to the teen brain.* Retrieved from teenbrain.drugfree.org.

Perry, B. D. (2001). The neurodevelopmental impact of violence in childhood. In D. Schetky & E. P. Benedek (Eds.), *Textbook of child and adolescent forensic psychiatry* (221–238). Washington, DC: American Psychiatric Press.

Philip, K., & Hendry, L. B. (2001). Making sense of mentoring or mentoring making sense? Reflections on the mentoring process by adult mentors with young people. *Journal of Community and Applied Social Psychology, 10,* 211–223.

Reilly, T. (2003). Transition from care: Status and outcomes of youth who age out of foster care. *Child Welfare, 82*(6), 727–746.

Rhodes, J. E. (2002). *Stand by me: The risks and rewards of mentoring today's youth.* Cambridge, MA: Harvard University Press.

Rhodes, J. E. (2005). A model of youth mentoring. In D. L. DuBois & M. J. Karcher (Eds.), *Handbook of Youth Mentoring* (30–43). Thousand Oaks, CA: Sage.

Rhodes, J. E., Contreras, J. M., & Mangelsdorf, S. C. (1994). Natural mentors' relationships among Latino adolescent mothers: Psychological adjustment, moderating processes, and the role of early parental acceptance. *American Journal of Community Psychology, 22,* 211–228.

Rhodes, J. E., & and DuBois, D. L. (2006). Understanding and facilitating the youth mentoring movement. *Social Policy Reports: Society for Research in Child Development,* 20(3), 3–19.

Rhodes, J. E., Ebert, L., & Fischer, K. (1992). Natural mentors: An overlooked resource in social networks of youth, African American mothers. *American Journal of Community Psychology, 20,* 445–462.

Rhodes, J. E., Grossman, J. B., & Resch, N. L. (2000). Agents of change: Pathways through which mentoring relationships influence adolescents' academic adjustment. *Child Development, 71,* 1662–1671.

Rhodes, J., Liang, B., & Spencer, R. (2009). First do no harm: Ethical principles for youth mentoring relationships. *Professional Psychology: Research and Practice, 40,* 452–458.

Rhodes, J. E., Reddy, R., Grossman, J., & Lee, J. (2002). Volunteer matching relationships with minority youth: An analysis of same- versus cross-race matches. *Journal of Applied Psychology, 32,* 2114–2133.

Robert Wood Johnson & Partnership for Solutions. (2004). *Chronic conditions: Making the case for ongoing care.* Baltimore: The Johns Hopkins University.

Sackett, D., Rosenberg, W., Gray, J., Haynes, R., & Richardson, W. (1996). Evidence-based medicine: What it is and what it isn't. *British Medical Journal, 312,* 71–72.

Sánchez, B., & Colón, Y. (2005). Race, ethnicity and culture in mentoring relationships. In D. L. DuBois & M. J. Karcher (Eds.), *Handbook of youth mentoring* (191–204). Thousand Oaks, CA: Sage.

Shlonsky, A., & Gibbs, L. (2004). Will the real evidence-based practice please stand up? Teaching the process of evidence-based practice to the helping professions. *Brief Treatment and Crisis Intervention, 4*(2), 137–153.

Sieh, D., Meijer, A., Oort, F., Visser-Meily, J., & Van der Leij, D. (2010). Problem behavior in children of chronically ill parents: A meta-analysis. *Clinical Child and Family Psychology Review, 13*(4), 384–397.

Sipe, C. L. (1996). *Mentoring: A synthesis of the P/PV's research: 1988–1995.* Philadelphia: Public/Private Ventures.

Smith, W. B. (2011). *Youth leaving foster care: A developmental, relationship-based approach to practice.* New York: Oxford University Press.

Spencer, R. (2007). "It's not what I expected": A qualitative study of youth mentoring relationship failures. *Journal of Adolescent Research, 22*(4): 331–354.

Spencer, R., Collins, M. E., Ward, R., & Smashnaya, S. (2010). Mentoring for youth leaving foster care: Promise and pitfalls. *Social Work,* 55(3), 225–234.

Spencer, R., Jordan, J. V., & Sazama, J. (2004). Growth-promoting relationships between youth and adults: A focus group study. *Families in Society, 85,* 354–362.

Spencer, R., Theokas, C., & Lerner, R.M. (2006). Promoting positive development in adolescence: The role of ecological assets in families, schools and neighborhood. *Applied Developmental Science, 10*(2), 61–74.

Teenage Research Unlimited, National Teen Dating Abuse Helpline and Liz Claiborne Inc. (2008). *Teen and tween dating violence and abuse study.* Retrieved from www.loveisrespect.org/wp-content/uploads/2008/07/tru-tween-teen-study-feb-081.pdf.

Theokas, C., & Lerner, R. M. (2006). Promoting positive development in adolescence: The role of ecological assets in families, schools and neighborhoods. *Applied Developmental Science, 10*(2), 61–74.

University of South Florida. (2003). *Mentoring.* Retrieved August 1, 2004, from www.aa.ufl.edu/aa/affact/ummp/mentoring.htm.

U.S. Census Bureau. (2009). *Internet use in the United States: 2009.* Washington, DC: Author.

U.S. Census Bureau. (2010). *The AFCARES report: Preliminary FY2009 estimates.* Washington, DC: Author.

U.S. Census Bureau. (2011). *Statistical abstract of the United States: 2011.* Washington, DC: Author.

U.S. Department of Education, Office of Safe and Drug-Free Schools (2009). Mentoring Resource Center Fact Sheet, *Research and Practice: The role of evidence-based program practices in the youth mentoring field.* Retrieved from www.edmentoring.org.

U.S. Department of Education. (2010). *What's possible: Turning around America's lowest-achieving schools.* Retrieved from www.ed.gov/blog/2010/03.

U.S. Department of Justice, Office of Juvenile Justice and Delinquency Prevention. (1995). *Delinquency prevention works: Program summary.* NCJ 155006. Retrieved from www.eric.ed.gov/PDFS/ED394115.pdf.

U.S. Department of Veterans Affairs, National Center for Post-Traumatic Stress Disorder. (2007). *Community violence: Effects on children and teens.* Retrieved from www.ptsd.va.gov/public/pages/effects-community-violence-children.asp.

Wheeler, M., Keller, T., & DuBois, D. L. (2010). *Is school-based mentoring effective? Making sense of mixed findings.* Presentation at the National Press Club, arranged by MENTOR. Washington, DC.

White, V., Chau, M., & Aratani, Y. (2011). *Who are America's poor children: The official story.* New York: National Center for Children in Poverty, Mailman School of Public Health, Columbia University.

Zimmerman, M., Bingenheimer, J. B., & Behrendt, D. E. (2005). Natural mentoring relationships. In D. L. DuBois & M. J. Karcher (Eds.), *Handbook of youth mentoring* (143–157). Thousand Oaks, CA: Sage.

INDEX

ABOUT THE AUTHORS

Gail Manza is a social worker and former CEO of MENTOR. For more than two decades, she led initiatives to focus the combined resources of the public and private sectors on helping America's young people succeed. She was also a founding chair of the Federal Mentoring Council and its National Mentoring Working Group, a co-founder of 1,000 Women for Mentoring, and continues to serve MENTOR as an *Emeritus Fellow*. Ms. Manza has a master's degree from the University of Maryland School of Social Work and Community Planning and is currently completing doctoral studies at the Bryn Mawr School of Social Work and Social Research.

Susan K. Patrick is a youth development and mentoring consultant with a passion for improving the lives of America's young people. She is the former president of the Governor's Prevention Partnership in Connecticut, a statewide public-private partnership, co-chaired by the Governor and a business CEO with a mission is to keep Connecticut's youth safe, successful, and drug free. She is the founder of the Connecticut Mentoring Partnership and has developed numerous mentoring guides and toolkits. Ms. Patrick has a master's degree in community psychology from Central Connecticut State University.